EDWARD K. BROWN, former Professor of English at the University of Chicago, was embarked on the only authorized, full-length critical biography of Willa Cather—what promised to be a work of major stature—when he died unexpectedly at the age of forty-five. Fortunately, Mr. Leon Edel, a long-time friend from his student days at the Sorbonne, was able to complete WILLA CATHER with the help of Brown's copious notes and correspondence.

LEON EDEL has been active as a critic, writer, and teacher for more than a quarter of a century. A renowned biographer, he was the 1962 winner of both the Pulitzer Prize and the National Book Award for Volumes II and III of his life of Henry James. Mr. Edel is the author of HENRY DAVID THOREAU, JAMES JOYCE: THE LAST JOURNEY, LITERARY BIOGRAPHY, and THE MODERN PSYCHOLOGICAL NOVEL. His five-volume HENRY JAMES, and BLOOMSBURY: A HOUSE OF LIONS are both available in Avon editions.

WILLA CATHER

A CRITICAL BIOGRAPHY

E. K. Brown
Completed by Leon Edel

Primus ego in patriam mecum . . .
deducam Musas.   VIRGIL

 A DISCUS BOOK/PUBLISHED BY AVON BOOKS

AVON BOOKS
A division of
The Hearst Corporation
959 Eighth Avenue
New York, New York 10019

Copyright 1953 by Margaret Brown
Published by arrangement with Alfred A. Knopf, Inc.
Library of Congress Catalog Card Number: 52-12204
ISBN: 0-380-49676-3

First Discus Printing, April, 1980

DISCUS TRADEMARK REG. U.S. PAT. OFF. AND IN
OTHER COUNTRIES, MARCA REGISTRADA, HECHO EN
U.S.A.

Printed in the U.S.A.

Primus ego in patriam mecum . . .
deducam Musas.

VIRGIL

Introduction

AND EDITOR'S FOREWORD

INTRODUCTION BY E. K. BROWN

IN the autumn of 1946 the *Yale Review* published an article of mine entitled "Homage to Willa Cather," in which I surveyed her fiction and tried to define its peculiar qualities and effects. Miss Cather liked the article and during the winter and early spring we exchanged a number of letters. Plans were laid for meetings in the summer of 1947 when I was to teach at New York University. It had always been Miss Cather's way to decide instantly and irrevocably whether she would give her confidence; to me she wrote warmly and vigorously, with no apparent shadow of restraint, concerning her books, the principles of her art, and the general values from which her achievement grew. Late in March she began to dictate a letter about the pleasure it gave her to have been visited by Yehudi Menuhin and his sister Hephzibah and their children—she was carried back to the time when the parents had come there to talk, play, and read Shakespeare with her more than a decade before. She hurried out of New York before she could finish the letter. It stopped in the middle of a sentence. Miss Cather died on April 24.

Her literary executrix, Edith Lewis, who had shared her life for forty years, remembered Miss Cather's pleasure in my article and was aware of the epistolary friendship that had begun and had grown to maturity so quickly. She asked me to write a study of her friend, a biography of the artist, and of the person, always keeping before me the principle that the person was to be studied not for herself but for the light her life and character might cast upon her art. In one of the stories in Willa Cather's first book, an admirer of the paintings of Sir Hugh Treffinger, visiting the studio soon after his death, grows curious about the life that lay behind the art and resolves to write a biography. "I mean," he says, "to touch only on such facts in his personal life as have to do directly with his work." It was a book of this kind that Edith Lewis had in mind. I had long believed that no American novelist since the death of Henry James was Willa Cather's equal in vision or in design and was joyfully ready to attempt it.

In an essay of which she thought well, T. K. Whipple described the literary development of Willa Cather as the victory of mind over Nebraska. Like many another capsule of criticism this has value only when its elements are clearly defined. It will not be sufficient to define *mind* and *Nebraska; victory* also will require a gloss.

In 1883 Willa Cather's parents took their four children to join more adventurous members of the family who ten years earlier had started a Virginia colony on the unbroken prairie. Willa Cather, who was not quite ten, was excited by two violent contrasts: between the tumultuous polyglot mass of pioneer life on farms within an easy ride of the colony, and the homogeneous, somewhat humdrum life of the farming community in the Virginia she had left; and between the wind-tormented flatness of south-central Nebraska and the rich hill-and-dale landscape of her corner of Virginia. Her friend Dorothy Canfield, who met Willa Cather before she was twenty, has said that an imaginative and emotional response to the great shift from Virginia to Nebraska is at the core of Willa Cather's fiction. Her own accounts of her response show that it gave her an awareness of her differentness from others, her individuality. Within a year or two of their coming to Nebraska the Cathers moved to town, to Red Cloud, a straggling village that was no more than a market center and a section point on the Burlington line from Kansas City and St. Joseph to Denver. Unlike the settlers on the prairie, most of the villagers were of old American stock and instinctively repeated in the appearance of the buildings and the way of life what they had known in small towns in Illinois, Ohio, and Kentucky, but in cheaper and rougher fashion. From her first visits to Red Cloud, Willa Cather had felt an unlikeness between the tight, rather mean aspect and pace of the village, and the vigorous, precarious, and in some ways exalting life of the farmers. When she began to live in the village, she threw herself impetuously against the way of the majority and sought out the exceptions, the dreamers, the nonconformists, the questioners. Visits to relatives who remained in the Virginia colony kept her sense of the land and its people vivid. In 1890 she began a five-year course at the state university in Lincoln, and this was to be the third and last tier in her experience of Nebraska. In Lincoln the dreary churchiness and bustling women's clubs could not repress the bold imagination of an occasional professor, or the theaters that gave Willa Cather so much pleasure, whether she was making friends with actresses backstage, seeing plays, or writing reviews of them for the *State Journal*. If Lincoln was very much a part of Nebraska, it also held a hint of the Eastern cities for which Willa Cather had begun to long.

In an obvious way Nebraska meant to her, when she was a girl and when she was a mature artist, the prairie and its foreign-born farmers, the crude village with its hard molds and its rebels, the college town where two worlds collided without requiring one to choose between them. In her early stories, a few of them recently accessible in James Shively's collection of Willa Cather's juvenilia, she rendered what was hard and bleak and cruel in the state's way of life—the collapse, for instance, of minds and bodies in the struggle with the land, the pressure of convention in the village, the imperviousness to art which was early and late for Willa Cather the chief expression of mind. Her first literary response to Nebraska was an almost unmitigated hate and fear: it was opposition to forces that seemed to her monstrously strong and a threat to her differentness, to the core of what she felt herself to be.

To look at Nebraska otherwise, to contemplate it with some objectivity and appreciation, Willa Cather needed to go away for a long time and to achieve success. She had gone east in 1896, and when twelve years later she was named managing editor of *McClure's Magazine*, she had finally the security of an established position and a firm foothold in the world of art. In "The Bohemian Girl," a long story published in the magazine in 1912, a new attitude toward Nebraska appears, and its main origin is plain. The young hero of the narrative, Nils Ericsson, returns to his home on a Nebraska farm after some years in a Norwegian port where he has had extraordinary success. He cannot persuade Clara Vavrika, who has married a stolid brother of his, to join him in admiring the vitality, force, and endurance of the pioneer grandmothers. She knows their thoughts of her, and feels in them a threat to her differentness. But she will find it an easy matter to recognize their values, Nils tells Clara, after she has gone away with him to Bergen—freedom and distance change the aspect of all things. So they did with Willa Cather.

Still, her new perspective toward Nebraska might never have been achieved, and would certainly have been retarded, if she had not come under the influence of an author whose name and work she had known when she was a child—the face appeared in a special pack of cards for the game of "Authors"—and whom she met in 1908. This was Sarah Orne Jewett. In 1908 Willa Cather was at the height of her enthusiasm for Henry James; some of the short stories she had been writing during the five preceding years were obtrusively Jamesian both in substance and in form, and in "Eleanor's House" she did what is really a pastiche of Jamesian implication. There is no record that Miss Jewett gave any warning against the cult of Henry James, whom she had known for some years; but her example and her precepts told powerfully against his influence. She showed to Willa Cather the possibilities of a simple rural subject, treated by an artist in profound sympathy with the places and the persons she dealt with, but also who, by a broad knowledge of the world, and of books, and by a habit of detached contemplation, could see her material from a distance. Miss Jewett was a supreme example of the artist who is both involved in her material and disengaged from it. Little by little Willa Cather's addiction to Jamesian substance and form wore off—there is a good deal of it surviving in *Alexander's Bridge*, written in 1911—and in her later years she would say that much as James had meant to her at one time, she knew that she would never reread his more complicated fictions. But there never came a time when she could not and did not reread the stories of Sarah Orne Jewett. The first sure evidence of the effect Miss Jewett had upon her was in the sketch called "The Enchanted Bluff," which appeared in *Harper's* in 1909, the year of Miss Jewett's death. It is severe in its treatment of Nebraska life, much more severe than "The Bohemian Girl"; and when one knows the works that were to follow, all of them seem implicit in this short piece about a few boys gathered by the river and what they made of their lives.

In the stories and novels that came after "The Enchanted Bluff" and "The Bohemian Girl," Willa Cather went far beyond those early works in the quality of her contemplation and appreciation of Nebraska. The dichotomy she had felt between the pioneer and the artist—one crucial form of the conflict between mind and Nebraska—began to disappear. The pioneer, it was true, did not often set any value on art, the old grandmothers would not have understood that art had much importance, would have agreed with the Northern Farmer that to stub Thurnaby waste was a prouder achievement than any bit of brain-work. Nevertheless the pioneer and the artist were generically one, they were both intent on creating. Underneath all the distinctions that separated them, and more telling than any, was the impulse they shared to turn from all the tracks of routine and convention to make a track of their own. A farmer like Alexandra Bergson in *O Pioneers!*, a farm-wife like Ántonia Shimerda in *My Ántonia* were creators just as surely as the artist in "A Sculptor's Funeral," at whom the villagers sneered while his body lay in his coffin. In later novels the conception of a pioneer broadened to take in those who planned the West and gambled fortunes on its future, building its railroads and filling its towns.

When Willa Cather lived in Red Cloud, the village had a number of extraordinary personalities who did not bend to the narrow standards of the majority. There was a dry-goods merchant whose *Iliad* in a Greek text lay on the counter before him and meant more than any number of customers, and a former Governor of Nebraska whose way of life had more to do with Denver and Omaha and Lincoln than with the little incidents of local progress. Everyone in the village who had an exceptional nature responded to that exceptional element in Willa Cather's, exactly as happened with Thea Kronborg when she was growing up in Moonstone in *The Song of the Lark*. Few of the dreamers or rebels read many books, but they had an obscure fellow-feeling for an artist's nature. In a sense, it was better to grow up in a Nebraska village just then than in one farther east.

In retrospect Willa Cather could see that she had never been quite so lonely or so different as she had supposed. Even in the university, crude and undiscriminating as it then was in so many important ways, there was a delight in originality, a welcome for promise, that would not probably have come in a more conventional institution committed to the usual stupid academic routines. From the beginning of her time there instructors and students saw and valued what was distinctive in her writing and in her personality; so did some people in the town—editors, clubwomen, exiles from Eastern cities, who stayed in Lincoln bewailing its rigidities but drawn to its vigor and daring.

As she matured, Willa Cather became the kind of artist to whom the past was important. She did not care to start from nothing—she wanted to start from the point art had reached in the sequence of great experiments, the chain of explorations, which make up tradition. Nor was her attachment to tradition any longer narrowly æsthetic. Art, she knew, was a flowering of fine personalities, and to their flowering the atmosphere of a fine society had brought much of the beauty and the strength. It began to appear to her that her art had been kept poor, and her personality clipped, by inadequacies in the society in which she had grown up. It was a society without a real past, and without much consciousness of what past it had.

In 1912 she made her first of many journeys to the Southwest. There she found a Western land with a past, with an interweaving of traditions complex, highly colored, and yet austere. The region began to press into her fiction, in the references to Mexico in *O Pioneers!*, in the long account of Thea's coming of age during her months in and near the canyon of the Cliff-Dwellers in *The Song of the Lark*, in the speculations about Coronado's expedition in a crucial scene of *My Ántonia*, in Tom Outland's record of his discovery of the Cliff-Dweller settlements in *The Professor's House*, and finally in the whole conception of *Death Comes for the Archbishop*. The persistence and the diversity of the references to the Southwest suggest—what is indeed the truth—that the discovery of this region was the principal emotional experience of Willa Cather's mature life. Not all the passages about the Southwest flowed from her stay there in 1912. She returned as often as she could, and when she came she remained for months. In that region she found a landscape with a beauty that was at once austere and spectacular, a proper setting for great emotions and great achievements; she found also a history of successive creations—the creation of the Cliff-Dwellers' villages, the establishment of another religion and civilization by the Spanish friars, and its re-creation by the French missionaries of the nineteenth century. In the Southwest the making of a society, a civilization, always went hand in hand with the making of beauty. Willa Cather found the artifacts of the Cliff-Dwellers as purely beautiful as any that remained from the old civilizations. With the creation of beautiful objects went appreciation of others that were old. The heavy bell that was the treasure of the Church of San Miguel at Santa Fe had been cast in Spain centuries before the discovery of America, and it was in the Southwest because someone had cared enough for its silvery tone to have it brought by cart all the thousands of miles from Mexico City across some of the most difficult country in the world. Nothing could be more unlike the early days in Nebraska than a story told in the prelude to *Death Comes for the Archbishop*. A Franciscan friar had begged a painting from one of the great collectors of Spain; the nobleman, thinking the friar would prefer a sentimental daub, had courteously bidden him choose which of his treasures the friar preferred; the choice fell on an El Greco, and somewhere in the Southwest that picture found its place. The preachers in Webster County would have chosen the daub. In the Southwest, layer upon layer of the past was visible, and each layer was an inexhaustible stimulus to the admirer of the pioneer and the admirer of art. All that Nebraska meant and all that mind meant were here reconciled in a synthesis for which no praise, no gratitude could be sufficient.

The effects of her discovery of the Southwest were complicated by her response to the First World War and its aftermath. Like many other American artists of her time she had a cult of France, and from the beginning she was attached to the cause of the Allies. The one saving element in the war was, in her opinion, that all the Americans she knew responded to it not as a matter involving dollars and cents, but in terms of emotions and ideas. Especially after the United States entered the war, what she heard and saw persuaded her that the heavy materialism that overlaid

American life, both on the prairies and in the large Eastern cities, had not crushed, though it had hampered and obscured, the life of the spirit, those forces within individuals which protect them from becoming mere economic units. The aftermath of the war depressed her as nothing had before: the heavy materialism had won out after all, it was the one genuine victor. She had never disliked the sight of a great railway-maker traveling in a special train and having the tracks cleared for his regal progress. He was a creator, and these accompaniments to his life were merely his due. The 1920's seemed to her the period not of great creative men of business, but of their lackeys, their secretaries, managers, lawyers, vice-presidents: these men were wholly uncreative, they exacted huge sums merely for keeping the wheels turning, spent them grossly, and nevertheless were commonly accepted as model products of the American way of life. In *One of Ours*, and in *A Lost Lady*, studying Nebraska in the decade before the war, she showed how uncreative, mercenary, odious men kept control once they had won it, and what they did to those who were finer than themselves; in *The Professor's House* she showed the hollowness of any pretensions they might make to interest in art or mind. She was now painfully disillusioned with the world about her, and for the first time suffered from a sense of being severed from it.

Her new anxieties coincided with middle life, and the very title and the substance of *A Lost Lady* suggested Willa Cather's sense of being adrift in a world with which she no longer felt in harmony. Her next three novels are a search for the meaning of this disharmony; they also may be regarded as the protest of one who has lived intensely and heartily against the advancing years. Her exploration led her to a deeper consideration than hitherto of the role of religion, its relation to art, to the mind, and to civilization. She had been brought up a Baptist; she had accepted this faith as she had accepted much else that being a member of her family had brought to her (and much as Thea accepts the Methodism of her family). It was not until after the First World War, when she was nearing her fiftieth year, that religion, in a broad sense, came to play a more significant role in her art. In 1922, with her father and mother, she was confirmed in the Protestant Episcopal Church. In part this was because this Church, more recently established in Nebraska, had won a distinct following in Red Cloud and obtained the adherence of her family; she had always maintained close links with her home and she wanted to share to the full the participation of her kin in the institutions of the town. In part it was an emotional response to religion, more keenly felt than before—although readers of *O Pioneers!* will recall the early pleasure she expressed in the color and ritual of the French Catholic settlement and her account of the cavalcade of forty French boys to meet the Bishop's carriage.

It would be a mistake to say that her entrance into the Episcopal Church brought her repose, and it is doubtful whether she expected it would. Her association with that Church shows only one of the directions in which she was seeking a solution and the repose a solution would bring. In the Episcopal Church there was no strain on the relation between religion and art, or on the relation between religion and civilization. The great prophet for Willa Cather's grandmothers had been John Bunyan; she never lost her feeling for his books, and never seemed to tire of reading *The Pilgrim's Progress*, about which many tender memories clustered; she had read also John Henry Newman. His name brings up powerfully the other great value Willa Cather found in the Episcopal Church; it was one of the great historic churches, and like all historic institutions that continue alive and faithful to their origins, it set a high value upon the past. So, of course, as she knew, did the Roman Catholic Church, for which she had such sympathetic insight that a great many of her readers, some of them Roman Catholics, supposed that she had become a member of that Church. The Episcopal Church was the historic church of America, and notably of Virginia, and it was natural she should turn to a church that appreciated and was of the past. . . .

EDITOR'S FOREWORD

The introduction that Edward Killoran Brown was writing to his critical biography of Willa Cather breaks off at this point. He had written to me in October 1950: "I may be close to the end by spring." In March 1951 he wrote: "I feel a bit written out with the Willa Cather and am taking a few weeks on odd jobs." A month later he was dead, in his forty-sixth year, and at a time when his life seemed to loom before him rich with the fulfilment of early promise —with a host of literary tasks remaining to be carried out and this one all but completed.

I have heard it said that the cruelest losses are those of the young, who are asked to yield so many of their years before they have had them. Certainly they are no less cruel when they strike in the prime of life, in the midst of creation and achievement, when the false starts and wrong turns, the trials and errors of youth, are behind and an accretion of wisdom and experience is being brought into fullest play. In the case of E. K. Brown, professor of English Literature at the University of Chicago, who had devoted almost a quarter of a century to teaching and writing, the loss seemed deeply cruel and wasteful; in the class, as in the study, he was in the very process of reaping the harvest of a rich life here and abroad that had practiced a close and exacting scholarly experience and discipline.

Fashioned in the schools of his native Canada, which maintained Old World traditions of scholarship and whose liberal-arts faculties even today are dedicated not to preparing young men to be competitors in a competitive society but to giving them wide cultural sympathies and interests, he had pursued his studies at the Sorbonne during the late 1920's. It was there that I first met him. When he arrived in Europe he possessed much more than a smattering of the Romance languages. He spoke French with admirable fluency, and a well-marked copy of Dante showed how assiduously he had cultivated Italian. We sat together on occasions in the classes of the venerable Émile Legouis, the French Chaucerian. I can see Legouis still, noble-browed and white-bearded, declaiming Chaucer in an English lightly touched with Gallic accents that rendered the Gallic in Chaucer admirably vocal. We listened to Louis Cazamian, Brown's principal master in Paris, expound the English humorists with subtlety and psychological insight, and to Charles Cestre of the pointed beard and New England manner, incumbent of the chair of American Literature and Civilization, who presided over textual analysis of Edwin Arlington Robinson's poems at a time

when the poet had not begun to be given his full due in the
United States. Or we sat before Fernand Baldensperger (he
looked then like a patrician painted by Rembrandt), to
whom all American students seemed to flock, as he ex-
pounded foreign influences in Balzac and gave us for the
first time a full appreciation of the values inherent in the
study of comparative literature. Or we might make our
way across the cobbled street to the Collège de France,
where in some unventilated room Joseph Bédier, Gaston
Paris's successor, was still lecturing on the *chansons de
geste*, and Paul Hazard could be heard in the sugared
cadences he brilliantly cultivated, demonstrating how
Pope's *Essay on Man* spread over the Continent to have
strange offspring in Madrid or Muscovy. Or, as was natural
in a great seat of medievalism, we listened to Étienne Gil-
son and marveled at the clarity with which he took us over
the difficult paths of faith and reason, under the illumination of the *Summa* of St. Thomas.

It seemed right and proper that we should have come
across the ocean to the Sorbonne to complete our education in our own literature, for a great school of English
and American studies existed there, set amid opportunities
for the study of other literatures, illuminated by many fine
European minds that had transcended national insularity
to grasp universal ideas and the universality of the creative
impulse. I invoke these memories to suggest the background that furnished the mind of E. K. Brown and
equipped him for his vocation.

From the first he had dedicated himself to literary study
and to teaching. He had many of the qualities of Willa
Cather's Professor St. Peter, and not the least of these was
a capacity alike for communicating ideas to young students
and unraveling the works of the mind. He was an authority
first and foremost in nineteenth-century literature in England and in France, as his painstaking study of Matthew
Arnold (1948) and his earlier examination of the textual
variants in Arnold's prose (1935) had shown. He had
begun with an interest in criticism and poetry but increasingly, during the 1930's, he turned to the study of the great
and capacious novel form which has harbored so much of
the life of three centuries. We lunched almost daily during
those Parisian days in a little *crémerie* on the boulevard
Saint-Michel where E. K. was particularly fond of their

omelette au confiture, and on that pleasant *terrasse* we talked much of Flaubert and James, of Joyce and Proust, of form, of architecture, of what Miss Cather came to describe as the novel *démeublé*; and in due course Brown took his doctorate—the *doctorat-ès-lettres* which is conferred by the French national ministry of education as distinct from that given by the university, and which is the degree sought by Frenchmen desiring to hold a chair in the institutions of higher learning. Brown wrote two theses, the minor on Arnold's texts, and the major on Edith Wharton's novels, which had interested him because of their craftsmanship and the moral values they reflected. But even before the completion of the book on Mrs. Wharton he had begun to read an American novelist he could admire even more. He read and reread the works of Willa Cather with an ever growing interest. His thumbed and worn copies of the novels are marked and underlined with the signs of his close perusal; and at the end of some of them he jotted down the dates of his rereadings. There is a characteristic expression of his firm belief in the value of rereading in the first of his Alexander lectures, *Rhythm in the Novel*, delivered in Toronto little more than a year before the end:

> One of the most illuminating remarks I remember was overheard at a public examination for the licentiate in English at the Sorbonne. The examiner was Émile Legouis. He asked a young man for his impression of education at English and American universities. The student replied that what had impressed him most was the amount of reading expected and accomplished. "Yes," said Legouis, "yes, they read, read, read." He was silent for a full minute. "It would appear," he mused, "that they find something magical in reading."

And Brown added his own comment that "there is nothing magical in reading: it is in rereading that some magic may lie."

Although he had read every novel of Willa Cather's several times, Brown reread them all once and some of them twice while he was writing this book; its pages show how close he always was to his texts. How he came to write this biography he has related in his uncompleted introduction. The story he could not tell was how, face to face with death, knowing that his years were to be shortened, he continued to write—and to write admirably—in the supreme belief that man must pursue his appointed task to the end. Like "Neighbour Rosicky" he had his intimation. There may have been moments of deep inner suffering, of fear before the unknown; but outwardly this was not visible. Scholars, by nature, are not addicted to heroic attitudes; they have none of the swagger of men of action or the boundless physical energy of indefatigable adventurers. The quiet corner, the book, an adequate supply of paper, a well-filled inkpot or convenient typewriter, a pipe or a cigarette and they can conquer worlds. But this doesn't mean that they lack the stuff of heroism. Edward Brown was made of such stuff: he did not allow the supreme warning to discourage him from writing the book he had planned. At his desk the work grew methodically and without a flagging of purpose or style; there was never any divergence from the high critical standards he had always set for himself and there is no trace of hurry in the manuscript. He wrote with all the craft and subtlety—and urbanity—he possessed, catching Willa Cather's "vision of essences" and noting all the little details—how for instance she had misquoted Longfellow's translation from the Anglo-Saxon:

> *For thee was a house built*
> *Ere thou wast born,*
> *For thee was a mould meant*
> *Ere thou of mother camest*

—lines that must have come to have a particular poignancy for him, as they do for us, in the light of what he knew might happen.

He began writing this book in the winter of 1949. Early in 1950 he had several warning bouts of illness, yet by Christmas of that year most of his chapters had been set down and some of them revised. There was additional work done during January and February 1951 and he apparently at that time completed the next to the last chapter. Only the Pittsburgh years and the final years were left unwritten; but detailed notes remained which, together with his well-marked books, have simplified my task. I have also added certain passages to the study of *Death Comes for the Archbishop*, as the notes disclosed Brown had intended to enlarge this chapter. In a number of instances I have grafted into the text, and into the conclusion, certain sentences and paragraphs from Brown's article on Miss Cather which appeared in the *Yale Review* in 1946. With these exceptions, the book follows the text set down by Brown as his widow found it among his papers and as she transmitted it to me for editing and completion.

It is not clear to what extent E. K. Brown intended to explain to his readers some of the problems he encountered in the writing of this biography. He had never met Willa Cather and remembered her only from having seen her aboard a ship in which they made the same crossing from France. The book was to be an account of Miss Cather's life, as he said, but only as it illuminated the art. Miss Cather believed intensely in the artist's right to a private life; her will contains an unqualified prohibition of the publication "in any form whatsoever of the whole, or any part of any letter or letters written by me." This may be regarded, in a very real sense, as a loss to the corpus of her writings, for Miss Cather gave freely of herself in her correspondence, and her letters are touched with the cadence, as with the radiance, of her style; they reflect also, as letters can, the directness and generosity and charm of the personality, its courage and steadfastness. To understand the art of Willa Cather, however, is to understand why she decided that her letters should not be published. She belonged to the addicted "revisionists" of art, and since she could not have the re-editing of her correspondence— moreover, since that correspondence was unrelated to her work except perhaps as furnishing occasional marginal comments on it—she imposed the testamentary restrictions. E. K. Brown was able, however, to read many of her letters and to assimilate the information they contained. His logical course was to use the process to which Boswell alludes—that is, to "melt down" his materials—and this is perhaps what Willa Cather intended. George F. Whicher has expressed the belief that as a result of the novelist's restrictions upon her personal papers "even a judicious examination of her career" is made difficult "if not impossible." He added that we must "resign ourselves to the probability that the critical study of her works cannot be supported by any but superficial understanding of her personality."

Professor Brown has demonstrated, it seems to me, that this need not be so. By the use of the time-honored *témoignage* in the manner of Boswell, and in particular that offered him by Miss Edith Lewis, Miss Cather's friend of many years, who has been virtually a collaborator in the work, by ranging freely into the Virginia background of Willa Cather's childhood, by his visits to Pittsburgh, to Red Cloud and Lincoln, E. K. Brown was enabled to gather up old threads, talk with old friends and with relatives, examine old houses, study the landscape and the scene; and having already saturated himself with the work—that work which Miss Cather chiseled from her life—he arrived at a striking and one might venture to say enduring critical portrait. Willa Cather was so recently in our midst that the portrait has still the aspect of contemporaneity. If he has painted a good portrait, all future material that will be uncovered about Miss Cather's life will heighten the likeness and the coloring, but will not change the countenance he has set down. This is not the commemorative biography of which Lytton Strachey wrote, more funeral oration than life; nor is it a paper figure, as so many biographies are, fashioned out of documents alone. It is the life of a great American novelist of the first half of the twentieth century seen through the windows of her work and through the eyes of those who knew her. It will be read also as the act of courage of a scholar for whom, like Willa Cather's protagonists, only death could be defeat—and even it was to be challenged to the last.

New York City

LEON EDEL

Contents

PART ONE

PART TWO

PART ONE

1

From Virginia to
the Divide

1873–1883

IN AN INTERVIEW that is often quoted, Willa Cather said in 1921—just before the publication of *One of Ours*—that the "years from eight to fifteen are the formative period in a writer's life, when he unconsciously gathers basic material. He may acquire a great many interesting and vivid impressions in his mature years but his thematic material he acquires under fifteen years of age. Other writers will tell you this. Lord Dunsany once told me that he believed he had never used any basic material he had acquired after his fifteenth year." It is a remarkable statement. What is most remarkable is not the obvious thing, the minimizing of the experiences of maturity, but the dismissal of the experiences of early childhood. The traces of the "years from eight to fifteen," roughly the years she had in Webster County, Nebraska, are almost everywhere in Willa Cather's fiction; but the traces of her early years in Virginia are few and faint. She left Virginia when she was nine, and until she wrote the last of her novels, *Sapphira and the Slave Girl*, the first nine years of her life gave her neither a subject nor a theme. There is an uncollected early short story, "A Night at Greenway Court," set at Lord Fairfax's great house a few miles to the southeast of Winchester; but this is only a routine cloak-and-sword piece written when Willa Cather was under the spell of *The Prisoner of Zenda*. Virginia is a somewhat unsubstantial standard of reference in the early chapters of *My Ántonia*, and, disguised as Tennessee, a more substantial standard in "Old Mrs. Harris." Not only does Virginia count for little; its fiction does not offer an important record of early childhood translated into Western terms. The novels are full of interesting adolescents, boys as often as girls, presented with a finely sympathetic understanding, seen very convincingly from within, and these adolescents are often devoted to younger children; but there is very little sense or feeling of what it means to be a young child.

The first nine years were passed in a society of extraordinary stability. Dorothy Canfield, who knew her well during her formative years, does not exaggerate when she says that Willa Cather "was born and lived for what is traditionally the period which most influences personality in a state which had the tradition of continuity and stability as far as they could exist in this country, and in a class which more than any other is always stubbornly devoted to the old ways of doing things." Continuity and stability were values that Willa Cather cherished, and the older she grew, the more she cherished them. It is easy to believe that they owed something of their hold upon her to the ways of life in the rural Virginia of her childhood; but except in *Sapphira* she never cared to link these values in her fiction with the first world she could remember. Edith Lewis, her friend of four decades, has said:

> Her Virginia life was one of great richness, tranquil and ordered and serene. With its freedom from all tension and nervous strain, it may have helped to give her that deep store of vitality which underlay her work. When her family . . . moved west, she felt the break cruelly. But in later years she believed that for her the move was fortunate. Even as a little girl she felt something smothering in the polite, rigid social conventions of that Southern society—something factitious and unreal. If one fell in with those sentimental attitudes, those euphuisms that went with good manners, one lost all touch with reality, with truth of experience. If one resisted them, one became a social rebel. She told once of an old judge who came to call . . . and who began stroking her curls and talking to her in the playful platitudes one addressed to little girls—and of how she horrified her mother by breaking out suddenly: "I's a dang'ous nigger, I is!" It was an attempt to break through the smooth, unreal conventions about little girls—the only way that occurred to her at the moment.

Neither the antebellum South, of which her grandparents and parents often spoke, nor the South in reconstruction which she had known as a child became a temple of her imagination. In the years when she was writing critical papers and reviews she scarcely ever chose a Southern subject or concerned herself with a Southern writer. Her Virginian childhood is a prelude to her years of experience and preparation, not a part of them.

Willa Cather was born in the house of her grandmother, Rachel Elizabeth Boak, in the Back Creek Valley, a little more than ten miles to the west of Winchester, in the Northern Neck of Virginia. Cathers had farmed among the hills of this region, near what was to become the border with West Virginia, since the latter part of the eighteenth century.

The clearest figure among the older generations of the family is James, who was Willa's great-grandfather, and a son of Jasper, who is believed to have emigrated from Ireland. According to manuscript family records, Jasper Cather was at Fort Redstone in western Pennsylvania in the early 1750's; in 1773 his name appears on a tax list of Farquhar County in that state; by 1786 he had come to the countryside west of Winchester and in that year married Sarah Moore in Frederick County. James, one of the seven children of this marriage, was born in 1795 in his father's farmhouse on Flint Ridge only a few miles from the birthplace of Willa. The historian of the Shenandoah Valley, T. K. Cartmell, knew him well. "Mr. Cather," he says, "was largely above the average farmer in intellect. Possessed with rare physical strength and wonderful energy, these qualitites gave him an advantage over weaker men. Always informed on the current topics of the day, his conversational abilities were admirable. Young men were always benefited by having him as a friend." One of the young men who felt the benefit profoundly was a son-in-law, John Purcell, who welcomed every errand that took him to the farmhouse on Flint Ridge—nowhere else in the district was there such talk, amusing, thoughtful, informed, alive. James Cather's grandson, Charles, who was Willa's father, admired him to the end of his days and appears to have taken him as his model in character and manner. James makes a fleeting appearance in *Sapphira and the Slave Girl*, where "his talk had a flavour of old-fashioned courtesy."

The fine strong quality of the man appears in his photograph: a broad brow, benignant eyes, resolute mouth, the set of head and shoulders expressing both firmness and ease.

Of his seven children the one who appears to have inherited the most liberal share of his intellectual energy, his power of speech, his happy unresented dominion over others, was his daughter Sidney. Born in 1828, she was married at nineteen to Mahlon Gore, who had come west from Loudoun County to buy a farm in northwestern Frederick. Fourteen years later Mrs. Gore was left a widow with the farm on the northwestern turnpike, three sons, and a load of unsuspected debt. She saw her opportunity in the reputation of the district as a health resort: sick people flocked there from Eastern and Southern cities, often in such pathetic weakness that they died on the trains, in the railway station at Winchester, in the carriages that took them over the rough twisting roads. Mrs. Gore was at various times postmistress and schoolteacher and farmer, but she was above all manager of the resort called Valley Home, her own house, expanded again and again until for some years it is said to have had as many as fifty rooms. Valley Home is only a couple of hundred yards to the west of Willa Cather's birthplace. It is still a charming house, almost at the center of the little village that is now called Gore because Sidney Gore was for more than a generation its natural and admitted chief. From "its shady front porch behind blooming honeysuckle vines" it looks out as it did in Sapphira's day, over the valley to the south and west and to the heights beyond.

Like many other farmers in the Northern Neck James Cather opposed secession. No dogmatic Unionist, a friend indeed of Henry Clay, who stayed at his house, he nevertheless believed that the special interests of the South could be assured without war, and without the threat of war. Frederick County was not to an important degree a slaveholding neighborhood. The land did not lend itself to the peculiar institution—much of it, like the Back Creek district, was hilly, rocky, and sandy. "Here there were no large, rich farms," Willa Cather says in *Sapphira*, "for the blacks to work, as there were in Loudoun County. Many fieldhands were not needed." Few of the farmers had capital; even before the War between the States most of them were chronically hard up. Many were recently arrived from

Germany or Ireland—there were more Germans and Irish in the valley of Virginia than in any other part of the dominion; others, like Rachel Boak's family, the Seiberts, had come from Pennsylvania. James Cather had twice represented the county in the Virginia House of Delegates; and he was speaking for the opinion that prevailed in western Frederick when as its representative at the secession convention he opposed a violent solution. He appears to have thought with another citizen of Frederick County, Robert Y. Conrad, who declared: "Our present difficulties could have been satisfactorily solved within the Union, but for the premature movements of the States farther south. If no attempt at coercion is made, the best course Virginia can take is to remain peaceably in the Union." That was Mrs. Gore's opinion; and it was her father's.

In the War between the States Winchester is said to have changed hands at least sixty-eight times. The great valley was crucial to both sides. Stonewall Jackson, who did most of his fighting in or near it, believed that "if this valley is lost, Virginia is lost"; while the valley was held, lower Pennsylvania was in constant peril. The valley, as one who fought in Jackson's army has said, "with its detached mountain chains and ranges" was "one of the most remarkable fields for military operations in the country." The main actions were contested from north to south or from south to north, and the Back Creek district was slightly west of the stubborn fighting. But the highway from Winchester to Romney, on which the settlement lay, sometimes saw an entire army; it was along this road that, early in the war, a Confederate force moved at highest speed in an attempt to surprise Lew Wallace.

Again and again bands of marauders, little knots of wounded men, solitary stragglers, passed in front of Valley Home. A group of trigger-happy Union soldiers shot down an elderly neighbor almost in Mrs. Gore's sight. The murder, license, and destruction she saw and the deaths of friends and neighbors fighting in the armies of the Confederacy slowly hardened her heart against the Northern cause; but as late as Gettysburg she could still be horrified and angry at reports of Southern looting and burning and worse across the Pennsylvania border. Her son Howard Gore has said: "She reasoned deeply and dispassionately about every topic that came under her observation and it is quite safe to venture the belief that her judgment called for a continuation of the Union while her heart was enlisted under the flag with a single star."

The journals of this remarkable woman are emphatic, and sometimes eloquent, on the trials she underwent in so exposed a place with no man to protect her or her house. It is clear that she did not need a defender: the simplicity of her character, her manifest kindness, and something that survived in her of James Cather's instinctive dominance of those around him gave her a safety no husband or brother could have assured. The face in her photographs is extraordinarily winning—it is an intelligent and determined face, the eyes suggesting also an intense inner life and the most active kind of sympathy. Looking at it one can understand how Mrs. Gore hated the institution of slavery, how she recoiled from the fact of war, how she lodged, fed, and tended the wounded of both armies with the unquestioning devotion of an evangelical Christian, and how she gave improving lectures to those whose conduct displeased her.

Her journals show that she was an evangelical Christian. Before she was out of her girlhood she experienced conversion, the great event of her life. Her first independent act, the first about which she did not consult her father, was to abandon the moderate Presbyterianism professed by the Cather family as by most of the Scotch-Irish people in the valley, and to become a Baptist. In her new faith she was followed somewhat tardily by her husband, and zealously by one of her brothers, William A. Cather, Willa's grandfather.

William A. Cather married Emily Anne Caroline Smith, also of the Back Creek district, on March 31, 1846. Caroline's father had a tavern known for its good fare and cleanliness far along the turnpike. Her mother, Ann Ellis, was a pattern of pioneer virtues. G. P. Cather, Willa's uncle, writes of her: "Her great and wonderful physique was fortified with perfect health, great strength, powerful endurance and unsurpassed industry, which carried with them a practical knowledge of the work in her line of duty. She would take the wool as it came from the sheep's back, card it, spin it, weave it into cloth, and make it into clothes; and weave it into nice bed clothes and blankets. She would take flax and hackle it, spin it, weave it into linen, and make it into clothes, tablecloths, towels, bedticks and thread. She was a good tidy housekeeper, and a grand good cook. She was scrupulously honest, despised a liar and detested a lazy person, kind to the poor and merciful to the unfortunate. . . . Let us give her credit for much of the good that is in us, and if by chance there should be something wrong about us let us say there is no Ann Ellis about that." Her daughter Caroline greatly resembled her. Caroline appears in her late middle age as the grandmother of Jim Burden in *My Ántonia*. At fifty-five she was still "quick-footed and energetic in all her movements. Her voice was high and rather shrill, and she often spoke with an anxious inflection, for she was exceedingly desirous that everything should go with due order and decorum. Her laugh too was high, and perhaps a little strident, but there was a lively intelligence in it." She was—like her mother— the passage ends, "a strong woman of unusual endurance." She was an ardent Baptist, a reader of the Bible, *The Pilgrim's Progress*, and of such religious tracts as *The Tinker's Blind Daughter*.

William too was strong, and of unusual endurance. Among the family photographs his is the only formidable face, the face of a zealot with cold fiery eyes. In later life he was to prove his strength on a Nebraska farm, but he had proved it much earlier: he was the only member of the family to give unreserved adherence to the Union cause throughout the War between the States, and as marshal after the war had ended. His Unionist belief was shared by his wife and his young sons, and a strong bond with his mother-in-law. He was ostracized by some of his sisters and brothers; but it was not in his nature to be deterred.

In 1851 William Cather settled on a farm a mile or so to the east of Valley Home. The property was known as the Willowshade Farm. At first it consisted of one hundred and thirty acres; but by 1863 it had more than doubled, and extended to three hundred and four acres, one rood, twenty-eight poles, "a tract of land situated in Frederick County, about 10 miles from Winchester, lying on both sides of the North Western Turnpike and on the East banks of Back Creek." On this farm, a large one for that time and place, William Cather built the large and solid house in which Willa lived as a child. The house at Willowshade, the scene of the epilogue in *Sapphira*, is on the north side of the turnpike just where it takes a sharp bend and the village of

Gore comes into sight. It rests at the foot of a gentle slope that begins to rise steeply a little behind the house. Willowshade is a red brick house of three full stories; it has a broad front in which large single windows are evenly spaced, each of them with twelve "lights"; and to the rear there is a brick extension of two stories. A few trees now stand between it and the highway; but in the last century it was indeed shaded by willows, and there was a somewhat formal front garden, and thick shrubbery. The house gives an impression of indestructible solidity; but the moldings, and the woodwork of the entrance lack the fineness as well as the elaboration that give to the old houses in the best streets of Winchester so graceful a charm. Willowshade has something of the pioneer roughness about it. Across the turnpike, limiting the view of the lower rooms, is a steep, almost perpendicular hill, the first in the series of "high hills which shut the winter sun . . . early" from the family at the Mill House in the closing pages of *Sapphira*. To the southwest, beyond the fields of the Back Creek settlement, rise the much higher heavily wooded hills and mountains that the miller's wife in *Sapphira* liked to gaze at in the late afternoons of her last winter.

Not much of the farm could be cultivated. It is chiefly hills, and rocks, and woods. Raising sheep for the Baltimore market was William Cather's main concern as a farmer; and in looking after them he soon had help from his sons.

Charles Fectigue Cather, Willa's father, was born in 1848; his unusual middle name honored his uncle Joseph Fectigue Smith, a doctor who lived in Back Creek Valley and served in the Union army. On December 5, 1872, he married Virginia, the daughter of William Lee Boak and Rachel Elizabeth Seibert. Charles Cather's appearance as a young man is caught up in the description of Mr. Templeton, the husband in "Old Mrs. Harris," one of the *Obscure Destinies*, with "his boyish, eager-to-please manner, his fair complexion and blue eyes and young face." Charles Cather had the courtesy and the gift of speech that marked his grandfather, his equitable mind and patience at work or in dealing with persons, but no great part of his energy. Virginia Boak, two years younger than her husband, was always to have more than enough energy for two. A handsome imperious woman, with a strong will and a strong nature, she was without effort a ruling personality. She had a great power, one who knew her well remembers, for caring about things, everything—whether the coffee was hot, whether a neighbor's child was ill, whether it was a pleasant day for a picnic or a pleasant evening for a dance at Winchester or along the highway to the west, at Capon Springs. She cared greedily for pleasure, but the simplest kinds of pleasure sufficed. She could make an ordinary social call an occasion, and read the most commonplace attention as a fragrant tribute. In the generation following the war, the young couples in rural Frederick, as in so many parts of the South, "were poor and extravagant and jolly. They were much given to picnics and camp meetings in summer, sleighing parties and dancing parties in winter." The war had impoverished a district that had never been rich, and had obscured, if not effaced, many social distinctions and assumptions. In this part of the Northern Neck Willa Cather could not recall any sense of melancholy or embitterment: people had always made do with what they had; now they made do with much less, and were happy.

At first the Charles Cathers lived with Mrs. Boak. William Lee Boak was not a native of the Back Creek district. He was born in Berkeley County in 1805 and married Rachel Elizabeth Seibert of the Back Creek district on May 6, 1830, when she was but fourteen years old. He had a career of some distinction far from Frederick County. He was a justice of the Berkeley County Court; three times a member of the Virginia House of Delegates; and in his later years an official of the Department of the Interior, resident in Washington. He died at his home there on November 2, 1854. Mrs. Boak returned to the Back Creek district, with a family of five—three sons born soon after the marriage, and two daughters much younger. Her father presented her with a house in the village.

Mrs. Boak is still remembered in the valley as a vigorous practical woman, always busy, always efficient, with a talent for being unobtrusively agreeable and helpful. Many of her traits are to be seen in Rachel Blake, the early-widowed daughter of the miller in *Sapphira*. She had Rachel's head and features, the "set of the head, enduring yet determined, the broad, highly coloured face, the fleshy nose, anchored deeply at the nostrils . . . grave dark eyes, too, set back under a broad forehead." She had a special aptness in caring for the sick. Like old Mrs. Harris, "many a time she had gone into a house where five or six children were all down with scarlet fever or diphtheria, and done what she could. Many a child and many a woman she had laid out and got ready for the grave. In her primitive community the undertaker made the coffin,—he did nothing more."

The Boaks had relations in the deep South. Cousins from Louisiana visited them in the Back Creek district. The three sons grew up strongly attached to the Southern cause. One of them died before he was twenty; the two others fought in the army of the Confederacy, and one was killed, William Lee Boak, to whose memory Willa Cather addressed a poem, "The Namesake," in 1902. Their sister Virginia shared their attachment, and to the end of her life cherished her brother's sword, and the Confederate flag. It was by her means that the breach between William Cather and some of his kinfolk and neighbors was finally repaired. Not long after her marriage she gave a large party, driving about the valley to issue her invitations and make sure they were accepted. The record of the Boak attachment to the Confederacy was so excellent that people who shared the Boak views did not care to decline the invitation. Probably the passage of years had made the ostracism of William Cather somewhat absurd, and it was highly inconvenient. At any rate, when the estranged kinfolk and neighbors met him at his daughter-in-law's party, the open quarrel ended.

Meanwhile one of William Cather's sons, George, had married a girl from the North and decided to settle in Nebraska. The climate of Virginia was thought to be perilous to those with weak lungs; at least one of William Cather's daughters was ill with tuberculosis, and other women in the family were threatened. The dry bracing air of Nebraska was an inducement; another was the prospect of living in a Republican state. George Cather took up land in the northwest part of Webster County in 1873. William Cather paid his son a long visit in 1874—5, and in 1877 acquired a farm two or three miles from George's, leaving to Charles the care of the farm at Willowshade. It would be wrong to suppose that William's main reason for emigration was the hostility of neighbors. It would not have been in his character to run from opposition: he was not a man who would, in a phrase of the region, let others "hate him out." No doubt he felt he would be happier in a Republican state; no doubt he wished to do the best he could for the health of sisters and daughters; another reason was the need he felt, as he grew older, to farm where land was level. The hills and vales of Back Creek were an increasing tax on his strength; but his zeal as a farmer was at its height.

II

Willa Cather was born on December 7, 1873,[1] and named after a sister of her father's who died young. All through

---

[1] During the 1870's births in Frederick County were reported by the tax collectors. Roscoe Boak Cather, Willa Cather's brother, is registered with the birth date of June 24, 1877. E. K. Brown confirmed by a search of the records that Willa Cather's name does not appear. In many current works of reference the birth date is given as December 6, 1876, a date incompatible with the registered date of her brother's birth. Brown was told that Miss Cather began to give 1876 as the year of her birth when she was on the staff of *McClure's Magazine* and that she did so because S. S. McClure advised her to subtract two or three years from her age. *Who's Who* from 1909 to 1919 gives Miss Cather's birth year as 1875 and from 1920 to her death as 1876. Brown was able finally to determine the date from a letter written by Willa Cather's father to his brother, George P. Cather, in Nebraska. It is dated January 22, 1874. "Jennie and I were at town today . . . the first time she has been out. . . . We left the baby at home with its Grandma; she said it did not cry once while we were gone. She grows very fast, and is just as good as she is pretty. She is not old enough yet to have that picture taken. We call her 'Willie' after our little sister." There is extant also a letter to George P. Cather of February 1, 1874 from a former schoolmate in Back Creek, who writes: "Charley and Jennie are getting along splendid. Charley don't get to Church till it is half out on account of having to rock the babe to sleep—that's the way of the world." This confirms the birth year as 1873. It is interesting to note that Lesley Fergusson, the young teacher in "The Best Years," the last story Willa Cather completed, made a change in her age: in the high-school records she added two years because "I didn't want to be the class baby, and I hoped I could get a school soon and help out at home." The compunction Lesley felt when she learned she had a school suggests that Willa Cather was not quite at ease about the harmless deception. On the other hand she could treat the same question with high good humor, as in the case of Doña Olivares of *Death Comes for the Archbishop*, who was born, like Willa Cather, in the South where "no birth records were kept; there was no document to prove the age of Isabella Olivares, and she could not be persuaded to admit her true age." How she is persuaded to give a reasonable if not entirely exact age is one of the moments of high comedy in the novel.—L. E.

her childhood and youth she was usually called "Willie," and she liked to think of her name as a bond with her grandfather William Cather and her maternal grandfather William Lee Boak, as well as with her mother's brother, William Lee Boak, Jr. Three more children were born to Charles Cather and his wife before they left for Nebraska: Roscoe Boak Cather was born at Willowshade June 24, 1877; next were Douglass, born in 1880, and Jessica, born in 1881.

The household at Willowshade was full of bustling and many-colored life. The Virginian virtue of hospitality was in force there: cousins came for a meal and stayed for a month. There were always, in the phrase of "Old Mrs. Harris," "plenty of helpers." The hills were "full of solitary old women or women but slightly attached to some household, who were glad to come . . . for good food and a warm bed, and the little present . . . slipped into their carpet-sack when they went away." When one of the children was ill, old Mary Ann Anderson was sent for because she was so kind, tactful, and understanding with a boy or girl obliged to stay in bed. It was almost worth the sufferings of croup, Willa Cather felt, to be able to count on Mary Ann's delightful coddling. The original of Aunt Till, the colored housekeeper at the miller's in *Sapphira*, was a woman of great firmness of character who used to live at Willowshade for weeks at a time, sometimes because she was needed, sometimes merely because she cared to stay.

Edmond de Goncourt remarks in *Chérie* that when one tries to recall one's childhood, it resembles a great empty space in which four or five little happenings start up with a sort of photographic clarity. For Willa Cather one of these happenings was a ride in a steamboat when she was not much more than a year old. She always remembered the terror with which she clutched her mother as she was carried aboard. The happening that in retrospect seemed most dramatic and most suggestive was the meeting described in the epilogue to *Sapphira*. A story had been repeated again and again to Willa Cather as a part of the district lore—of the flight of a beautiful young mulatto slave, the daughter of the woman from whom Aunt Till was drawn. Now this girl was to return after a quarter century of being away from the valley. Her meeting with her mother took place in Mrs. Cather's room at Willowshade, where Willa Cather lay in bed convalescing; it took place there because Mrs. Cather, knowing how much it would mean to the child to look on, arranged that it should. About this meeting between a woman who was now grown old and her daughter, who had passed into a prosperous and alien middle age, Willa Cather's ideas concerning the institution of slavery and other kinds of oppressive relationship often gathered.

Another incident in which her imagination had its part depended on her memory of a passage in *Peter Parley's Universal History*, a work from which Mrs. Boak often read to her. When she was four or five, one way to assure her being quiet and immobile for a long time was to reverse a chair, place it on another, and set the child on the upper chair. This became her chariot, and she would sit upon it in complete silence, listening to an imaginary slave who was repeating to her at intervals: "Cato, thou art but man!" Willa Cather's absorption in this private situation may have suggested to her father and mother that she was perhaps a remarkable personality; they never forgot the picture of the child guiding her chariot and listening to the attendant spirit.

The farm was as pleasant to Willa Cather as the roomy, cheerful house. She did not attend a school—her Grandmother Boak taught her. Mrs. Boak had gone to a good school in Baltimore, she had read much and carefully, and she had an alert mind. Much of the day, in all seasons, however, the girl spent out in the fields with her father. She liked to help herd the sheep, and shared his affection for his favorite shepherd dog, Vic, for whom he made little leather shoes to save her feet from the sharp rocks. He would often carry her on his shoulder, like the grandfather in her poem "The Swedish Mother," which is rich in memories of Willowshade:

> We go big field, 'way up on hill,
> Ten times high like our windmill.
> One time your grandpa leave me wait
> While he call sheep down. By de gate
> I sit still till night come dark;
> Rabbits run an' strange dogs bark,
> Old owl hoot, an' your modder cry,
> She been so 'fraid big bear come by.

> *Last, 'way off, she hear de sheep,*
> *Li'l' bells ring and li'l' lambs bleat.*
> *Then all sheep come over de hills,*
> *Big white dust, an' old dog Nils.*[2]

She had rabbit traps in distant spots in the woods, and when she revisited Willowshade about twelve years after the family had left for Nebraska, the first thing she did was to walk straight to where she had left them, and find them intact.

A hundred yards or so to the west along the road to the village was Back Creek, a sluggish stream except in spring, crossed then by an old suspension bridge. She liked to hang on this bridge and sing: "I stood on the bridge at midnight," though that was scarcely the time she chose. Less than a mile to the southwest was the mill of the Seiberts, where Mrs. Boak had grown up, and there were few things that gave Willa Cather so much pleasure as to talk with the miller in his cool dark mill, or watch the great wooden wheel turning hour by hour.

With Margie Anderson, a young girl who had come to Willowshade as nursemaid and general help, she would go as far as Timber Ridge to visit Margie's mother, Mary Ann, the Mrs. Ringer of *Sapphira*, who "was born interested," had a gift for telling stories, and a homely wisdom about people. She knew the histories of all the families in the region, rich and poor, and all the dramatic events that had become legends among the country people. Her talk was full of wit and fire, it was shot through with the vivid native idiom; and the stories she told, Willa Cather remembered all her life, as she remembered the drives along the mountain roads when she accompanied Mrs. Boak on errands of mercy or medicine, or her mother on visits to cousins, neighbors, or dependents.

The Virginia years ended in 1883, when Charles Cather was persuaded to join his parents and his brother in Nebraska. In February of that year the Willowshade property was sold for six thousand dollars. Most of the furnishings were auctioned. Even Vic, the shepherd dog, was given to a

---

[2] Willa Cather omitted the last two lines here quoted, when she revised the poem for the collected edition of her works.

farmer who lived near by. Parting with almost everything that she knew and cared for made this a time of heartbreak for Willa Cather. There was a climax of sorrow when, just as the family was about to board a train—at that time there was a railroad running through the Back Creek settlement—Vic tore herself free and came running across the fields, dragging her broken chain.

2

Red Cloud:
the Wild Land

1884–1890

THE DESTINATION OF the Cathers was the farm of Willa's grandfather in Webster County, Nebraska. Webster County is in the southern tier, and about halfway across the state. In 1884 it still had the aspect and character of the frontier. The first settlement within its boundaries had been made only fourteen years before. In the summer of 1870 Silas Garber, a captain in the Northern armies in the War between the States, had led a handful of associates and dependents overland southwest from Omaha. The pioneers at once saw that the land in the southern part of Webster County was the best and built their first stockades at Guide Rock in its southeastern corner, and at Red Cloud, some ten miles farther to the west.

Red Cloud was named after a famous and friendly Sioux chief. By the time the Cathers arrived in the county, it was a bustling and promising town, with a population about one half of its present two thousand. It had grown on a slight rise a mile or so to the north of the shallow, broad, and sandy Republican River, which at this point flows only a few miles to the north of the Kansas line. Much of the surrounding countryside had been settled, and here and there tracts were in pasture or under cultivation. The town had its stores and hotels, its smithy and mill, its newspapers and banks. A brick opera house, soon to be a magnet for Willa Cather, stood beside a brick bank. A school had been opened the year after settlement began—many of the newcomers were from New England—and soon after a Methodist church. In 1879 the Republican Valley Railroad had been extended south from Hastings to serve Red Cloud and continued to the west on the present line from St. Joseph to Denver. Soon afterward the eastward line to St. Joseph and Kansas City was completed.

The Virginia colony, in which Cathers were the leaders, had taken up land to the northwest of Red Cloud, close to the western border of the county; and long before 1884 they had a post office called, significantly, Catherton. Into other townships Europeans were flocking, as into almost every region in the state. "Nebraska," it was said in a proclamation from the state department of immigration, "is the last agricultural state in America offering cheap and good homesteads to the landless. . . . Nebraska is the only remaining state wholly and richly agricultural and pastoral where millions of acres are almost donated to the brave pioneers of the world by the generous government of America." Men and women of almost every European nationality were trying to make cornfields where there had been for centuries a sweep of high, rough, shaggy red grass, the "colour of wine-stains." To the north of Catherton there was a settlement of French Canadians holding apart from their neighbors. Spotted across the northern and central tiers of the county were colonies of Germans, Bohemians, Swedes, Danes, and Swiss. All but the Swiss were within a morning's ride of Catherton; and all but the Swiss have important roles in Willa Cather's fiction. In the richer southern parts of the county, near the river, where the cottonwoods grew more luxuriantly, there were families of native American stock.

Charles F. Cather, though he continued to own a large farm and added steadily to his holdings, remained on the land for little more than a year; but his eleven-year-old daughter made an extraordinarily full use of the time. A merchant in Red Cloud who met her during her first years in the state described her to his daughter as "a young curiosity shop." It was the best kind of curiosity, the omnivorous artist's, that took her out delivering mail on horseback, with a pretext for entering many a lonely sod farmhouse in which few native Americans ever cared to set foot. In her essay on Nebraska, written more than twenty-five years after she had left for the East, Willa Cather was still impatient of the incuriosity of her family and other native groups.

Unfortunately, their American neighbors were seldom open-minded enough to understand the Europeans, or to profit by their older traditions. Our settlers from New England, cautious and convinced of their own superiority, kept themselves isolated as much as possible from foreign influences. The incomers from the South—from Missouri, Kentucky, the two Virginias—were provincial and utterly without curiosity. They were kind neighbors—lent a hand to help a Swede when he was sick or in trouble. But I am quite sure that Knut Hamsun might have worked a year for any of our Southern farmers, and his employer would never have discovered that there was anything unusual about the Norwegian. A New England settler might have noticed that his choreboy had a kind of intelligence, but he would have distrusted and stonily disregarded it. If the daughter of a shiftless West Virginia mountaineer married the nephew of a professor at the University of Upsala, the native family felt disgraced by such an alliance.

Willa Cather's own kin conformed to the Southern pattern. Like the grandparents of Jim Burden in *My Ántonia* they were kind to luckless neighbors and sought to encourage those who despaired; but neither Bohemian nor Scandinavian aroused their curiosity or taught them anything about the nature of man or of this prairie country in which European and Eastern American were at first equally alien.

The Bohemians at once drew Willa Cather. It was in the first of her years in Nebraska that she met and admired the girl from whose character and appearance she drew Ántonia Shimerda, and the old man who suggested to her Anton Rosicky. In the Bohemian settlements there were families that had come to America for political and ethical reasons, and some of the older men had the impress of a high European culture. But Willa Cather did not require that for her interest to stir. Simpler men like Rosicky were enough. In a leading editorial devoted to the story that centers on him, Anton Rosicky was described in the *Omaha World-Herald* as "the very stuff of which Nebraska was builded . . . the love of the land . . . combined with hard work . . and a great spirit, and the will to take a beating and do battle again." In foreign-born men and women of this stripe Willa Cather found the most interesting people in her new home.

The old farmwomen, Bohemian and Scandinavian, moved her imagination. In a long story that she did not care to collect, "The Bohemian Girl," she presents the grandmothers gathered at a barn-raising in the northwest part of Webster County. It is the fullest of many such pictures in her fiction:

> The older women, having assured themselves that there were twenty kinds of cake, not counting cookies, and three dozen fat pies, repaired to the corner behind the pile of watermelons, put on their white aprons, and fell to their knitting and fancywork. They were a fine company of old women, and a Dutch painter would have loved to find them there together, where the sun made bright patches on the floor and sent long quivering shafts of gold through the dusky shade up among the rafters. There were fat, rosy old women who looked hot in their best black dresses; spare alert old women with brown, dark-veined hands; and several of almost heroic frame, not less massive than old Mrs. Ericson herself. Few of them wore glasses, and old Mrs. Svendsen, a Danish woman, who was quite bald, wore the only cap among them. Mrs. Oleson, who had twelve big grandchildren, could still show two braids of yellow hair as thick as her own wrists. Among all these grandmothers there were more brown heads than white. They all had a pleased, prosperous air, as if they were more than satisfied with themselves and with life.

Nils, the sensitive and traveled narrator, asks his brother's wife:

> Aren't they the Old Guard? I've just counted thirty hands. I guess they've wrung many a chicken's neck and warmed many a boy's jacket for him in their time.

As he spoke,

> He fell into amazement when he thought of the Herculean labors those fifteen pairs of hands had

performed: of the cows they had milked, the butter
they had made, the gardens they had planted, the
children and grandchildren they had tended, the
brooms they had worn out, the mountains of food
they had cooked. It made him dizzy.

As a young girl Willa Cather felt the vigor and energy in
these old women from Europe; it was later, when she came
out from Red Cloud to stay with her aunts, that she saw
something that in her maturity she set even higher than
vigor or energy—endurance.

When she was a girl, as in her later years, she cared as
much about places as about persons. The high plains between the valley of the Republican and the valley of the
Platte are not conventionally beautiful. In winter they are
as dreary as a desert. "The variegated fields," Willa Cather
wrote in *O Pioneers!* "are all one colour now; the pastures,
the stubble, the roads, the sky are the same leaden grey.
The hedgerows and trees are scarcely perceptible against
the bare earth, whose slaty hue they have taken on. The
ground is frozen so hard that it bruises the foot to walk in
the roads or in the ploughed fields. It is like an iron country, and the spirit is oppressed by its rigour and melancholy. One could easily believe that in that dead landscape
the germs of life and fruitfulness were extinct forever."
"In the cold light," she wrote elsewhere, "even the fresh
snow looked grey, and the frozen weeds sticking up
through it." In all seasons, the Divide (as the high plains
between the Republican and the Blue and between the Blue
and the Platte are often called) was "one of the loneliest
countries in the world."

If it was lonely, it was spacious; and even when Willa
Cather was a little girl she was pleased with broad vistas
and turned to places where her privacy was secure. In the
more hospitable seasons the high plains had a vigorous
beauty to which she responded with joy. The red grass, the
rustling corn (Naples-yellow as she later learned to call its
color in the end of summer), the sunflowers and ironweed
along the soft dirt roads, skies "bright and shadowless,
hard as enamel," were strange to a girl from Virginia, but
delightful. The warm southwest wind that blew with the
beginning of spring was another exhilarating discovery.
"There were none of the signs of spring for which I used to

watch in Virginia," Willa Cather wrote in *My Ántonia*, "no budding woods or blooming gardens. There was only—spring itself; the throb of it, the light restlessness, the vital essence of it everywhere; in the sky, in the swift clouds, in the pale sunshine, and in the warm, high wind—rising suddenly, sinking suddenly, impulsive and playful like a big puppy that pawed you and then lay down to be petted. If I had been tossed down blindfold on that red prairie, I should have known that it was spring." In the heat of summer Willa Cather "used to love to drift along the pale-yellow cornfields, looking for the damp spots one sometimes found at their edges, where the smartweed soon turned a rich copper colour and the narrow brown leaves hung curled like cocoons about the swollen joints of the stem." Trees led a precarious life on the Divide, and Willa Cather "used to feel anxious about them, and visit them as if they were persons."

The stay in the Virginia colony, so rich in impressions that were to pour out in novels and tales, ended sometime in 1885, when Charles F. Cather, who was not born to be a farmer on the prairie, opened an office in Red Cloud where he dealt in loans and mortgages on farm property. He leased a house, which remained the family's home until long after Willa Cather left Nebraska for the East. This house is at the southwest corner of Cedar Street and Third Avenue, one short block from the main street. It is a long, narrow frame house, painted white, one and a half stories high. Something of the rooms downstairs and the life that went on in them has been recorded in "Old Mrs. Harris," the longest of the stories in *Obscure Destinies*. The Cathers' was a crowded household: to the four children they brought with them from Virginia three were added in Nebraska—James, Jack, and Elsie; Mrs. Boak continued to live with them; and Margie Anderson continued to be their servant until her death well on in this century. In the back rooms there was the confusion that numbers always bring unless the mistress of the house is an adroit manager of detail, and Mrs. Cather was never that, though her firm will, supported by her rawhide whip, arrested disorder when it became a tumult. The parlor was always a pleasant room. "The hard-coal burner threw out a warm red glow. A faded respectable Brussels carpet covered the floor, and an old-fashioned wooden clock ticked on the walnut book-

case. There were a few easy chairs, and no hideous orna-
ments about." For Willa Cather the attic with its bare
rafters was the most important part of the house. Her
memory of it is in the description of Thea Kronborg's attic
room and in one of the last of her writings, "The Best
Years," the one Nebraska story in *The Old Beauty and
Others*.

> "Upstairs" was a story in itself, a secret romance.
> No caller or neighbour had ever been allowed to go
> up there. All the children loved it—it was their very
> own world where there were no older people poking
> about to spoil things. And it was unique—not at all
> like other people's upstairs chambers. . . .
>   Lesley and the boys liked space, not tight cubby-
> holes. Their upstairs was a long attic which ran the
> whole length of the house, from the front door
> downstairs to the kitchen at the back. Its great
> charm was that it was unlined. No plaster, no
> beaver-board lining; just the roof shingles, supported
> by long, unplaned, splintery rafters that sloped from
> the sharp roof-peak down to the floor of the attic.
> Bracing these long roof rafters were cross rafters
> on which one could hang things—a little personal
> washing, a curtain for tableaux, a rope swing. . . .
>   In this spacious undivided loft were two brick
> chimneys, going up in neat little stair-steps from the
> plank floor to the shingle roof—and out of it to the
> stars! The chimneys were of red, unglazed brick,
> with lines of white mortar to hold them together.

The children's beds stood side by side; and on a winter
night, with hot bricks at their feet, while the snow sifted in
through cracks in the shingles and sprinkled their faces and
the covers, and through the single small window at the end
of the loft "the white light from the snow and the half-
strangled moon" shone on the floor, the children had some
of their happiest moments. Willa Cather regretted a change
that her mother insisted on as the girl grew older. "Her
mother had said she must have a room of her own. So a
carpenter brought sheathing and 'lined' the end of the long
loft—the end over the kitchen." The little room was "very
like a snug wooden box"; but she could "leave her door

open into the long loft, where the wood was brown and the chimneys red and the weather always so close to one." The loft was no common bedroom—she thought of it as a feudal hall and associated it with lines in Grimm's *Fairy Tales*.

In the Virginia colony Willa Cather had been taught by her grandmother Mrs. Boak and others in the family. In Red Cloud she began to attend school and had extraordinary fortune in her teachers. With three of them, all people of remarkable gifts, she remained in touch for many years, and one was an intimate friend for life. Mrs. Eva J. Case, who is still recalled in Red Cloud as a teacher of literature and foreign languages and a woman of great charm, was one of Will Cather's first teachers. It was probably with her that Willa Cather read *Paradise Lost*, one of her first literary experiences. Mrs. Case later was Superintendent of Public Instruction for Webster County, and something of her nature and her work is recorded in the character of Miss Knightly in "The Best Years." Mrs. Case had a remarkable perception of the moral and intellectual flaws in the town's way of life and was an ally in Willa Cather's efforts to find an environment in which her mind could grow more freely. The other teachers to whom Willa Cather was specially drawn were Mr. and Mrs. A. K. Goudy, and it was an agreeable coincidence that when she was graduated from the Red Cloud high school in June 1890, the two signatures on her diploma were theirs, Mr. Goudy as county superintendent, Mrs. Goudy as principal. The Goudys moved to Lincoln in 1891, when Mr. Goudy became state superintendent, and Willa Cather was much in their company and confidence during the years when she was a student at the University of Nebraska. She admired Mr. Goudy's union of quietness with force, and until Mrs. Goudy died, in 1930, she was one of Willa Cather's intimates.

From gifted people in the town Willa Cather learned more than her teachers could tell her. Not far from the Cather house lived Mrs. Charles Wiener, a brilliant Frenchwoman, married to one of the merchants of Red Cloud. The Wieners spoke French and German and had collected a library extraordinary both in size and in quality. They soon gave Willa Cather the run of it and of their house. What the privilege meant to her she has recorded in

"Old Mrs. Harris," where the Wieners were the models for the Rosens. Willa Cather began to read French and to wish that she could read German; and she began to inform herself about life in France and Germany and in Europe generally. On hot afternoons, when her attic retreat was stifling, she would go over to the Wieners. "She would take a sofa pillow and lie down on the soft carpet and look up at the pictures in the dusky room [the shades were drawn], and feel a happy, pleasant excitement from the heat and glare outside and the deep shadow and quiet within." Mrs. Wiener's house exemplified a kind of culture she had not known, and at once recognized as akin to her spirit. In this household she also found intellectual encouragement: Mrs. Wiener was among the first to appreciate what a remarkable mind Willa Cather had and to urge her to hard work.

A German music teacher music from whom she drew Wunsch in *The Song of the Lark* was another source of information about European life and culture. Willa Cather was no Thea Kronborg: if she delighted in listening to music and in talking about it, she had no interest in learning to play or to sing. The old music teacher used to ask the mother of another and more docile pupil what he should do with "that Cather girl," for he could find no argument that would induce her to practice as she must if she would become even a mediocre musician. Wisely he decided that he would give her her head, overlook what she could not or would not do, and spend his time with her playing or talking about great music and musicians, or about the life and culture he had known in European cities.

William Ducker, "Uncle Billy" to so many children in Red Cloud at the time when Willa Cather knew him, was the first to make Greek and Latin literature come alive for her. Of English birth, he had come to Waukegan, Illinois, when he was eighteen to join older brothers who had a store there. His formal education was slight, but he had a passion for learning and a love for poetry seldom found together. His brothers allowed him a good deal of leisure, and much of this he gave to reading ancient writers, particularly the poets. When he was fifty he came to Red Cloud with members of his family, who opened a store in which he might sometimes be found leaning over a counter with the *Iliad* or the *Æneid* or the *Odes* of Anacreon lying open before him. The schools of Red Cloud did not satisfy him; and he gave his own children lessons in the classics and other subjects to supplement the meager official schedule. He too found something remarkable in Willa Cather, and he supervised her reading as closely as if she were a daughter. After she had begun to study at the University of Nebraska, she continued to read Latin and Greek with Mr. Ducker in the vacations; and she contrasted his passion for poetry with the somewhat arid scholarship she found in the classical instructors in Lincoln. Ducker's sudden death in the terrible drought-ridden summer of 1893 was one of her first deep griefs. Willa Cather had just left his house one afternoon when she was suddenly summoned by one of his children who came running after her. Mr. Ducker was dead when she reached him. He lay on the couch with the *Iliad* open on the floor beside him. "There are always dreamers on the frontier," she wrote in *O Pioneers!* He was one of the most memorable.

The pleasure that Willa Cather found in the company of older people, and the readiness with which they accepted her, appear very sharply in "Two Friends," the story with which *Obscure Destinies* closes. The two middle-aged men —one of them was the merchant Mr. Miner—pass the early part of their evenings together; it is the only time they see each other. In colder months they sit in the store that one of them owns; on any night that is warm enough they draw two chairs out on the broad sidewalk. They allow the narrator of the story, from the time she was ten years old, to sit within hearing of their wide-ranging talk and to make what she can of it. A whole evening's discussion might pivot on a scientific novelty, a play, a reminiscence of the older and better West, or the life-history of a remarkable farm family in this or a neighboring county.

I liked to listen to those two because theirs was the only "conversation" one could hear about the streets. The older men talked of nothing but politics and their business, and the very young men's talk was entirely what they called "josh"; very personal, supposed to be funny, and really not funny at all. It was scarcely speech, but noises, snorts, giggles, yawns, sneezes, with a few abbreviated words and slang expressions which stood for a hundred things.

The original Indians of the Kansas plains had more
to do with articulate speech than had our promising
young men.

It is a revealing passage. There was scarcely a man or a
woman in Red Cloud who had any "conversation," who
knew anything worth hearing and could tell something of
it, whom Willa Cather did not frequent. Doctors, lawyers,
clergy, men of affairs, she listened to them all; and when
there was a woman such as Mrs. Miner, whom she drew as
Mrs. Harling, Ántonia's employer, Willa Cather never tired
of eliciting her experience of life and the conclusions she
had drawn from it.

Just beyond the southeastern edge of the town, in a
house much larger and much more grandly furnished than
any in Red Cloud, lived the most famous man in Webster
County, the leader in the first settlement at Guide Rock
and Red Cloud, Silas Garber. In 1873 he had been elected
to the state legislature to represent Webster and adjacent
counties; and in 1875 he became Governor of Nebraska.
(He passed, said a local paper, the *Nation*, "in three years
from a 'dug-out' on yonder bank to the Capitol at Lincoln,
from the organization of Webster County to the reorgani-
zation of the State of Nebraska.") In 1879 he was thrown
from a carriage and suffered injuries that condemned him
to an inactive life. Silas Garber and his wife, a Southern
woman of extraordinary charm and color, took little part
in the life of the town; but he had broadly scattered invest-
ments in land and was the principal power in a local bank.
Presidents of railroads, politicians from Lincoln, and other
notables stayed at the Garber house. It was the center of a
larger kind of life than any other that Willa Cather knew.
She was often in it, and as she came to know Governor
Garber and to hear the story of his life, he symbolized for
her the ideal pioneer. Red Cloud and Webster County were
passing into another phase, in which Silas Garber was a
relic of a bolder past, full of a promise that was not to be
realized. From him she drew Captain Forrester in *A Lost
Lady*, who "looked like the pictures of Grover Cleveland"
and whose "clumsy dignity covered a deep nature, and a
conscience that had never been juggled with."

The cemetery of Red Cloud lies at the southwest of the
town on a wind-swept height from which the ground drops

sharply to the south and the west. The tombstones are conventional and most of them small; but at the center of the cemetery rests a rugged reddish granite boulder of massive size with the name and dates of Silas Garber. The boulder would stir the imagination of a casual visitor: it has a place in *A Lost Lady*. Captain Forrester, ailing like Governor Garber, and like him impoverished in his last years, sits for hours in his garden by "a red block of Colorado sandstone, set on a granite boulder in the midst of the gravel space around which the roses grew." The red block was a sun-dial; and block and boulder were removed to mark the captain's grave. Governor Garber was the largest personality to come within Willa Cather's view when she was a girl. In her own generation she found no one with his stamp, and she never resigned herself to the disappearance of the generation of the founders. "The Old West had been settled by dreamers, great-hearted adventurers who were unpractical to the point of magnificence; a courteous brotherhood, strong in attack but weak in defence, who could conquer but could not hold."

II

Persons were the most important aspect of the town to Willa Cather in her girlhood. But they were not her sole resource. The opera house was a magical place, and the actors and actresses who played there were an enchantment. "Half a dozen times during each winter, a travelling stock company settled down at the local hotel and thrilled and entertained us for a week." As soon as posters began to appear "on the side of a barn, on the lumberyard fence, in the 'plate-glass' windows of drug stores," the children on their way home from school would pause and study them, choosing which plays or operas they would ask to see, and debating whether their parents would allow them to go only on the first and last nights or whether they might hope to attend every other night during the company's all too brief stay. The company usually arrived on the evening train from the east; and the children would walk the mile to the station—along a sidewalk that crossed the fields—often drawing younger brothers and sisters on sleds. The actors and actresses seemed like creatures from another planet.

"If by any chance one of the show ladies carried a little dog with a blanket on, that simply doubled our pleasure." Everything the company did during their stay at the hotel evoked curious and favorable comment. They were almost as much a show as the plays and operas they performed, such plays as *The Corsican Brothers, Damon and Pythias, The Count of Monte Cristo*, such operas as *The Mikado, The Chimes of Normandy, The Bohemian Girl*. This last was, in memory at least, the one that most affected Willa Cather; it found a way into more than one of her stories.

The companies were not of the first order, but when "old Frank Lindon in a frilled shirt and a velvet coat blazing with diamonds, stood in the drawing room of Madame Danglars and revealed his identity to Madame de Morcerf, his faithless Mercedes, when she cowered and made excuses, and he took out a jewelled snuff-box with a much powdered hand, raised his eyebrows, permitted his lip to curl, and said softly and bitterly—'a fidelity of six months,' then we children were not in the opera house at Red Cloud, we were in Madame Danglars' salon in Paris." In a nostalgic letter to the *Omaha World-Herald*, written as long afterward as 1929, Will Cather recalled the effect of the old operas and plays and affirmed that they were one of the great imaginative elements in her youth. No movie, she thought, not even a Chaplin comedy, could do for a later generation what the plain old opera house with its scratch companies of beginners and veterans had done for hers.

Books of many kinds mattered to her, even more than the operas and the plays. She was interested in the history of the Western plains and the Mississippi Valley; and in Parkman's volume on La Salle and in his *Oregon Trail* she found aspects of this described in a prose that delighted her. The main paths of English fiction in the nineteenth century were another resort—George Eliot, Hardy, Stevenson, and Kipling in especial. She had already begun to take what proved to be a passing pleasure in Tennyson—the Tennyson of the *Idylls*—and in Byron's narratives. *Sartor Resartus* and *The French Revolution* were to exercise an influence the most decisive of all.

There was also the river. The Republican has often changed its course and there is no trace above water of the

pirate headquarters on a large sandy island in which Willa
Cather, her two brothers next in age, Roscoe and Douglass, and many friends spent pleasant summer days. Stevenson, Mark Twain, and many a humbler source combined with the misshapen roots of trees, the odd configura-
tions of sand and the grotesque contours of the island to
make of this retreat a place of high childish romance.
Much of what the river and the island meant to her is
recorded in an early story, "The Treasure of Far Island":

> Of all the possessions of their childhood's Won-
> derland, Far Island had been dearest. . . . Long be-
> fore they had set foot upon it the island was the goal
> of their loftiest ambitions and most delightful im-
> aginings. . . . They had even decided that a race of
> kindly dwarfs must inhabit it and had built up a
> civilization and historic annals for these imaginary
> inhabitants, surrounding the sand bar with all the
> mystery and enchantment which was attributed to
> certain islands of the sea by the mariners of Greece.

It was Willa Cather who gave imaginative names to the
several parts of the long sandy island—and to many other
places of adolescent resort: the Silvery Beaches, the Ut-
termost Desert, the Salt Marshes, the Huge Fallen Tree.
"The Treasure of Far Island" was later to be remolded into
a different tale, a little masterpiece, "The Enchanted Bluff."
The hold the memory of river and isle had upon Willa
Cather's imagination as a place where her childhood was
eternally enshrined may be judged by the dedicatory lines
she inscribed in the first edition of her poems, to her brothers, in which she remembered the "Odysseys of summer
mornings" and the "starry wonder-tales of nights in
April. . . ."

> *Of the three who lay and planned at moonrise,*
> *On an island in a western river*
> *Of the conquest of the world together.*

Another kind of romance entered into the children's explorations of the countryside when they learned at school
about Coronado's expedition in quest of the seven golden

cities. The orthodox view was that Coronado had not come as far north as the Nebraska line; but there were many in the state then, and there are some now, who believed that he had traveled along the Republican River. The children had no doubt that he had done so; they were convinced that the great captain had paused within sight of their citadel. The debate concerning Coronado was the first link in the long chain that was to bind Will Cather to the Southwestern country and the Spanish explorers and missionaries.

Opera house and river island were invitations to her imagination. So were the European families she always saw when she visited her aunts Mrs. G. P. Cather and Mrs. Andrews in Catherton township, and on the streets of Red Cloud, where on many evenings there were more farmers than townsfolk.

The town as she knew it in the 1880's has been described in *The Song of the Lark* with the name of Moonstone. Approached from the river, it began with the red Burlington "depot" and the settlement that had grown up about it—a roundhouse, a restaurant or two, and some modest houses. A boardwalk and dirt road led north across the fields and up a hill close to the Catholic church and the cemetery. It rose past some small houses until on a slightly higher rise it reached the main part of Red Cloud, where there was a occasional house of two full stories, and on the main street an impressive expanse of brick. To the west of the main street lived the important and more or less wealthy, the Cathers among them; to the east, on streets that have altered little in half a century, "the humbler citizens, the people who voted but did not run for office." Those who lived to the west had the usual indifference to the homes and ways of the respectable poor; but Willa Cather preferred the eastern streets when she took one of the younger children for a walk or for a ride in carriage or express wagon. She had a strong pleasure in the unpretending simplicity—old women washing clothes in back yards, men sitting at front doors smoking a pipe. In the quiet streets there were few of the elms and pines that dragged out a somewhat precarious life in front of the larger houses to the west. Instead the cottonwood, one of her great pleasures, "had its way and spread in luxuriance."

III

Among many of the poorer people her curiosity was not disliked, but in both east and west there were some families stirred to disapprove, after the fashion of a small town anywhere, of a young girl who was obtrusively unconventional. Much of the disapproval centered in one peculiar pursuit, which began with the arrival of the personal belongings of an uncle who had died not long after he became a doctor. The presence of medical instruments in the household strengthened her already lively interest in zoology, a pursuit that fascinated Mr. Ducker about as much as epic poetry. She had more than a passing wish to become a doctor, and she understood that she could not progress in zoological science unless she performed experiments on animals. Her medical interest extended beyond the usual terminus of a physician's care and curiosity to include embalming.

The echo of the conflict between the young experimenter and the stuffily correct townsfolk is clearly to be heard in the remarkable high-school commencement address that Willa Cather, aged sixteen, delivered in the opera house on June 5, 1890. Her topic was "Superstition versus Investigation." These forces, she declared, had contended for mastery since the dawn of history. "The ancient orientals," she continued in language that must have been all too clear to the conservatives in her audience, "were highly civilized people, but were dreamers and theorists who delved into the mystic and metaphysical, leaving the more practical questions unanswered, and were subject to the evils of tyranny and priestcraft. Those sacred books of the east we today regard as half-divine; we are not apt to think as we read those maginficent flights of metaphor that the masses of people who read and believed them knew nothing of figures. It is the confounding of the literal and the figurative that has made atheists and fanatics throughout the ages." After an allusion to Carlyle, who was for more than twenty years to be her special modern prophet, she contrasted the Greeks with the ancient Hebrews. "The Greeks lacking the intense religious fervor of the Orient entertained broader views. Their standard of manhood was one of practical worth. They allowed no superstition, religious, political or social, to stand between them and the truth, and suffered exile, imprisonment and death for the right of opinion and investigation." In the Middle Ages, superstition regained the mastery. "All the great minds were crushed for men were still ruled by the iron scepter of fear and it was essential that they should remain ignorant. Superstition has ever been the curse of the church and until she can acknowledge that since her principles are true, no scientific truth can contradict them, she will never realize her full strength." Superstition sustained a major defeat from Francis Bacon. "In the Elizabethan age, a book was written asserting that nature is the only teacher, that no man's mind is broad enough to invent a theory to hold nature, for she is the universe. With the publication of the *Novum Organum* came a revolution in thought, scientists ceased theorizing and began experimenting. Thus we went painfully back to nature, weary and disgusted with our artificial knowledge, hungering for that which is meat, thirsting for that which is drink, longing for the things that are. She has given us the universe in answer."

Against this vast background Willa Cather began to deal with the issue on which she had offended local opinion:

It is the most sacred right of man to investigate; we paid dearly for it in Eden; we have been shedding our heart's blood for it ever since. It is ours; we have bought it with a price.

Scientific investigation is the hope of our age, as it must precede all progress; and yet upon every hand we hear the objections to its pursuit. The boy who spends his time among the stones and flowers is a trifler, and if he tries with bungling attempt to pierce the mystery of animal life he is cruel. Of course if he becomes a great anatomist or a brilliant naturalist, his cruelties are forgotten or forgiven him; the world is very cautious, but it is generally safe to admire a man who has succeeded. We do not withhold from a few great scientists the right of the hospital, the post mortem or experimenting with animal life, but we are prone to think the right of experimenting with life too sacred a thing to be placed in hands of inexperienced persons. Nevertheless, if we bar our novices from advancement, whence shall come our experts?

But to test the question by comparison, would all the life destroyed in experimenting from the beginning of the world until today be as an atom to the life saved by that one grand discovery for which Harvey sacrificed his practice and his reputation, the circulation of the blood? There is no selfishness in this. It came from a higher motive than the desire for personal gain, for it too often brings destitution instead. Of this we have a grand example in the broken-down care-worn old man who has just returned from the heart of the Dark Continent. But perhaps you still say that I evade the question, has any one a right to destroy life for scientific purposes? Ah, why does life live upon death throughout the universe?

Investigators have styled fanatics those who seek to probe into the mysteries of the unknowable. This is unreasonable. The most aspiring philosopher never hoped to do more than state the problem, he never dreamed of solving it. Newton did not say how or why every particle of matter in the universe attracted every other particle of matter in the universe. He simply said it was so. We can only judge these abstract forces by their effect. Our intellectual swords may cut away a thousand petty spiderwebs woven by superstition across the mind of man but before the veil of the "Sanctum Sanctorum" we stand confounded, our blades glance and turn and shatter upon the eternal adamant. Microscopic eyes have followed matter to the molecule and fallen blinded. Imagination has gone a step farther and grasped the atom. There, with a towering height above and yawning death below even this grows sick at soul. For over six thousand years we have shaken fact and fancy in the dice box together and breathlessly awaited the result. But the dice of God are always loaded, and there are two sides which never fall upward, the alpha and omega. Perhaps when we make our final cast with dark old death we may shape them better.

This discourse, which like Jim Burden's "stated with fervor a great many things" the speaker "had lately discovered," is still remembered as a startling dissonant note in a conventional program. Among the flowers and the evergreens, with a festoon bearing the legend "1890," a male quartet and a female duet had rendered appropriate music and song. There were three graduates. A boy developed the theme of "Self-Advertising," with which "he was thoroughly conversant"; and his counsels "if followed generally would be a great boon to those men who think that advertising doesn't pay." Another boy, the son of a rich moneylender, addressed himself to the topic "New Times Demand New Measures and New Men," proving "what close application to study in early childhood will do for those who improve the opportunity." We are in the world of Bayliss Wheeler in *One of Ours*, and of Ivy Peters in *A Lost Lady*. "They would drink up the mirage, dispel the morning freshness, root out the great brooding spirit of freedom, the generous, easy life of the great land-holders. The space, the colour, the princely carelessness of the pioneer they would destroy and cut up into profitable bits, as the match factory splinters the primeval forest. All the way from the Missouri to the mountains this generation of shrewd young men, trained to petty economies by hard times, would do exactly what Ivy Peters had done when he drained the Forrester marsh." Between the addresses of the two boys and Willa Cather's there was an interlude of music and song. Then came the "masterpiece of oratory," with "its line of thought well carved out," in which Willa Cather linked her defiance of local currents of opinion with the history of genius and of heresy.

Will Cather was already beginning to feel that the conventionalism of Red Cloud was a denial of life itself, a network of caution, evasion and negation. In a chapter of *My Ántonia* which was much resented in the town she recalls that the girls refrained from exercise as from something inelegant if not indecent, and "stayed indoors in winter because of the cold, and in summer because of the heat." Even when they danced, their bodies seemed not to move inside their clothes—"their muscles seemed to ask but one thing—not to be disturbed." What kind of life would they have in comparison with the sturdy pioneers who had founded the town? "The Black Hawk boys looked forward to marrying Black Hawk girls, and living in a brand-new little house with best chairs that must not be sat upon, and hand-painted china that must not be used." Willa Cather had no intention of taking the mold that was prepared for her generation. She offered a challenge that was much more obtrusive than her preoccupation with zoological experiments. In her high-school days she wore her hair shingled, shorter than many of the boys. Her clothes and hats were also boyish: a starched shirt, a tie, and a hat almost like a boy's. She did not care to be called Willa; many of her friends used Willie, but to this she preferred Will or Billie; and it gave her a particular satisfaction when a perceptive, appreciative person would call her Dr. Will.

A young girl who dressed like a boy, preferred the conversation of unusual older men to most of the pleasures sought by the other boys and girls of the town, and was reputed to hold dangerous opinions about religion as well as to enjoy cutting up animals, was an alien creature in what she was to call a "bitter, dead little Western town." About her, as about Jim Burden, circulated the whisper that there was "something queer" and unsound in so complete a rebel. Willa Cather was under the spell of the Nebraska countryside, and she was under the spell of philosophy, science, history, and the arts. The town was not a place where either spell could work. In 1890 she made a choice between the two kinds of interest which were to divide her being for the rest of her life, and it is recorded with modifications in "Old Mrs. Harris": she went to Lincoln to complete her preparation for the University of Nebraska.

3

Lincoln: the Striving
Years

1891–1895

WILLA CATHER ARRIVED in Lincoln at the end of the
summer of 1890. She still wore her hair very short and
straight, her hats and clothes were boyish, and in more
important ways she was determined to obey what she
thought to be the law of her individual nature. She came
expecting to encounter teachers as speculative as William
Ducker and as responsive to beauty in literature; as civilized as Mrs. Wiener; and above all with a store of scientific knowledge far beyond that in any mind in Red Cloud.

A full year was to pass before she could become a student in the University of Nebraska. Like many of the
smaller institutions in the state the high school at Red
Cloud did not offer adequate preparation for a university
course. It was especially weak in scientific instruction. The
Latin School, a preparatory academy with a two-year program, had been established at Lincoln primarily to enable
students from other parts of the state to make up their
deficiencies. Willa Cather was enrolled in the senior year,
or "Second Prep." Members of the university faculty
taught most of the courses, and their teaching has been
remembered as effective and stimulating. William Linn
Westermann recalls that while the "preparatory" class in
Greek was waiting for the instructor to begin the first
lesson the door opened and a head appeared, with short
hair and a straw hat; a deep masculine voice inquired
whether this was where the class in elementary Greek was
meeting; a boy nodded that it was; and as the newcomer
opened the door wide and revealed a girl's figure and skirts,
the entire class burst into laughter. Willa Cather, unruffled,
quietly took her place.

Willa Cather's instructor in English, Professor Ebenezer Hunt, who was soon to say to her: "Life is one damned grind, Cather," was alert for signs of originality in writing. Late in the winter he assigned a long theme on the topic: "The personal characteristics of Thomas Paine as judged from his writings." There was alarm among some of Hunt's friends and colleagues. The "filthy little atheist," as a President of the United States was to call him, was an inappropriate theme for the speculations, or studies, of preparatory students in pious Lincoln. Hunt yielded to advice, and scoring out "Paine," he substituted "Carlyle." Members of the class recall that on the day when Hunt returned to the themes, he wrote on the blackboard a sentence from one of them, Willa Cather's: "Like the lone survivor of some extinct species, the last of the mammoths, tortured and harassed beyond all endurance by the smaller though perhaps more perfectly organized offspring of the world's maturer years, this great Titan, the son of her passionate youth, a youth of volcanoes and earthquakes and great unsystematized forces, rushed off into the desert to suffer alone." This sentence, surviving in yellowed notes at Lincoln, and still repeated when classmates meet at street corners, reveals much more about Willa Cather than about Thomas Carlyle. So does the rest of the theme: there is scarcely a mention of his "personal characteristics." Like the essential parts of the graduation address of the preceding spring this paper is intensely emotional; but here the emotion is almost unrestrained, though far from the ebullience of Carlyle. In a deeper likeness to the graduating address, the theme expresses Willa Cather's sense of being at variance, even at war, with the world surrounding her and pressing upon her. In what Hunt shrewdly took to be the key sentence she has translated into general terms her individual problem—that of nonconformity in a small town—which later was to be retranslated into the larger sense of tragedy in the supersession of the heroic pioneer generation of Nebraska by the neat petty generation of Ivy Peters and Bayliss Wheeler.

Hunt was so pleased by the theme that without consulting its author he arranged for its appearance in the local paper, the *State Journal*, where it was published on March 1, 1891. A note on the editorial page drew attention to "Some Personal Characteristics of Thomas Carlyle" as the work of a student at the university, "a young girl sixteen years of age who comes from Webster County." "A careful reading," Charles H. Gere, the editor, declared, "will convince any student of literature that it is a remarkable production, reflecting not a little credit on the author and the university."

Thirty years afterward the appearance of her theme in print at that time seemed to Willa Cather to have been a decisive event. She had come to Lincoln intending to take a chiefly scientific course, and later to specialize in medicine. The sight of her work in print, and no doubt the commendation it drew, had an effect upon her which she could only describe as "hypnotic." Henceforth it was clear that her aim must be to write. Miss Mariel Gere, a classmate and lifelong friend, who followed a scientific program, cannot recall among "numberless discussions of various topics" from 1891 to 1895 any that touched on science. She does not believe that Willa Cather retained "any interest in science worth mentioning."

The courses Willa Cather attended in her four years at the University of Nebraska were primarily literary. In her first and second years her principal studies were in classics and in English. The records of the university do not include her grades. It is clear that her ability continued to be recognized in the department of English: in each of these years she was permitted to substitute advanced courses in literature for the courses normally required. Her interest and competence in Greek are shown by her election in her second year of a course in the Greek lyric; and she was prone to quote Greek on unlikely occasions. If there are no records of her grades, her contemporaries recall her in those years as working very long hours, and distinguishing herself in both the linguistic and the literary courses that constituted most of her program.

She had no intention of becoming a scholar, and some of the courses she took seemed to her pedantic and sterile. What she desired from the classics was the experience of great literature and the knowledge of great civilization. In the classical courses at Nebraska, as at most universities, there was altogether too much gerund-grinding, too much about *hoti* and the enclitic *de*. The great initiation promised for the truly elect was into the mysterious classifications of Sanskrit verbs. Even the classicist from whom she learned most, James T. Lees, was notable for precision rather than insight. What she had hoped the teachings of the classics would give in terms of literature and civilization she has shown in *My Ántonia* in her rendering of Jim Burden's response to the inspired teaching of Gaston Cleric, an imagined figure, superior to any of Willa Cather's instructors.

> He could bring the drama of antique life before one out of the shadows—white figures against blue backgrounds. I shall never forget his face as it looked one night when he told me about the solitary day he spent among the sea temples at Paestum: the soft wind blowing through the roofless columns, the birds flying low over the flowering marsh grasses, the changing lights on the silver, cloud-hung mountains. . . . I remember vividly another evening, when something led us to talk of Dante's veneration for Virgil. Cleric went through canto after canto of the "Commedia," repeating the discourse between Dante and his "sweet teacher," while his cigarette burned itself out unheeded between his long fingers. I can hear him now, speaking the lines of the poet Statius, who spoke for Dante: "*I was famous on earth with the name which endures longest and honours most. The seeds of my ardour were the sparks from that divine flame whereby more than a thousand have kindled; I speak of the 'Aeneid,' mother to me and nurse to me in poetry.*"

The words from the twenty-first canto of the *Purgatorio* are very close to Charles Eliot Norton's translation. The sort of teaching that Willa Cather desired she might have had if Norton's favorite pupil, George Edward Woodberry, had found Lincoln and the University of Nebraska agreeable to his temper and his aims. In 1882, after three years as professor of English, he was engaged in such spirited controversy with the chancellor that both parties were encouraged, if not required, to leave the institution. In the year that Willa Cather arrived in Lincoln, Woodberry became professor of comparative literature at Columbia, and his course on the Epic was exactly what Willa Cather longed for, and indeed required—a study of ideas, person-

alities, and forms conducted by a man to whom all three
were living realities.

His successor at the University of Nebraska was a man
of very different stamp, and Willa Cather's aversion from
his approach to literature became an important fact in the
history of her mind and art. Lucius A. Sherman, a graduate of Yale, had taught in an Eastern school for a few
years before coming to Nebraska in 1882 as head of the
department of English. His interest was about as wholly
literary as Woodberry's; but, as his books make very plain,
it was not the ideas, the personalities, and the forms, but
the laws he could frame that really interested Sherman. He
made an exhaustive study of sounds as expressions of emotion. "The vowel of pain," he wrote in his *Elements of
Literature and Composition*, is $\bar{o}$, and its best supporting
sounds are *g* hard, *r*, and *w*, with the vowel accompaniments of *uo*, *au*, *a*, *u*, and *oi*." He devised elaborate dia-
grams for the analysis of words, in which such a term as
bicycle was judged by two tests, "ideals of the beautiful"
and "ideals of the true." The ideals of the beautiful he
described as "adornment," "symmetry," "pleasure," and
"form"; the ideals of the true as "construction" and "reliability." "A bicycle," he opined, "is not a thing of beauty,
although every effort has been made, in its construction, to
secure symmetry and comfort for the eye. After the sensation of the outline, and of the lacquer and polish, we
recognize the proportion, and the finish of the instrument,
and begin to be conscious of the pleasure of the motion it
invites." The bicycle satisfies more nearly the tests of "construction" and "reliability": it is indeed notable for "its
staunchness and safety." Sherman worked out similar tests
for more complex kinds of form in art, for the organization of incident and the revelation of character. He delighted in long sets of minute questions. About the mother
of Coriolanus he inquired, Miss Olivia Pound remembers,
in one seemingly interminable test: "What did the noble
matron Volumnia say then?" Willa Cather's answer ran:
"The noble matron Volumnia then said 'Bow-wow.' " She
had many courses with Sherman, but this was her essential
judgment of his mechanical approach to literature. When a
younger member of the Cather family enrolled more than a
decade later in a course of Sherman's, Willa Cather tele-
graphed to insist on cancellation. It gave her great pleasure

when, during her years in Pittsburgh, she met Ian Mac-laren newly returned from Lincoln and conversation with Sherman, to find that he dismissed Sherman's analysis of his own work in terms of "effects of degree" and "effects of tone" as fantastic and sterile, as well as comic.

Sherman's systematic studies seem silly enough; but there is scarcely a chapter in any of his books that does not have a valuable perception. The perceptions are not wholly independent of his systems. His weakness was that he could not discern when his systems led him into the rigidities of pedantry; he lacked to a startling degree what Matthew Arnold called literary tact. Unfortunately Willa Cather rejected him entire. Forever after she was suspicious of complicated or systematic literary analysis. In general, criticism, as she practiced it, was but purely personal response, unsupported by argument and occasionally veering into fantasy.

This was the kind of criticism she wrote in "Shakespeare and Hamlet," a remarkable paper prepared when she was a student in Sherman's class in Shakespeare, a course for juniors to which she was admitted in her freshman year. The paper was printed in the *State Journal*, in the Sunday issues of November 1 and 8, 1891. Her method appears in her account of Shakespeare's interest in the material:

> I don't think Shakespeare had any definite purpose even in writing Hamlet. It was not like him to write a play that should be a puzzle for all time to come. He probably read the legend, felt sorry for the young prince, and as an expression of his sympathy wrote about him. He probably had no intention of giving the drama any more of himself than he gave to any other of his plays. The Danish prince had nothing in common with him except that both were misunderstood. He gradually grew into the play as he wrote it, without any special reason. Perhaps outside matters bore more heavily upon him than usual. It may be his feeling and individuality were wrought up intensely and crept into the play which he happened to be writing.

This has the genuine mark of Willa Cather. It is the kind of explanation that she often gave in later years for her own interest in subjects, and for the way in which she had dealt with the subjects once they had demanded expression.

II

At the beginning of her sophomore year, in the fall of 1892, Willa Cather became one of the editors of the undergraduate literary periodical, the *Hesperian*, and shortly afterward its mainstay. One of her associates remarked years later: "The truth is the *Hesperian* was Willa practically. . . . The rest of us looked wise and did nothing. The sheet would have been rolled into a scroll and gone *thither* if Willa had not worked like a nigger." Willa Cather contributed verse, criticism, dialogues, satirical sketches of students, and, above all, stories. It is the stories that matter.

Her first published story had appeared six months earlier, on May 21, 1892, in a Boston literary weekly called the *Mahogany Tree*. It was probably submitted on Willa Cather's behalf by her English instructor, Herbert Bates, a young New Englander and a Harvard graduate who held the faith of his teacher, Barrett Wendell, on the importance of courses in composition. In her mature years Willa Cather believed that Bates had stimulated her to publish stories in the magazines before she had the command of her craft; but the encouragement he gave her, if it may have been somewhat uncritical, helped a great deal more than it hurt. The brief tale published in the Boston magazine—it is little more than a sketch—was titled "Peter" and it is the episode that will become the suicide of Mr. Shimerda in *My Ántonia*. Indeed, Peter Sadelack differs from the amateur fiddler Shimerda only in being more of a professional musician who is also strongly addicted to drink. Their longing for the past is the same. Peter lives in his memories and these are of his days as second violin in the big Prague theater where he "wore a dress coat every evening and there were always parties after the play." He had watched the great Rachel and heard Liszt perform when the Countess d'Agoult sat in the stage box and threw white lilies at the master. But now in the bleak Western winter he makes his irrevocable decision:

> . . . He took Antone's shot-gun down from its peg,
> and loaded it by the moonlight which streamed in
> through the door. He sat down on the dirt floor, and
> leaned back against the dirt wall. He heard the
> wolves howling in the distance, and the night wind
> screaming as it swept over the snow. Near him he
> heard the regular breathing of the horses in the
> dark. . . . He held his fiddle under his chin a mo-
> ment, where it had lain so often, then put it across
> his knee and broke it through the middle. He pulled
> off his old boot, held the gun between his knees with
> the muzzle against his forehead, and pressed the
> trigger with his toe.

This is sufficiently remarkable narrative for a young college student.

Willa Cather republished the story in the *Hesperian*, where it appeared in the issue of November 24, 1892. Before that she had published another tale in the college magazine; probably both had served first as compositions for Herbert Bates's class. "Lou the Prophet" in the October 15 number, is an outcome of her life on the Divide; in substance and attitude, though not in art, it is akin to the presentation of Ivar in *O Pioneers!* or the two aloof Russian farmers in the first book of *My Ántonia*. A young Danish farmer, Lou works with a peasant's laboriousness until his spirit is broken by the desertion of the girl he expected to marry, and by the death of his mother. He develops a religious mania, buries himself in solitude, broken only by the sympathetic company of young boys, and at the end rushes away across the prairie to avoid the police who have come to remove him to an asylum. The last scene is as melodramatic in its own way as the sentence quoted from the theme on Carlyle. But there are passages that might appear in any of the Nebraska novels without disharmony. The descriptive touches are often precise and striking in a manner that is a rough anticipation of *O Pioneers!* "When the moon came up, he sighed restlessly and tore the buffalo pea flowers with his bare toes." The phrase is not satisfactory; but like many of the unsatisfactory phrases in *Endymion*, and for the same reason, it is full of promise. Willa Cather's lifelong attachment to the very old and the very young appears in the opening reflection: "Among the northern people who emigrate to the great west only the children and the old people ever long much for the lands they have left over the water." The figures of Mr. Shimerda and Ántonia are distinctly on the horizon.

Another story, "The Clemency of the Court," appearing a year later, October 26, 1893, is more elaborate. It is about Serge Povolitchky, a Russian who grew up as an orphan on a farm in the western part of Nebraska; he was even more of a solitary than Lou, since the only creature ever to show him affection was a farm dog. When out of mere passing bad temper the farmer splits the dog's head with a hatchet, Serge, now a young man, kills him "even as the man had struck the dog." (This episode emerged later in *Death Comes for the Archbishop*, transformed into the story of a man and his rooster bred for cockfighting.) Condemned to imprisonment for life, he is set to factory tasks that he cannot perform. After a long stay in a dark cell, during which he is "roped up" tight against a wall night and day, he dies, alone. The grimness of this story is without relief except for the quiet treatment of the emotion the Russian feels for the dog, and for rare notations of the prairie landscape, with its buffalo grass, wild roses, and "a little marshy pool, grown up in cat-tails and reeds." The extension of meaning beyond a horrifying individual case comes through an ironic treatment of the idea of the State. The old Russian woman on whose farm Serge spent his childhood had heard in a Fourth of July oration of a beneficent power in America to which there was no parallel in Europe: here there was a benevolent State, and all were her beloved children. In Serge's starved inward life the idea of the maternal State became an obscure but powerful consolation. "About his trial Serge remembered very little, except that they had taken him to the courthouse and he had not found the State." Even in prison he trusted serenely that "the State would come some day and explain, and take him to herself." As he strangled he was still expecting the arrival of his savior the State. Many of the elements in Willa Cather's novels about Nebraska are already present: there is the deep concern over the plight of the foreign-born in a society that requires them to conform and has no generosity of spirit, no perception of their troubled frame of mind; there is the sympathy with people rooted in the land to whom confinement and city labors are intolerable; and there is the governing emotion of so much she was to write already governing here—an alarm and dislike at the pressure of a community on a personality which, like Lou's, is essentially at variance with it and has a central core the community will never rightly value.

Whatever the false notes in these stories, written before Willa Cather was twenty, they point forward to the substance of her first great novels, and to an element in the attitude with which she would always view the American community.

During her last two years at the university Willa Cather's interest in her studies declined. Exact scholarship, represented in a conventional way in the professors of Greek and Latin, and with peculiar personal additions in L. A. Sherman, irked her more and more. She was eager to explore authors who had special value for her personal life, and for the practice of fiction and poetry. She is remembered in Lincoln as a devotee of Flaubert, and of *Madame Bovary* in particular: she often carried a copy of that novel. In the sketch "A Chance Meeting," written in the early 1930's, she speaks of Flaubert as one in whom and near whom "lay most of one's mental past." From Flaubert she passed to Mérimée, to whom she came, as so many American undergraduates have come, by way of *Colomba*. She felt a close, lasting and at first sight rather surprising, affinity with his mind and his art, with his critical writings as much as with his fiction. She also read Maupassant and Ibsen, and the *Dame aux Camélias* of Dumas *fils*. Her enduring pleasure in Stevenson began in these years, encouraged perhaps by Bates, who was strongly drawn to him—to the stylist even more than to the creator of character, teller of tales, and commentator on life. She bought Stevenson's complete works, the first large set she acquired, paying for it at the rate of a dollar a month. At the time of her death the "Stevenson" occupied a shelf conveniently accessible to casual reading in the living-room of her apartment. Like the rest of the reading that was important to her as an undergraduate, it was important to the end.

She was active in one of the undergraduate literary societies, the Union, which was at that time more intellectually disposed than its principal rival, the Palladian. She edited

the senior yearbook or annual of 1894, *The Sombrero*.
Dramatics interested her, and she was especially effective
in comic and in masculine roles, though she had ceased to
wear strikingly masculine clothes and had let her hair grow
and even submitted to having it curl. Her recitation of
"Curfew Shall Not Ring Tonight" was a hilarious success
she was called on to repeat.

III

She was often in the houses of interesting Lincoln families.
Among her principal friends were Louise and Olivia
Pound, the sisters of Roscoe and daughters of Judge Stephen M. Pound, and Mariel and Frances, the daughters of
Charles H. Gere of the *State Journal*. Sarah B. Harris,
editor of the Lincoln *Courier*, and Mrs. Gere were no less
important to her: she was drawn to these older women
much as she had been drawn to Mrs. Miner in Red Cloud.
She was especially devoted to Mrs. Emma Tyndale Westermann, the mother of six young men, students or recent
graduates, and the center of a circle of young people attracted to her by the richness and warmth of her nature
and the range of her culture. Mrs. Westermann's brother,
Dr. Julius Tyndale, had recently come west from New
York, seeking a drier climate. He was a man of great
personal and intellectual force, and as keenly interested in
music and letters as in medicine and science generally.
With him she formed the same kind of association she had
enjoyed with the gifted, experienced men in Red Cloud.
His stories about the literary and musical world of the east
coast and his opinions about contemporary movements in
the arts became an important element in her growth.

The Westermanns occupied a large and striking house
on S Street near Sixteenth, on the edge of the campus. (It
had been occupied during Willa Cather's earlier years in
Lincoln by the chancellor of the university, James H. Canfield.) A studio had been added, and it is this room Willa
Cather describes in the sixth chapter of *One of Ours*, "all
windows on three sides above the wainscoting." This and
all the other details about the house, William Linn Westermann declares, have been recaptured in that novel with
a precision of visual memory startling in its sureness. The

bust of Byron, the portrait of Napoleon were recalled, one may suppose, because the quality in the family life of the Westermanns, so intense, and so deeply marked by European culture, had meant so much to the young girl from Webster County. The Westermanns represented in these years in a more developed form the same values she had found in the Wieners, whose house was recalled with equal fullness in "Old Mrs. Harris."

Willa Cather's relation with the family of James H. Canfield was just as intimate. Dorothy Canfield was several years younger than Willa Cather—she was in primary school when Willa Cather came to Lincoln—but a son, James Canfield, was in Willa Cather's class. Dorothy Canfield Fisher describes the response to Willa Cather by the members of the family: "It was through what my parents and my brother who was in her class thought of Willa that I saw her, I think, as I look back on those years—my father an impassioned educator, always a flame of hope and eager, forward-looking, when some student showed rare gifts; and my erratic highly talented artist-mother rejoicing in any young person who spelled Art with a capital, as Willa certainly did. And my brother, a lively, tennis-playing, dancing, extremely social-minded party-loving undergraduate." Mrs. Canfield's cult of art, nourished by her association with French artists and her broad reading in French literature, was important to Willa Cather—it strengthened her in the æsthetic attitude she was forming in her years at Lincoln. Before long the two novelists-to-be had found each other. A short story on a football game, submitted in a competition for a prize of ten dollars and published in *The Sombrero*, was the fruit of a collaboration between Dorothy Canfield and Willa Cather. It is uncharacteristic of either. It is indeed the least promising of all Willa Cather's juvenilia.

In the 1890's students at the University of Nebraska lived in various parts of the town—"where we could and as we could," Willa Cather says in *My Ántonia*. There were no dormitories and few fraternities or sororities. Willa Cather's room was not far from the central business district, and remained bare and austere, more like a boy's than a girl's. She spent much more time at her desk than most students cared to do, but in the evenings she would very often go out for long talks in the houses of her friends, and usually would return on foot and alone through the silent streets as late as one or two o'clock. Lincoln might be the state capital and a vigorous commercial town; to her it was as manageable and familiar as Red Cloud.

Her later years at the university fell in one of the most difficult periods in the history of the state. Its "rapid industrial development," as she says in her essay on Nebraska, "was arrested in the years 1893–1897 by a succession of crop failures and by the financial depression which spread over the whole country at that time—the depression which produced the People's Party and the Free Silver agitation." The first Nebraska district was represented in Congress from 1891 to 1895 by a Lincoln lawyer who made the issues of Populism and free silver plain across the state before he became the Democratic candidate for the Presidency in 1896. There are echoes of William Jennings Bryan in Willa Cather's fiction: the issues that he dramatized appear movingly in "Two Friends" and to a lesser extent in "The Best Years." Willa Cather's own family suffered heavily in the years of agricultural failure. Charles F. Cather had acquired a great deal of land in Webster County, and much of it was heavily mortgaged. A large farm that he had under cultivation was abandoned. A bank with which he had dealings failed. He was in desperate straits to keep the land and to meet the expenses of a large family, even though Roscoe and Douglass, the next in age to Willa, taught school and helped to the utmost.

IV

A chance to help came to her in the autumn of 1893. Willa Cather enrolled for a course in journalism with Will Owen Jones, the managing editor of the *State Journal*, who for a few years gave special instruction at the university. She was invited to become a regular contributor to the Sunday issues of the *State Journal* at a dollar a column, and the prodigious number of columns she filled gave her literary earnings sufficient to meet many of her expenses.

In the contributions to the *State Journal* it is possible to follow many of Willa Cather's early enthusiasms, and to discover her artistic aims. C. H. Gere and Will Owen Jones left her free: she could say what she would and say it as she would. In later years she was grateful for the privilege of "stepping as high as she cared to" in her rhetoric, and thus working out a rhetorical vein which was so rich that otherwise she might never have come to the end of it. A slight smile, stopping short of the sarcastic, was all she had to endure when she had been particularly outrageous or Corinthian.

The most explicit statement of her conception of art is this:

> The further the world advances the more it becomes evident that an author's only safe course is to cling to the skirts of his art, forsaking all others, and keep unto her as long as they two shall live. An artist should not be vexed by human hobbies or human follies: he should be able to lift himself into the clear firmament of creation where the world is not. He should be among men but not of them, in the world but not of the world. Other men may think and believe and argue, but he must create.

The stress upon the sufficiency and separateness of the artist's function appears again in a review of Paul Bourget's volume of impressions of America:

> It is rather a pity that Paul Bourget should have written *Outre Mer*, thoroughly creditable book that it is. . . . Mr. Bourget is a novelist, and should not content himself with being an essayist, there are far too many of them in the world already. . . . When God has made a man a creator, it is a mistake for him to turn critic. It is rather an insult to God, and certainly a very great wrong to man.

Perhaps the writer of these lines addressed them more to herself than to Paul Bourget; but if she believed that she should be about her creative business, she could reflect that at twenty she was not ripe for the kind of fiction she cared to write:

> A man cannot write a novel before he has grown a mustache. . . . O for the good old days of Thack-

eray and Dickens when a man did not dare to write
a novel before he was thirty. . . . A man must live
and know and labor and endure before he can write
a book that purports to tell of life.

At least one of the columnist's examples was dubious;
when Dickens reached thirty he had behind him the *Pick-
wick Papers, Oliver Twist, Nicholas Nickleby, The Old
Curiosity Shop*, and *Barnaby Rudge*. But Dickens is not a
writer that a novelist beginning his craft in the 1890's
would be likely to study. He was never to be an enthusiasm
or a model with Willa Cather.

Her most pungent articles were reviews of plays. In an
interview that appeared in the *State Journal* on February 3,
1895, Gustave Frohman remarked: "Lincoln newspapers
are noted for their honesty in dramatic matters, and it is
the best advertisement of intelligence and refinement that a
town can have. I have heard of it from professionals and
non-professionals all along the road, and poor companies
begin to tremble long before they get here. That kind of
respect is worth something." From an impresario this was
a generous way of putting a good face upon a characteristic histrionic malaise. By "Lincoln newspapers" Frohman
really meant Willa Cather's columns in the *State Journal*.
A retrospective editorial appearing in that paper on November 1, 1921, and probably written by Will Owen Jones,
leaves an impression that not all the theatrical visitors to
Lincoln took her criticisms so urbanely. "Many an actor of
national reputation wondered on coming to Lincoln what
would appear next morning from the pen of the meat-ax
young girl of whom all of them had heard. Miss Cather did
not stand in awe of the greatest actors, but set each one in
his place with all the authority of a veteran metropolitan
critic." It has been said that a *State Journal* reporter who
presented a pass at a theater in Chicago was contumeli-
ously refused admission to the play, which was one that
Willa Cather had excoriated.

How pointed her criticism could be appears in a comment on the acting of Lillian Lewis:

She will next year stage a magnificent spectacular
production of *Cymbeline*, in which she will play

Imogen. When one knows Lillian, her nose and her
emotions, one hopes they dug Shakespeare's grave
very deep.

She could be equally pointed in a comment on a playwright. In a review of *Lady Windermere's Fan,* published
on June 5, 1894, almost a year before the first trial of
Oscar Wilde, Willa Cather remarked:

Mr. Wilde is afraid to be coarse, so he is insinuat-
ing. . . . He does not attempt to apotheosize filth,
he plays with it because he likes it when it is pretty.
. . . To hear Mr. Wilde, on [motherhood] is like
hearing one of the very little Satans philosophizing
on Calvary.

It is the slashing passages that are most vividly and long
remembered in a dramatic critic. But Willa Cather's best
reviews in the *State Journal* are admirably balanced. There
is for instance an estimate of Julia Marlowe. Marlowe
seemed to Willa Cather to carry grace, delicacy, and
beauty to perfection. It was a distinguished æsthetic pleasure to see her move and hear her speak. "A sort of warm
rich delight will hover about us for days." But for all the
fascination, there was a reach beyond Marlowe, a reach
she never attempted. "She lives too beautifully to live very
hard, dies too gracefully to die very effectively." The reservation about Marlowe is generalized in a way that relates
Willa Cather's critical principles to her own early attempts
in fiction:

After all the supreme virtue in art is soul, perhaps
it is the only thing which gives art the right to be.
The greatest art in acting is not to please and charm
and delight, but to move and thrill; not to play a part
daintily and delightfully, but with power and passion.
All prettiness for its own sake is trivial. No matter
how dainty, how refined, how spirituelle, it is still a
thing of the sense only.

The insistence on the grave, hard core of all great art is
often repeated in the dramatic reviews. She found this core
in Clara Morris's rendering of Camille:

Camille is an awful play. Clara Morris plays only awful plays. Her realism is terrible and relentless. It is her art and mission to see all that is terrible and painful and unexplained in life. It is a dark and gloomy work that has been laid upon more geniuses than one.

In her own fashion, in the stories of Lou and Serge Povolitchky, Willa Cather had written awful works. Some of the readers of the *Hesperian* found the stories "morbid" and "brutal"; they were instead "painful" and "relentless," the product of a mind that was already committed to a work which, though it was seldom dark and gloomy, had its dark depths and gloomy passages. The spirit of Carlyle was still her spirit; what she has to say about books is much nearer to his kind of judgment than to that of the critics who in the 1890's had authority and disciples—Matthew Arnold, for instance, or Henry James, or the impressionists native and foreign. It is not known when Willa Cather first discovered Tolstoy, but it could be predicted that when she did, *War and Peace* and *Anna Karenina* would be among the chief literary experiences in her life, as indeed they were. Already, however, her primary care for the grave, hard core of art went along with a delight in exquisite form; and she would not easily be content unless she found both the hard core and the perfect form. Her period of apprenticeship would inevitably be a long one.

V

In June 1895 she was graduated. Like many another artist she had had her struggles with mathematics; not until the end of her senior year had she succeeded, and then only by special instruction, in removing her deficiency in the first-year course in that discipline.

The year 1895–6 was spent at home in Red Cloud. It was a year of recovery and preparation. Willa Cather left Lincoln very tired, much more tired than she knew. Her first three years had been a time of most assiduous study, in which she rose as early as a farmer on the Divide and went to bed long after midnight. In the last two years she kept the same exhausting hours, though not so many of them went to reading for her courses. Much of her time was given to writing for the *Journal*, and during the dramatic season to haunting the theaters; much went to writing done for her own satisfaction or experiment. These were the years in which she began to discover what art meant, and the process of discovery was attended with great emotional excitement and disturbance. Her mind and spirit now required a fallow season.

Red Cloud was at the bottom of its depressed period. Charles Cather kept afloat only because he had become the representative in south-central Nebraska of R. E. Moore, one of the most successful financiers in the state, whose headquarters was at Lincoln. The father had begun to spend more of his time in Lincoln than he did at home; and Willa Cather's presence in the house on Cedar Street, and often in her father's local office, allowed Mrs. Cather to accompany her husband to Lincoln. She gave her father some help in his work, which at this time had to do mainly with land-titles and mortgages. It was some reassurance to feel that she was partly paying her way when the family was short of money. She tried to pick up the threads of her friendships, but some of the older friends were dead, others had moved away, and among those of her own age she could not overcome the feeling she attributed forty years later to Lucy Gayheart, that "she was not there in the old way . . . scarcely herself at all . . . trying to feel and behave like someone she no longer was; as children go on playing the old games to please their elders, after they have ceased to be children at heart." She believed that her family and friends, who had heard so much of her writing at Lincoln for undergraduate magazines and for the *State Journal*, were expecting her to make some dazzling success, to place stories in some popular journal or bring out a brilliant novel. She was writing stories, but they seemed jejune and superficial—how, she wondered, could they seem otherwise, coming from one who had seen so little of the world? If only she might travel, as Stephen Crane had done, and quickly accumulate a knowledge of cities and men; but first there were debts to pay, some of them incurred in helping actresses she had met in Lincoln to some tawdry pleasure, paste jewelry, or champagne. During the winter of 1896 Herbert Bates resigned from the University of Nebraska and recommended that she be named in his place. Her age and her sex were, she knew, against her; and she also knew that Lucius Sherman had a low opinion of her abilities. She enlisted friends in Lincoln in support of her application, but she was not surprised when it was unsuccessful. She was able to make a number of visits to Lincoln during the year—the *State Journal* was always ready to supply free transportation—but, just as Claude Wheeler in *One of Ours* found the trips he took to Lincoln after he had dropped out of college ended with acute depression when he was once more at home, Willa Cather felt that the few days she could spend among stimulating people like the Geres and the Westermanns served mainly to make her months at a stretch in Red Cloud a greater trial.

By one of her visits to Lincoln, however, she was able to make her escape not only from Red Cloud but from Nebraska. Once when she was visiting the Geres she met Charles Axtell, a Pittsburgh businessman, with his wife and daughter. Axtell appears to have been struck by her experience as a journalist—no doubt Charles Gere spoke golden words of her—and late in the spring of 1896 he offered her a position in the editorial office of a "family" magazine he was founding, the Pittsburgh *Home Monthly*. Before the end of June Willa Cather was in Pittsburgh.

4

Pittsburgh: the Bright
Medusa

1896–1901

WILLA CATHER HAD had a foretaste of the world beyond the prairies during the spring of 1895 after her graduation. To mark the end of her college years she traveled to Chicago for a week of opera—an expedition arranged with the sympathetic aid of Dr. Tyndale. Like Thea Kronborg, she boarded the train in elaborate attire, more feminine than she allowed herself to wear in her everyday life in Lincoln, and before the week was out she was surfeited with music, dazzled by the glittering audiences, and exhausted by her tramping of Chicago's streets. The successive evenings at the opera were to find their way many years later into a dramatic portion of Lucy Gayheart's adventure in Chicago.

Perhaps more significant for Willa Cather's future was the arrival in Lincoln, also during that spring, of "the first man of letters I had ever met in the flesh." He was scarce a man, barely twenty-four, just two years older than she was. He seemed to come out of nowhere. But he brought a glimpse of distant things and the aura of struggle and fame. The author of *The Red Badge of Courage* walked one day into the office of the managing editor·of the *Journal*, where Willa Cather happened to be. He was slender and narrow-chested and wore shabby gray; his soft felt hat was low over his eyes. He had on a flannel shirt and a "slovenly apology" for a necktie. His shoes were dusty, worn about the toes, badly run over at the heel. Only his gloves contradicted his general shabbiness, and when he took them off to search his pockets for his credentials, Willa Cather noticed that his hands were singularly fine, "long, white and delicately shaped, with thin nervous fingers."

Stephen Crane was on his way to Mexico. He wanted to get rid of his cough and to try to do some work there. He was waiting in Lincoln for some money to catch up with him. In the ensuing days Willa Cather repeatedly sought to draw from him his literary opinions and an account of how he practiced his craft. She asked him about Maupassant. His unhelpful rejoinder was "Oh, you're Moping, are you?" as he buried himself in the little volume of Poe he always had with him. Then, one hot evening, sitting on the ledge of the window in the newspaper office, Stephen Crane finally—

> Quite without invitation on my part . . . began to talk, began to curse his trade from the first throb of creative desire in a boy to the finished work of the master. The night was oppressively warm; one of those dry winds that are the curse of that country was blowing up from Kansas. The white, western moonlight threw sharp, blue shadows below us. The streets were silent at that hour, and we could hear the gurgle of the fountain in the Post Office square across the street, and the twang of banjos from the lower veranda of the Hotel Lincoln, where the colored waiters were serenading the guests. The drop lights in the office were dull under their green shades, and the telegraph sounder clicked faintly in the next room. In all his long tirade, Crane never raised his voice; he spoke slowly and monotonously and even calmly, but I have never known so bitter a heart in any man as he revealed to me that night. It was an arraignment of the wages of life, an invocation to the ministers of hate.

Crane spoke of how he led a double life: he wrote the matter that pleased himself slowly and with care; he dashed off anything he could sell. "He declared," Willa Cather remembered, "that his imagination was hidebound; it was there, but it pulled hard. After he got a notion for a story; months passed before he could get any sort of personal contact with it, or feel any potency to handle it." And then he pronounced these words, of the greatest significance for the future art of Willa Cather: "The detail of a thing has to filter through my blood, and then it comes out like a native product, but it take forever." The young-old Stephen Crane did not have forever. But Willa Cather was to have many years in which to ponder and cherish these words.

II

Willa Cather threw herself into her Pittsburgh life with all the young ardor she possessed. The Eastern city meant what Chicago was to mean to Thea Kronborg and Lucy Gayheart, "the freedom to spend one's youth as one pleased"—freedom to live according to one's measure of life, a degree of economic security, access to the arts, liberation from the ceaselessly active tongues in Red Cloud that had given her an acute sense of being an outcast among her own people. Yet Willa Cather was soon to discover that the price of her new-found freedom was long and unremunerative hours in an office and printing shop which could not be reconciled with the art she wished to practice. When the young narrator in *My Mortal Enemy* is asked why she does not turn to journalism, and is warned that teaching is a cul-de-sac in which generous people use themselves up, she replies with a vehemence that eloquently proclaims the author's feeling: "I hate journalism. I know what I want to do, and I'll work my way out yet, if only you'll give me time." It took Willa Cather a rounded decade to work her way out of journalism and teaching in Pittsburgh.

She spent the first few days after her arrival as the guest of her employer. The Axtells seemed to Willa Cather rigorously and comically puritan; in her room there were three Bibles and a shelf full of novels of the Reverend E. P. Roe. If the Axtells had known of her belief in artistic creation as the first of the values, she was sure they would not have had her under their roof; she thought they suspected her of Bohemianism, for shortly before she arrived they had sent their daughter, whom she described as the "Puritan Maid," to stay with relatives at a safe distance. In this household she discovered what was characteristic of one side of Pittsburgh: an alliance between business and an unpleasant religious formalism. "Presbyterianism of that day," Elizabeth Moorhead has observed in writing of the city, "offered little encouragement to any sort of artistic activity. Physical comfort was admissible, yes—the good Presbyterian was by no means an ascetic—but duty was the law of life. Aesthetic impulse too often led to a dangerous laxity." Willa Cather was to make the same observations in a much more mordant way in an article she wrote for the Lincoln *Courier* in the autumn of 1897 on the Pittsburgh horse show. "Of course the most sensible beings present were down in the horse stalls. They were not Presbyterians, nor were they covered with diamonds, and everything they did was in good taste. . . . There is no getting away from a Presbyterian environment, no getting around it, or behind it or above it."

To this environment the *Home Monthly* was dedicated— to "more than half a million firesides" within a hundred miles of downtown Pittsburgh. It offered "entertainment for the idle hour . . . pure and clean in tone" and purveyed by "the best story writers in the country." There were departments devoted to floriculture, fashions, the nursery, Christian endeavor; articles on cycling for pleasure, Angora cats, Harriet Beecher Stowe, and the care of the children's teeth. The stories offering the "entertainment for the idle hour" in the first number—issued in August 1896— were "A Modern Elaine," a stereotype of moderate realism (an English boy of gentle manners and refined character becomes a farm laborer in America, the farmer's daughter is charmed, and so on); "The Lovely Malincourt," a romantic stereotype (noble families, virtuous lovers separated by a cruel worldly mother, one of them dying of despair and reviving when the mother relents, etc.). A third story, "Tommy the Unsentimental" by Willa Cather, as its title suggests, is a revolt against the stereotype. It is not a revolt against Barrie, who was a lifelong admiration of Willa Cather's (the admiration was returned—for more than twenty years Barrie asked her to autograph her books for him); it is a revolt against the conception of the young girl which ruled the magazines and most of the national thinking at the turn of the century. Willa Cather is writing, as in the grim stories in the *Hesperian*, about her own corner of Nebraska. Her heroine is a sketch of herself:

> Needless to say, Tommy was not a boy, though her keen gray eyes and wide forehead were scarcely girl-

ish, and she had the lank figure of a half-grown lad. Her real name was Theodosia, but during Thomas Shirley's frequent absences from the bank she had attended to his business and correspondence signing herself "T. Shirley" until everyone in Southdown called her "Tommy." That blunt sort of familiarity is not unfrequent in the West, and is meant well enough. People rather expect some business ability in a girl there, and they respect it immensely.

Tommy is in love with a feckless and effeminate cashier in her father's bank, "the only foolish man" she knew; the other men she cared for were among her father's middle-aged or elderly friends, "who had seen a good deal of the world and were very proud and fond of Tommy." A touch in the drawing of Tommy's relationship with them must have been passed when Axtell was nodding; it must, indeed, have startled subscribers at a thousand firesides:

> She played whist and billiards with them, and made their cocktails for them, not scorning to take one herself occasionally. Indeed Tommy's cocktails were things of fame in Southdown, and the professional compounders of drinks always bowed respectfully to her as though acknowledging a powerful rival.

No evil fate overtakes her because of pursuits so abhorrent to the Presbyterians of Pittsburgh and western Pennsylvania. Tommy dispatches the cashier to his Eastern girl, who is his true mate; she remains to the end a sharply drawn portrait, framed to excellent effect by brief realizations of the Nebraska landscape. If "Tommy the Unsentimental" was one of the stories Willa Cather wrote and was unhappy about during the year at Red Cloud, the move to Pittsburgh may have been a mistake. Not until she wrote "The Sculptor's Funeral" did she achieve anything better— and that remarkable story lay nine years ahead.

She found, indeed, little time for writing fiction. The *Home Monthly* made great demands on her, and Willa Cather was soon managing editor of the journal in everything but name, with only a stenographer to help her. She read manuscripts and proof, presided over the make-up in the hot composing-room until all hours of the night, and wrote articles and small fillers for gaps in the dummy. She learned to discipline herself and, what was hardest of all, to keep still and do what she was told. She wrote her Nebraska friends that she had never worked so hard and so consistently in all her life. While there was a certain relish in some phases of her work, and a very real sense of achievement, she found the journal's conventionality and parochialism increasingly stifling. She made a virtue of the drudgery, however; it was a question of maintaining her as yet uncertain foothold in the East; and it was a question of demonstrating to the doubters back home that she could "win out."

III

In Pittsburgh Willa Cather rode to work on her bicycle from her boarding-house in Craig Street to the *Home Monthly* office at Pennsylvania and Eighth Street. She said the only excitement she allowed herself was her daily race with the tram; however, everything at first was rather exciting. She enjoyed the coal-smeared aspect of the city, its hills and rivers and the flaring skies and plumes of gas flame ("the very incandescence of human energy") that reflected the spectacular sources of Pittsburgh's wealth. Early in her stay she visited, with a group that included her Lincoln friends George W. Gerwig and Dorothy Canfield, the great Homestead steel mills, where they saw fountains of flame and the workers moving like ants in a clanging inferno. She was to catch the city's rhythm and tone and the "legends of the iron kings" in one of her best-known stories, "Paul's Case," in which she drew on many elements of her life in Pittsburgh. Unlike the Western silver kings in Colorado and Nevada, whose conception of art was the building of palatial and grotesque homes with ornate bathrooms, the iron kings were endowing museums and concert halls and turning grimy Pittsburgh into one of America's centers of culture; steel and oil, coal and gas were transmuted into vast fortunes, and the overflow of this money became painting and music, literature and opera. The iron kings had blasted their way deeply into that earth whose surface on the frontier was being tamed by quite another type of pioneer. Willa Cather had a profound admiration for both.

This, then, was the dichotomy of Pittsburgh: out of its ugliness and slums, its industrial smoke and flame sprang the beautiful things that were the breath of life to Willa Cather. And her own life there had the same dichotomy. "It was at the theatre and at Carnegie Hall that Paul really lived; the rest was but a sleep and a forgetting." Willa Cather's work and the lonely drabness of most of the boarding-houses in which she lived were things to run away from, and the avenues of escape were there: in the newly inaugurated Carnegie Institute with its library, its art gallery, and its concert hall. In the library she could have more books than had ever been available to her on the prairie and she could meet librarians such as the sensitive and discerning May Willard, who was to become a lifelong friend. At Carnegie Hall she could hear Victor Herbert conduct the symphony orchestra and like young Paul feel that some hilarious spirit in her was freed by the first sight of the instruments, "something that struggled there like the Genius in the bottle found by the Arab fisherman." Paul felt "a sudden zest of life; the lights danced before his eyes and the concert hall blazed into unimaginable splendour." Something of that splendor touched the artists and composers she began to meet, among them Ethelbert Nevin, whose dazzling success and whose kindness to Willa Cather made him one of the heroes of her early Pittsburgh days, so that to her Red Cloud and Lincoln friends she evoked him as a young prince or a king, almost a fairy-tale figure, who lived with a devoted wife in a beautiful suburban home named Vineacre, where he entertained the girl from the prairie, treating her with a generous and disarming gallantry that endeared him to her. The author of "The Rosary" dedicated a song to Willa Cather and showed her warm friendship and an appreciation of her talents that she never forgot. Like Crane, he was to die young, and many years later Willa Cather put her recollections of him into the story "Uncle Valentine," where Vineacre is barely disguised as Greenacre.

The flight from ugliness and monotony to things of beauty and enchantment led Willa Cather to the Pittsburgh stock company, where every week a new play enabled her to cross that "boundary line beyond which dreams came true and lost illusions live on, forever young." Here too she found a loyal and devoted friend in one of the artists. Lizzie Hudson Collier was the leading lady, and this meant that her audiences would find her there on the stage every week in a new role, with the same warmth, charm, and dignity that had made her almost a legendary institution in Pittsburgh. Dorothy Canfield Fisher remembers her as "singularly decent and straight-fibred." For Willa Cather the stage-door leading to Mrs. Collier's dressing-room was "the actual portal of Romance"; she was an increasingly frequent visitor there, and an attentive watcher from the wings of the way in which the theater's "lost illusions" were created. Memories of those evenings, as so much of the emotion of those days, are to be found in "Paul's Case." When Paul went to visit his young friend backstage at the stock company and crossed its portal, "the moment he inhaled the gassy, painty, dusty odour behind the scenes, he breathed like a prisoner set free, and felt within him the possibility of doing or saying splendid, brilliant, poetic things. The moment the cracked orchestra beat out the overture from 'Martha,' or jerked at the serenade from 'Rigoletto,' all stupid and ugly things slid from him, and his senses were deliciously, yet delicately fired."

> Perhaps it was because, in Paul's world, the natural nearly always wore the guise of ugliness, that a certain element of artificiality seemed to him necessary in beauty. Perhaps it was because his experience of life elsewhere was so full of Sabbath-school picnics, petty economies, wholesome advice as to how to succeed in life, and the unescapable odours of cooking, that he found this existence so alluring, these smartly-clad men and women so attractive, that he was so moved by these starry apple orchards that bloomed perennially under the limelight.

The table of contents of the *Home Monthly* and the boarding-houses are in this paragraph.

This harder side of Willa Cather's Pittsburgh life was not so readily apparent to those who had an opportunity of seeing only what might be called its softer side—that side which she recounted to her friends in animated letters or which was visible to Dorothy Canfield, who occasionally stopped off in Pittsburgh and stayed with her college friend. For her young visitor she provided concerts, and the glamour of her celebrated friends, after-theater suppers, and access to the friendly houses in which she herself was often a guest—the homes of George Gerwig or Edwin Hatfield Anderson, the chief librarian at the Carnegie, or the European-like home of George Seibel, where music and pfeffernüsse were somehow mingled and where she went regularly to improve her French. Seibel too was a librarian. "She came once or twice a week to read the French classics," he remembers, "and always helped to trim our Christmas tree as long as she lived in Pittsburgh." She had known the Gerwigs during her *Sombrero* days in Lincoln and at their home met a number of persons who became good friends during her Pittsburgh days, including Preston Farrar, head of the English department at Allegheny High School, where she was later to teach.

IV

Willa Cather resigned from the *Home Monthly* during the summer of 1897 while she was vacationing in Red Cloud. The journal was to change hands at the end of its first year and this seemed the appropriate moment to withdraw gracefully. Her resignation did not mean that she was abruptly burning her valued Pittsburgh bridges. As far back as the previous January she had investigated the possibility of finding work on one of the city's dailies. Before the summer's end a telegram arrived offering her a position with the *Daily Leader*, the largest evening paper in Pennsylvania, at a salary of seventy-five dollars a month.

During the four years Willa Cather worked for the Pittsburgh *Leader* her principal task was the editing and rewriting of telegraphic news as well as copy-reading and headline-writing. This was drudgery of a different sort from that of the *Home Monthly*, but here, at least, she had no disagreeable editorial responsibilities and did not have to write what she considered to be quite simply "trash." At times the tedium of the telegraph desk was relieved by the interest of the news—as when she handled the story of the bottling up of Cervera's fleet in Santiago Harbor during the

Spanish-American War—but even the excitement of head-lines and newsflashes can pall, and it did for Willa Cather once the novelty wore off.

The *Leader*, however, gave her a sense of permanence and security she had never enjoyed at the *Home Monthly*, and presently she was able to resume the writing of dramatic criticism, which had been the form of journalism she had enjoyed most in Lincoln. It was still marginal to her routine duties but offered a welcome relief from them. Her first drama notices appeared early in the autumn of 1897 signed "Sibert"—a variant of her grandmother's name which she later adopted as a middle name, only to drop it in 1920 to become again simply Willa Cather. Dramatic criticism for her was still often the wielding of a sharp hatchet rather than of an urbane pen: she could still describe a play as "awful" or "terrible." What she lacked in finesse, however, she made up in vigor and conviction; and she never lacked the capacity to formulate and frame her strong opinions with complete clarity and often with charm, as when she characterized the miscasting of Julia Marlowe in a melodrama as "trying to force the notes of a 'cello from a violin" or when she dismissed Cora Tanner as an actress who could "shed more pearly tears to the minute and still remain more perfectly calm than any other woman on the stage—or off it."

One suspects on reading Willa Cather's metropolitan drama reviews that her emotions often ran away with her critical sense at a performance and that her interests more often lay in the players than in the play. She believed the drama's laws to be inflexible, in common with many nineteenth-century critics: "the demands of the drama are rigidly exacting, and chief and foremost among them is this—that the chief persons of the play shall be identified with some great purpose or strong passion." Her association with Mrs. Collier gave her a sense of being in possession of the practical side of the theater as well as understanding the histrionic temperament. It was this saturation with the theater frontstage and back that led her two years later to the preparation of what she hoped would be her first book. She had been writing a series of open letters to living actors, the soliloquies of a critic offering praise and blame (and tending to pontificate at moments rather freely). Nothing could be calculated to touch—and hurt—the special vanity of the stage-folk more than to have gratuitous counsel offered them on how to play their roles; and perhaps for this reason publishers did not warm to the book that Willa Cather tentatively spoke of as *The Player Letters*. A few of these letters appeared as separate articles in the Nebraska newpapers, and we can discover the writer's intention in the directness of her communication to Joseph Jefferson:

> The enormous financial success of *Rip Van Winkle* checked your career gloriously, but finally your ambition went to sleep with Rip upon the mountain top, and though thirty years have passed, it has never awakened. You have chosen the placid waters and sheltered harbors. . . . Unlike Richard Mansfield you have risked nothing and lost nothing. In our hearts, sir, you reign always, the Prince of Players, best loved, most honored of them all. . . .

She might call him a Prince, but if so she was scolding royalty; and this compound of stricture and accolade was hardly likely to be received with favor. It was one thing to criticize a specific performance and a specific play; it was another to address the actors directly in terms of an uncompromising schoolmistress talking to her pupils. The manuscript lingered in a few publishers' offices and then was quietly withdrawn; and from this distance the circumstance may be judged a happy one. Had the book been published, Willa Cather's emergence in letters would have been somewhat stormy, we suspect, and certainly heartbreaking. As it was, she was destined to make a much more modest and indeed a happy debut.

V

It is not, however, in Willa Cather's dramatic criticism that we can obtain a coherent picture of her slowly maturing personality and of her growing confidence in her artistic future. That picture emerges rather from the series of columns she wrote, first for the Nebraska *State Journal* and then for the Lincoln *Courier*, under the rubric "The Passing Show." The column lived up to its name, and if it is not quite a diary of Willa Cather's activities in the East, it

permits us to follow her to play and opera, to art gallery
and horse show; whatever seized her interest—the latest
book, the latest literary gossip, the life of Pittsburgh's Bohemia—was grist to her productive and lively mill. She
read A. E. Housman's poems in their freshness of first
appearance and promptly communicated her elation of discovery to her Western readers. She discoursed on John
Philip Sousa and described a reception tendered Anthony
Hope Hawkins, whose *Prisoner of Zenda*, no less than the
spectacle of Richard Mansfield in the then comparatively
new *Cyrano*, touched the deepest well of romanticism in
Willa Cather. The young woman who had trailed wistfully
after Stephen Crane now chatted informally with Rudyard
Kipling (for forty-six minutes, she informed her readers
with precision) and Marion Crawford, Fridtjof Nansen,
and Minnie Maddern Fiske—whose performance of Tess
Willa Cather saw four times in one week. And there was
the first discovery by her as yet unsophisticated musical
taste of Dvořák's *New World* Symphony, which she translated promptly into a prose picture:

> the Largo . . . before you stretch the empty, hungry
> plains of the middle west. Limitless prairies, full of
> the peasantry of all nations of Europe . . . and it
> seems as though from each of those far scattered
> lights that at night mark the dwellings of these peo-
> ple of the plains, there comes the song of a homesick
> heart.

Thea Kronborg found in the same movement, during her
first evening at the symphony in Chicago, the "immeasura-
ble yearning of all flat lands," and this yearning was now
being gratified in Willa Cather by such experiences. Piece-
meal in these running chronicles written for her home
papers Willa Cather was setting down material that would
in time filter into her novels.

"The Passing Show" is alike a record of experience and
a revelation of Willa Cather's artistic growth. If we set
aside those portions of her columns written with an eye to
her Western audience, we have a substantial quantity of
lively reflection on the arts and the personalities who practice them, and a consistent effort to define—and to refine—
her critical views. The element of hero-worship is strong.

Willa Cather never overcame it. But mingled with much biographical matter concerning the personalities of the artists, we find discussions of realism in the novel, critical evaluation of dramatic and lyric poetry, and frequent consideration of the art of the actor and the playwright. She praises Zola and admires his young American disciple Frank Norris; her literary interests reflect her reading of the French novelists, but also show the closeness with which she followed the new English writers and dramatists. If the columns reflect in part Willa Cather's playgoing and her nights in Carnegie Hall, they provide also a glimpse into her extensive raids on the shelves of the Carnegie Library.

Most important for the furture of Willa Cather's novels were the nights in Carnegie Hall and at the opera. She heard the great voices of the era—Melba and Nordica, Schumann-Heink, Sembrich, Calvé, Campanari, the de Reszkes. They interested her not only as musicians but as figures who had acquired their artistry by long discipline and tenacity of purpose, and who had finally, like her own heroines later—Thea, or Cressida Garnet, or Kitty Ayrshire—conquered. Concerts and opera were a ritual, occasions for dressing up, for brilliant gatherings, for discussions during intermissions; they possessed a dramatic quality of their own—applause and curtain calls, artistic triumphs and artistic failures. Willa Cather liked the artist's "indefinable air of achievement"—but the time was to come when it would be defined and was, in her longest novel, a study of the growth and development of a great singer.

VI

During her years on the *Leader* Willa Cather wrote very little fiction. The process of day-to-day living, the round of plays and celebrities, the act of absorbing experience, preempted all her energies. Moreover, she had begun to range out from Pittsburgh, traveling to New York to see Broadway plays—and one summer to act as guest drama critic for the New York *Sun*—and in the spring of 1898 paying a protracted visit to Washington. Here she obtained that glimpse of bureaucracy and the routinized life of the civil servants of which she wrote with a biting pen in her story of Tom Outland. During one of her visits to New York she had lunch with Helena Modjeska, whom she judged one of the greatest actresses of the time, and this experience too was to be translated into fiction. It forms a dramatic scene in *My Mortal Enemy*.

These forays beyond Pittsburgh, and her immersion in the life of art, only made her work on the telegraph desk seem increasingly oppressive and mechanical. Her imagination soared from the city room, beyond the prosaic literalness and perishable content of the daily newspaper, and there began a process by which she sought gradually to disengage herself from the pressure it imposed upon her. The Pittsburgh directory of 1900 still listed her as reporter for the *Leader*, but during that year she undertook no tasks outside her regular routine and there are no signed articles by her. She devoted her free time instead to writing for a short-lived periodical, the *Library*, founded by a wealthy Pittsburgh citizen who dispersed a legacy of twenty thousand dollars to foster literary talent. When the money was spent, the journal suspended publication. The *Library's* twenty-six numbers contain some two dozen items by Willa Cather—reportage, poetry, stories. Much of the reportage, including her reminiscences of Stephen Crane, is under the pseudonym of Henry Nicklemann; the literary material, however, with the exception of one tale, carries her own name. She reprinted one story of 1896 from the *Nebraska Literary Magazine*, "A Night at Greenway Court," and she wrote one tale, "The Sentimentality of William Tavener," in the vein of the early *Hesperian* pieces; save for a few descriptive touches, it showed that Willa Cather had made little progress in the writing of fiction during her first three years in Pittsburgh. Nevertheless what she did write, in this return to imaginative prose, was beginning to find favor with editors. Not only the *Library* was publishing her during the new year of the new century. In addition to verses placed in the *Critic*, the *Criterion*, and *McClure's*, there was a story in *Cosmopolitan* and an illustrated article in the *Ladies' Home Journal*. It was this ever increasing acceptance of her work that demonstrated to Willa Cather that she could ultimately hope to free herself completely from the demands of newspaper work. She could not yet be sure of her capacity to earn a livelihood as a free lance, and after a long trip to the West she was led to a decision that marked a turning-point in her life. She applied for a position in the Pittsburgh school system. Aided by Mr. Gerwig's connection with the Allegheny Central Board, she received a post in the Central High School as a teacher of English and Latin at an annual salary of $650. This was three hundred dollars a year less than what the *Leader* paid her; but in reality she had never worked the year round at the newspaper, taking leave of absence regularly to spend her summers at home. Consequently her earnings in both positions were roughly the same and quite sufficient for her modest needs.

Willa Cather taught at Central High during 1901–2, and from 1903 to 1906 at Allegheny High, where she was given the post vacated by her friend Preston Farrar, who left to pursue further studies. In 1902 her salary was advanced to $750, and by 1906, when she resigned, it had increased to $1,300. Her first year in school convinced her that the step had been wise. Newspaper work had drained her energy, strained her eyesight, and kept her from her own writing. Now she taught only three or four hours a day and had a theme-reader to assist her. She took her duties as teacher seriously, however, and believed that she succeeded better at teaching than in anything else she had ever done before she became a writer. Her work, moreover, was recognized and appreciated. One of her students, who was later to become a teacher himself and a distinguished critic, has recorded his recollections of this time:

> I first knew her [writes Norman Foerster] during my two years, 1902–04, at the Central High School in Pittsburgh. This was a regular academic high school —with ancient history, for example, as a freshman requirement—in distinction from the Commercial High School a mile or so away. The Central High School building was a dismal, grimy structure on a bluff looking down on the Union Station. The darkness of fog and smoke in fall and winter, the dirt of the squalid streets that led up to it must have made Willa Cather feel that the great plains and skies of Nebraska were very far away—as they were. Miss Cather was my freshman teacher only. . . . Her voice was deeper than is usual; she spoke without excitement; her manner was quiet, reposeful, suggesting

reserves of energy and richness of personality. Her teaching seemed natural and human, but without contagious sparks. . . . She liked some of my own themes. I remember one, which I believe I still have, on my memory of the dreamy summer time while I lay in bed during a blizzard that beat against the windows. On her advice I submitted it to the High School Journal where it appeared, to my great delight, with my name in print for the first time. . . . What could I do but respect and admire her? This attitude was heightened in my second year (when I no longer had her as a teacher) by the publication of her *April Twilights*. I thought it wonderful of her to write a book. . . .

Willa Cather thus turned her back forever on journalism. Edith Lewis says that "it never gave her any pleasure to remember her newspaper work." Perhaps for this reason it never figured in her novels. It was not a part of her life she could draw upon in recapturing the past; indeed, it did not seem worth recapture. Journalism had been a means to an end. It could never be for Willa Cather an end in itself.

5

Troll Garden, Goblin
Market

1902–1905

THE DECADE Willa Cather spent in Pittsburgh—from her twenty-third to her thirty-third year—fell evenly into two periods devoted to the two careers; she was a newspaperwoman for five of these years and a teacher for the remaining five. As if to establish, also, a difference between the unsettled, exacting journalism and the settled life of the classroom, the second half of the decade was marked by a change from boarding-house life to residence in a sedate mansion, in Pittsburgh's finest section, where Willa Cather found herself surrounded by the luxuries she had craved when young and a warm friendship that was devoted to providing her with an environment helpful to creative writing.

Willa Cather met Isabelle McClung in Lizzie Collier's dressing-room backstage at the stock company apparently in 1901, and it took very little time for the two to become close friends. Isabelle McClung was the daughter of a conservative Pittsburgh judge, a strict and upright Calvinist of considerable dignity and affluence, who lived with his wife, son, and two daughters in a large house at 1180 Murray Hill Avenue. She had revolted early against the rather rigid pattern of life in her home and gravitated toward the arts. She did not care for the society in which it was thought fit the daughter of a judge should move; she preferred the company of players, singers, writers. She shared Willa Cather's passion for music and the stage. And she was an avid reader. Elizabeth Moorhead, who has written of Willa Cather's life in Murray Hill Avenue in *These Too Were Here*, thought Isabelle McClung "the most beautiful girl I had ever seen . . . large of mind and heart, entirely frank and simple with natural dignity of manner. Not an artist in the sense of producing, she could identify herself wholly with the artist's efforts and aims. She had an infallible instinct for all the arts. She never mistook the second-best for the best. She became for Willa Cather what every writer needs most, the helping friend."

Isabelle McClung proposed to Willa Cather that she leave her boarding-house and come to live in the McClung mansion. Dorothy Canfield Fisher remembers:

> The McClungs had a great rich house, with plenty of servants, conducted in the lavish style of half a century ago. Isabelle was simply devoted to Willa always, and was sweet, warm-hearted and sincere— as well as very beautiful, at least I used to think her so, in a sumptuous sort of way. There was a good deal of stately entertaining carried on in the Mc-Clung house too, the many-coursed dinners of the most formal kind, which seemed picturesque (and they really were) to Willa.

For Willa Cather the invitation must have been a welcome one. It meant release from boarding-house life and greater freedom to write in ideal surroundings. In a sense she was achieving a childhood dream and reliving a childhood experience; there had always been in Red Cloud the other house, the house where there were books and pictures and cultivated manners—that of the Wieners—which had later been translated into the Westermann home in Lincoln. The McClung residence was the Wiener or Westermann house many times more spacious and elegant. Isabelle McClung offered Willa Cather a quiet room at the back of the house; it had, like the study in *The Professor's House*, been the sewing-room. Here she could work in peace, looking down over garden and trees to the Monongahela and the hills beyond. It is of this that she wrote when she dedicated *The Song of the Lark:*

To
Isabelle McClung

On uplands,
At morning,
The world was young, the winds were free;

> *A garden fair,*
> *In that blue desert air,*
> *Its guest invited me to be.*[1]

Judge McClung's house stood high on the top of a hilly street, on a little ridge with steps leading to a front porch banked with honeysuckle.

Isabelle McClung's parents at first wondered at the propriety of having Willa Cather come to reside in the household, though they welcomed her as their daughter's friend. The daughter promptly threatened to leave home if she could not have her way; her parents yielded and Willa Cather settled in Murray Hill Avenue as a temporary guest. She remained there, at Isabelle McClung's urging, during the rest of her Pittsburgh stay. Life for her now became even-paced and less driven; she could spend precious hours in her room writing in a more sustained fashion than hitherto. Elizabeth Moorhead, who called at Murray Hill Avenue after the publication of "Paul's Case," and became a friend of both Willa Cather and Isabelle McClung, says that evening after evening the two young women would forsake the McClung family group and spend their time reading Tolstoy, Turgenev, Balzac, and Flaubert. This was the way Willa Cather appeared to her when she first called at the house:

> Short, rather stocky in build, she had a marked directness of aspect. You saw at once that here was a person who couldn't easily be diverted from her chosen course. "Pretty" would indeed be a trivial word to describe a face that showed so much strength of character as hers, yet she was distinctly good-looking, with a clear rosy skin, eyes of light grey and hair a dark brown brushed back from a low forehead—an odd and charming contrast in color. They were observant eyes, nothing escaped them. . . . She looked me straight in the face as she greeted me, and I felt her absolute frankness and honesty. She would never say anything she didn't mean. . . .

---

[1] Willa Cather retained the dedication but eliminated these lines in the collected edition of her works.

To the years in Murray Hill Avenue belong the poems that constituted Willa Cather's first book and the tales that were incorporated in her first volume of prose fiction, *The Troll Garden*.

II

Before Willa Cather published her first two books she had to undergo one further experience; she had to discover the world that lay beyond the Eastern seaboard, beyond the Atlantic. Her first journey to Europe was made with Isabelle McClung during the summer of 1902 when she had completed her first year of teaching. To go to the sources from which much in America was derived, to discover links with a distant past, made the journey a time of exciting intellectual and æsthetic discovery. In England it was not only the present that interested her—and she saw it with the open eyes of a newcomer in its ugliness as well as its beauty—it was the evidence that still remained of the Imperial Rome of her Latin excursions with Mr. Ducker in Red Cloud. So in France later she discovered the sources from which sprang not only New France but the missions of the Southwest. In later years Willa Cather was to say that it takes the right kind of American to go to France— one with character and depth and a passion for the things that lie deep behind French history and French art. In a sense she was describing the qualifications of Claude Wheeler, her hero in *One of Ours*, and indeed her own. Grounded deeply in American soil, the novels of Willa Cather nevertheless are attached also by visible threads to roots in the Old World. The journey of 1902 was a landmark in the formation of the novelist.

It is possible to follow Willa Cather's European itinerary in the series of vivid letters which she contributed to the *State Journal* during her travels. She sailed with her companion in June. Presently they were in Chester, where three decades earlier another American novelist, Henry James, had begun his English tour recorded in *Transatlantic Sketches*. We catch the note of Willa Cather's mood from the first as she and Isabelle spent half of a June day "in utter solitude" at the foot of Chester's reconstructed tower:

"The rains and winds of a thousand years have given the masonry of the tower a white clean-washed look, like the cobble-stones of the street after a shower." The solitude is complete, the swallows nest serenely in the embrasures and loopholes, past and present merge in a timeless synthesis.

Speedily the journey becomes a pilgrimage to literary scenes, to the graves of the great. Under the impulse of Willa Cather's admiration for A. E. Housman there was a lively and enthusiastic trip through Shropshire, and later, as we shall see, a call on the poet himself. But Willa Cather did not confine herself to the arts in her European reportage; her jounalistic training enabled her to gather information rapidly and translate it into readable narrative; thus, at this point, she reported to her fellow Nebraskans in a lively and circumstantial manner on English canals, boats, crews. In London they stayed in a comfortable little hotel in King Street off Cheapside and Willa Cather's transition from the world of castles and romance and the English countryside to the sharp Hogarthian picture was complete:

> . . . the living city and not the dead one has kept us here, and the hard garish ugly mask of the immediate present drags one's attention quite away from the long past it covers. If the street life . . . is in any city more gloomy, more ugly, more grimy, more cruel than in London, I certainly don't care to see it. . . . Of all the shoddy foreigners one encounters there are none so depressing as the London shoddy. We have spent morning after morning on High Holborn or the Strand watching this never ending procession of men in top-hats, shabby boots, ragged collars; they invariably have a flower in their buttonhole, a briar pipe between their teeth, and an out-of-the-fight look in the eyes that ranges from utter listlessness to sullen defiance. . . . But very few of these night birds are fond of water and next to gin they are enamoured of life; of these muddy skies and leaky night skies, of their own bench along the embankment, of the favorite neighbor they beat or chew or claw, of the sting of cheap gin in empty stomachs and the exciting game of chess they play with the police back and forth across the marble squares.

Willa Cather observed the London shop girl: "She wears flowers and paste jewels but she seldom bathes, never has enough hair pins and considers tooth brushes necessary only for members of the royal family"; and the flower girl: "We have nothing at all at home to correspond with her. Her voice is harder than her gin-sodden face, it cuts you like a whip lash as she shouts 'Rowses! Rowses! penny a bunch!' " *Rowses! Rowses!* The cry was to be remembered and despite its whiplash was to acquire a romantic connotation for Willa Cather as the theme for a poem:

> *Roses of London, perfumed with a thousand years . . .*
> *Roses of London town, red till the summer is done. . . .*

Joined by Dorothy Canfield, Willa Cather and Isabelle McClung traveled to Paris at the Bank Holiday in August. They took the overnight boat from Newhaven to Dieppe. "Certainly so small a body of water as the English Channel never separated two worlds so different." In the dawn they had their first glimpse of the twinkling lights of France. Presently they were breakfasting at a Dieppe hotel, and on its stone terrace Willa Cather caught the glare of the sun on white rock and yellow sand and "a little boy . . . was flying a red and green kite, quite the most magnificent kite I have ever seen, and it went up famously, up and up until his string ran short and of a truth one's heart went just as high." This vision of escape from the things that bound one to earth was always to haunt Willa Cather. In "Coming, Aphrodite!" the pigeons wheeling out of the dust of Washington Square into the sky were described in the same way, and in the opening pages of *Lucy Gayheart*, from her sleigh Lucy sees the first star in the frosty sky and it "brought her heart into her throat. . . . That joy of saluting what is far above one was an eternal thing, not merely something that had happened to her ignorance and her foolish heart."

On that memorable day Willa Cather saw from the doorway through which she entered France the play of light and color, the reach of something for the sky, even though but a child's kite, and warm impressions flooded upon her, lighting up France for all the years to come. They proceeded to Rouen with its many associations of Flaubert. Willa Cather's report was sharply personal:

"Late in the day we arrived at Rouen, the well-fed, self-satisfied town built upon the hills beside the Seine, the town where Gustave Flaubert was born and worked and which he so sharply satirized and bitterly cursed in his letters to his friends in Paris. In France it seems that a town will forgive the man who curses it if only he is great enough." She might be writing of Rouen, but she seems to have thought of Red Cloud. "The Sculptor's Funeral" was already in her pen.

They viewed the Flaubert monument and the bust of Flaubert's protégé, Maupassant, and continued their travels. Looking at Paris from a terrace in Montmartre, Willa Cather saw it gleaming and purple across the ribbon of the Seine "like the city of St. John's vision or the Heavenly City that Bunyan saw across the river." The pilgrimages to the graves of the great continued: Heine's, which Willa Cather found covered with forget-me-nots, Musset's, Chopin's, the Balzac monument, "conspicuously ugly and deserted, but Balzac seems more a living fact than a dead man of letters. He lives in every street and quarter; one sees his people everywhere. He told the story not only of a Paris of yesterday, but of the Paris of today or tomorrow." To Willa Cather he seemed second only to Napoleon himself.

A visit to Barbizon caused her to reflect that creative artists had worked there leaving "intact the beauty that drew them there. They have built no new and shining villas, introduced no tennis courts, or golf links, or electric lights." Looking beyond the town, she translated a French *paysage* into familiar terms for her readers:

> The wheat fields beyond the town were quite as level as those of the Nebraska divides. The long even stretch of yellow stubble, broken here and there by . . . Lombard poplars recalled not a little the country about Campbell and Bladen and is certainly more familiar than anything I have seen on this side of the Atlantic.

She was interested in discovering in the field a reaper of American make.

In September they journeyed into the south, into the warm land of Alphonse Daudet, where the mistral blew "more terrible than any wind that ever came up from Kansas." Willa Cather drank in the warmth and color of the land and rejoiced in its people. The impressions of Provence garnered now were ineffaceable to the last. She rejoiced in the landscape, the history, the architecture, the food, the wine; she stayed at the hotel in the ancient Papal city of Avignon, which Henry James had affectionately praised in his travel writings. Willa Cather and Isabelle McClung were the only English-speaking people in the town; there seemed to be no other tourists and Willa Cather enjoyed saturating herself with the life and aspect of the place. Here on the bank of the Rhône the young woman from the Divide had found something that touched her more deeply than the metropolitan density of London or the luminous quality of Paris; a life rooted in the centuries—what she later had in mind when she spoke of the things that lie deep behind French history and French art. That art extended to the sense of well-being that comes from sun and light and artfully cooked food; it is reflected in Bishop Latour's remark when he tastes the soup cooked by Father Vaillant: ". . . a soup like this is not the work of one man. It is the result of a constantly refined tradition. There are nearly a thousand years of history in this soup."

A rapid trip to Nice and Monte Carlo was followed by a return to the heart of Provence, to Arles, where Willa Cather again could discover the Roman past:

> It is with something like a sigh of relief that one quits the oppressive splendor of Monte Carlo to re-trace one's steps back into Daudet's country. I am sure I do not know why the beauty of Monte Carlo should not satisfy more than it does. . . . I had a continual restless feeling that there was nothing at all real about Monte Carlo; that the sea was too blue to be wet, the casino too white to be anything but pasteboard, and that from their very greenness the palms must be cotton . . . nothing at all produced or manufactured there and no life at all that takes hold upon the soil or grapples with the old conditions set for a people.

In Arles she found no pasteboard. The Roman ruins had withstood the centuries; the Roman colonists had "a sort of

Chicago-like vehemence in adorning their city and making it ostentatiously rich," and the great eagle with a garland in its beak mounted on a section of cornice, "the one bird more terrible in history than all the rest of the brute creatures put together," had the inscription above him: "Rome Eternal"—amid ruins! Willa Cather wondered, as she described this, whether the Latin peoples, inheritors of the Romans, "must wither before the cold wind from the north, as their mothers did long ago." It was a pity. "A life so picturesque, an art so rich and so divine, an intelligence so keen and flexible—and yet one knows that this people face toward the setting, not the rising sun." It was difficult for Willa Cather to accept anything that did not endure.

III

The visit to A. E. Housman during the English phase of the European journey deserves to be chronicled apart since Ford Madox Ford made the episode the occasion for one of his finely spun imaginative anecdotes of his late years and because it reflected some of the passion and intensity Willa Cather brought to poetry and to literary achievement during this period of her life. She had discovered Housman's poetry long before he became a celebrated figure. As early as 1900 she had written in her Nebraska column: "I wonder who and what this man Housman may be." She found his touch "as genuine as Heine's" and its quality "as unmistakable as it is rare." In writing from Ludlow to the *State Journal* she observed that anyone "who has ever read Mr. Housman's verse at all must certainly wish to live awhile among the hillside fields, the brooklands and villages which moved a modern singer to lyric expression of a simplicity, spontaneity and grace the like of which we have scarcely heard in the last hundred years." She related that she went to Shrewsbury "chiefly to get some information about Housman—and saw the old files of the little country paper where many of his lyrics first appeared as free contributions and signed *A Shropshire Lad*. There was one copy of his book in the public library, but no one knew anything in particular about him." The Western countryside was full of reminders of the poems; her original enthusiasm for them was natural enough in one for whom Stevenson's verse had so great an appeal. The Housman poems and the Housman countryside, reacting upon each other, produced an excitement that was different from any she had experienced in the work of other living poets. She determined to see the writer.

Ford Madòx Ford in his *Return to Yesterday*, with that fondness for spinning stories which H. G. Wells characterized as "a copious carelessness of reminiscence," turned the story of Willa Cather's visit into a veritable saga. She and Isabelle McClung are here described not merely as curious young American women seeking out their favorite poet, but veritable emissaries sent abroad by the "Pittsburgh Shropshire Lad Club" to present a solid gold laurel wreath to Housman; Ford tells in detail of their wandering across England and their calls at innumerable parsonages in search of the writer of the lyrics. To make Ford's long story short, they ultimately discovered Housman, laid the wreath on his grand piano, and departed after he had mistaken them for American cousins.

As with all of Ford's elaborate reminiscences, there was only a germ of truth in the story and even that was not accurately recounted. What actually happened was that Willa Cather began to inquire, when she reached London, where Housman lived (he was then teaching Latin at University College). One afternoon, accompanied by both Isabelle McClung and Dorothy Canfield, she made the trip to his lodgings in Highgate. On the bus she was still wondering what he would be like. "We may find he's a blacksmith, working at his trade, or perhaps a retired officer living on half pay." This was the image his poetry had created in Willa Cather's mind. Dorothy Canfield Fisher remembers:

> I think from what he turned out to be in personality that nothing would have induced him to let in three young American women, entire strangers to him, on an incense-burning trip. He came racing down the stairs full of cordiality, holding out both hands, thinking that we were three Canadian cousins whom he was expecting and whom he had never seen. It was a shock to him to find who we were, and I think if he could have managed it without actually

pushing us out of the house he would have been very glad to get rid of us with no delay.

What followed was a little comedy of manners, a veritable scene out of Molière. The man envisaged by Willa Cather as a robust retired officer or a brawny blacksmith who could write immortal lyrics appeared to be more prosaic than the Browning of the London drawing-rooms. He had for the young women a reticent presence, perhaps an awkward charm, but a minimum of conversation. Shabbily dressed, as withdrawn as only Englishmen can on occasion be, he lamely, in a flat accent of conventional acceptance of an unexpected social situation, asked his visitors upstairs.

While Dorothy Canfield, who had not had a sight of Shropshire and to whom Willa Cather had not imparted the full extent of her enthusiasm, was looking at their reluctant host, the academically shabby furnishings (totally unendowed with the grand piano Ford Madox Ford later moved into the rooms), and the commonplace books on the shelves, Willa Cather and Isabelle McClung tried to convey to him what the poems had meant to them. This was not a kind of conversation that Housman found easy or even agreeable. Soon an awkward silence enveloped the group. Willa Cather in her newspaper days had met celebrities and knew how to cope with them. But how cope with this shy and seemingly aloof English professor who was not then a celebrity and seemed to be the very opposite of all his poetry suggested? As the silence grew thicker, Dorothy Canfield mentioned her work at the British Museum. Housman was interested; French drama, the study of dubious and corrupt texts, the relation between French and Latin poetry, the kinds of Latin poetry and the difficulties they offered to the research student—on topics like these Housman could be expansive and was. It was the opportunity he needed to depersonalize the situation, to lower a protective curtain between himself and his admiring guests. Indeed, nothing could persuade him to abandon the discussion, which became a dialogue between Dorothy Canfield and the poet. There was no more said about his lyrics or about himself. When the three left, Dorothy Canfield was embarrassed at having monopolized the conversation. Magnanimously Willa Cather said: "But Dorothy, you saved the day." And then on the bus-top as they rode back to the city she suddenly burst into uncontrollable sobs. They were tears of rage and of exasperation—and of disillusionment. Years later she told the anecdote with amusement and spoke of it as "my very pleasant visit with Housman," told it, indeed, once too often, to Ford one day at *McClure's*. To Carl J. Weber, of Colby College, who questioned her about the Ford version, she said that it had all happened "many years ago when I was very young and foolish and thought that if one admired a writer very much one had a perfect right to ring his doorbell. On the occasion of that uninvited call—certainly abrupt enough—Housman was not in the least rude, but very courteous and very kind. I judged he was not accustomed to such intrusions, but he certainly made every effort to make one feel at ease." And she added: "Some day I intend to write a careful and accurate account of that visit for persons who are particularly interested." Unfortunately the account was never written. Yet it had undeniably been an emotional experience. The poet Willa Cather imagined in the work seemed, perhaps, difficult to reconcile with the poet she met that day in the flesh.

IV

Willa Cather's first book was published in 1903, the year after her return from abroad. Like the debut of many a writer it was a slim volume of poetry. It bore the title *April Twilights*, and most of the poems had been published in the preceding months in magazines; the dedicatory verse to her brothers recalled the mood of "Far Island," and the twilights alluded to belonged to Nebraska, not to Pittsburgh. Twenty years later, when it was reissued under the same title with thirteen additional poems, she discarded the verse dedication and inscribed the book "To my father for a Valentine." The poems, early and late, show Willa Cather's verbal skill and her firm grasp of prosody. There are echoes in them of her readings of Virgil and Horace; there are other echoes of Rossetti, and the inevitable influence of Housman emerges in stanzas such as

> *Lads and their sweethearts lying*
> *In the cleft of the windy hill;*

> *Hearts that are hushed of their sighing,*
> *Lips that are tender and still.*[2]

We find, however, at every turn a curious poetic rigidity
and we discover the anomaly that one who could infuse a
page of prose with the cadences of poetry grew self-con-
scious and artificial in the writing of verse. The reader
today can glean at best from *April Twilights* certain lines
filled with delicate music:

> *Flutes for the feathery locusts,*
> *soft as spray*

and an occasional bright image. Willa Cather came closest
to the contemporary idiom in "Prairie Dawn" or in the
flatness of "Macon Prairie" or "Going Home":

> *How smoothly the trains run beyond the Missouri;*
> *Even in my sleep I know when I have crossed the river.*

Largely we catch from the poems those subjects and moods
which will find their way into the novels. Spanish Johnny
("those were golden things he said, To his mandolin") is
there; the poem "Grandmither, think not I forget" heralds
"Old Mrs. Harris"; the picture of "The Swedish Mother" is
painted in early pigments she will use in *O Pioneers!* or
later with rich tones in *Sapphira*; and there is the general
note of the elegiac, the ache of things dead and gone, the
"incommunicable past," which will be struck repeatedly
and in particular in *My Ántonia*. All her life was a quest
for the *neiges d'antan*:

> *Where are the loves that we have loved before*
> *When once we are alone and shut the door?*

and finally that sense of time immutable, the cave-dwellers
and the Rock; touched perhaps with the accent of Yeats:

> *The old volcanic mountains*
> *That slope up from the sea—*
> *They dream and dream a thousand years*
> *And watch what-is-to-be.*

---

[2] From "On Media Vita." This poem was not included in the collected edition.

> *What gladness shines upon them*
> *When, white as white sea-foam,*
> *To the old, old ports of Beauty*
> *A new sail comes home!*

It is when we catch in the early poems the foreshadowings of mood in the novels, or echoes of them contained in the later poems, that we can endow them with an added quality of feeling that was not originally evoked. *April Twilights* remains a part of the *œuvre* of Willa Cather largely as gleams and flashes from the mind that wrote the fiction.

V

Publication of *April Twilights* won Willa Cather a measure of recognition and a marked degree of respect from her fellow teachers and pupils. Ethel Jones Litchfield, a musician and a friend of Willa Cather's for almost half a century, remembers her at this time, when she first met her, as busy with her school work, her writing, her friends, and caught up in the web of calculated social life provided by Isabelle McClung. Yet she found time always for music and the theater and in particular liked to listen until all hours of the night to chamber-music rehearsals, in which Mrs. Litchfield, an accomplished pianist, participated with Pittsburgh's leading musicians as well as guest artists. One such guest, at a later date, was Jan Hambourg, the violinist, who was to marry Isabelle McClung and to whom Willa Cather dedicated two of her later novels. Jan Hambourg was a cultivated musician of a mixed Russian-Jewish-English background, a sensitive performer, an avid reader, particularly fond of the French novelists and a man of considerable general culture. He lived in Canada, in Toronto, where he and his brother Boris, the cellist, and their father taught music. The time was to come when Hambourg would sit for a not wholly flattering portrait as Louie Marsellus in *The Professor's House*.

Willa Cather's literary output during the three years that followed the European journey was modest. She wrote slowly and with great care and had little difficulty in placing her work in the larger magazines. She appeared in

Lippincott's, the *New England Magazine, Scribner's, Everybody's*, and *McClure's*, and the publication of "Paul's Case" in the last in 1905 gave her a foretaste of the interest her work would arouse increasingly with an ever-growing public. In retrospect it seems fitting that she climaxed her stay in Pittsburgh by producing her first volume of short stories; when she was assembling it she did not know that it would mark the end of a decade, and indeed of a distinct period of her life; but with the appearance of *The Troll Garden* in 1905, published by McClure, Phillips & Company, Willa Cather closed a door upon her formative years and by the same token opened another upon her future.

Her first book in prose contained two groups of stories. Three of the stories, the first, the third, and the fifth, present artists in relation with persons of great wealth. Alternating with these sophisticated tales is another series, comprising the second, fourth, and sixth stories, in which an artist or a person of artistic temperament from the prairies returns to them in defeat. The collection closes with "Paul's Case," the story of a sensitive Pittsburgh youth, for which there is a subtitle: "A Study in Temperament." The book, dedicated to Isabelle McClung, carries two epigraphs. The first, facing the title page, is a quatrain from Christina Rossetti's "Goblin Market":

> *We must not look at Goblin men,*
> *We must not buy their fruits;*
> *Who knows upon what soil they fed*
> *Their hungry, thirsty roots?*

The second epigraph, on the title page, is taken from Charles Kingsley:

> A fairy palace, with a fairy garden . . . inside the trolls dwell . . . working at their magic forges, making and making always things rare and strange.

When Willa Cather brought out her second collection of stories, *Youth and the Bright Medusa*, fifteen years later, she discarded the sophisticated stories of the artists living amid wealth and the troll epigraph, but retained the tales of artistic defeat in the West and the epigraph from the

"Goblin Market," thus ratifying the inescapable conclusion that *The Troll Garden* consists of two interwoven themes, with "Paul's Case" as a sort of coda.

Willa Cather was under the spell of Henry James at this time and quite possibly was struck by the manner in which he always arranged his short-story collections thematically. If one were to seek a parallel to *The Troll Garden* in James, it is to be found in his volume *The Two Magics*, published while Willa Cather was in Pittsburgh, in which he juxtaposed a tale of black magic ("The Turn of the Screw") with what might be considered a tale of white magic ("Covering End")—the one baleful, filled with suggestions of nightmare and evil, the other bright, sunny, cheerful, fairy-tale-like in substance and denouement. So Willa Cather's two strands in *The Troll Garden* are the baleful and the sunny, the evil-working goblins and the industrious trolls. Her stories of artists creating "things rare and strange" amid the wealthy belong to the trolls and to that "fairy garden" which was also the "garden fair . . . On uplands" to which Isabelle McClung had invited Willa Cather. The fairy palace and the fairy garden are the preserves of art; and the trolls are artists or persons with artistic temperament. In each of the stories the trolls come into relation, and usually into conflict, with those who live outside the preserves of art or trespass upon them. The tales of the defeated artists from the prairies are tales filled with an undercurrent of malaise and a sense of nightmare: those who venture into the goblin market, that great and exciting yet treacherous world beyond the prairies, risk eating of the poisoned fruit. The goblins will "get them"—if they don't look out! The sensuous fruits of life and of luxury can be tainted with evil. Success somehow exacts an ominous price. There is always the danger of having to retrace one's steps, back, back into the open stretches. This is the equivalent of death: the stony death that lies in the deceptive stare of the Bright Medusa. The attitude toward the aspect of the prairies, toward the people who live on them and form the ideas that prevail there, is still hard.

VI

The first of the three tales of the "troll" series, "Flavia and Her Artists," is the story of the wife of a manufacturer of threshing machines. Lacking any æsthetic responses, and unaware of her lack, she collects artists and intellectuals so that from the phrases she forces from them she can make an appearance of cleverness before the rest of the world. An ironic story might have been written about Flavia's parasitic relation with her artists; and that story is in fact here, but entangled with much else. It is entangled, for instance, with the presentation of her artists—some of them persons of the first rank in performance—as sorry, stunted human beings. The crux of the story comes when a French novelist, just after he leaves the house-party, gives an interview in which Flavia's type is ridiculed; everyone who remains, except Flavia, sees the report of the interview; and her loyal husband, believing that what Monsieur Roux has said the rest of the artists think, rebukes them at his own table. "As for M. Roux," Arthur Hamilton says, "his very profession places him in that class of men whom society has never been able to accept unconditionally because it has never been able to assume that they have any ordered notion of taste. He and his ilk remain, with the mountebanks and snake charmers, people indispensable to our civilization, but wholly unreclaimed by it; people whom we receive, but whose invitations we do not accept." An ironic story might have been written also about the chasm between the artist's devotion to beauty and what is sordid and trivial in the rest of his life; there are fragments of that story here, in the crude manners of one, the simper of another, the "malicious vulgarities" of a third; but only fragments, for just where this story required definition and elaboration, in the rendering of Roux, it evaporates. There does not seem to be anything wrong with Roux except that he is candid where the laws of hospitality require silence or a lie. The center shifts from Flavia to her artists and then to her husband, not with development, but only with vacillation.

The second in the series, "The Garden Lodge," is essentially a record of an inner conflict. Caroline Noble questions whether the practical stodgy life she lives in reaction against the fecklessness of her musician father and painter brother is not a negation of life. In the rendering of Caroline's bitter, anxious mood one can feel not only Willa Cather's personal sense of the value for one's life of devotion to art, but no less, and for the first time in her writing, a sense that sustained labor, when forced upon one by ambition and determination and directed toward a nonartistic goal, threatens the very core of personality. This was an opinion that Sarah Orne Jewett was soon to preach to her; her own experience was already leading her to feel its force.

The third and most Jamesian of the tales, "The Marriage of Phaedra," tells of an artist's visit to the studio of a fellow artist after his death and his discovering there an unfinished masterpiece. He decides after talking with the late Hugh Treffinger's servant, whose name is James, to write a biography of the artist. This leads to a meeting with Treffinger's widow. As later, in "Coming, Aphrodite!" he discovers the woman understood neither the artistic aims nor the temperament of her husband. In the end she sells the great unfinished picture to a dealer in a distant land. The story is filled with Jamesian echoes, and notably of those of his tales of artists and writers which appeared during the 1890's. As in "Flavia," the author writes from a recent superficial absorption of the material. The process Stephen Crane described, the "filtering through the blood," had not occurred, had not begun to occur.

From the group, the work of an author who had been thinking about the arts more than about anything else for fifteen years, it is unexpectedly difficult to derive any theory, any general idea. Artists do not often appear practicing their art, or theorizing about it, and never do they attempt either theory or practice at length; they appear in their relations with others, usually either with nonartistic persons or with persons who are merely appreciative. One may safely derive the idea that artists are crucially unlike other beings; Roux's discourtesy is an outcome of his radical honesty, his need to tell the truth whatever may fall; Treffinger loved his wife, but he sacrificed her as he sacrificed everything else that threatened his art; the emphasis on the unlikeness of the artist runs through all the stories. The unlikeness often brings havoc into the lives of those who surround the artist. The emphasis on the enriching force of an artist's personality also runs through the stories, and Willa Cather has made no attempt to weigh the havoc and the enrichment in the balance: she is content to suggest that both are real, both weighty.

The most promising source for a general idea about art

is "The Marriage of Phaedra," for here one artist is seeking to unravel the artistic method as well as the personality of another. The narrator discovers that Treffinger was guided toward his method and the range of his subjects by an older painter from whom he learned as much as an artist of genius can learn from anyone; in order to paint his masterpiece he needed to add to what he had learned the fruit of painful intimate experience. The clue to Treffinger's greatness as an artist is in the fusion of experience with instruction. Simple as this formula may be, it is not superficial. It applies generally to Willa Cather's writing—to the few promising pieces she had done before "The Marriage of Phaedra" and to the works she was to do.

The stories in which art and the prairies are brought together were of quite another sort, as Willa Cather herself recognized when she reincorporated them into *Youth and the Bright Medusa*. These stories arise from old memories, they have the richness that long preoccupation can give. They have been filtered through the blood. In "A Wagner Matinée" the deep source is in Willa Cather's brooding over the life of an aunt for whom the years on a farm in Webster County were a form of slow suffocation to which she was almost inhumanly resigned; in "The Sculptor's Funeral" the source is in her sense of her own differentness, vulnerability, and value during her years in Red Cloud. The incidents scarcely matter, and there is no contrivance in the arrangement of them: the stories take their life and also their shape from the force and fineness of the feelings poured into them. The quality that animated those passages in "The Garden Lodge" where the theme is the woman's feelings about the crucial and irremediable mistake in her management of her life sweeps through "A Wagner Matinée" and "The Sculptor's Funeral." For "A Death in the Desert"—the title derived from Browning— one cannot say the same. It is like the other two stories about art and the prairies in the rendering of the foreground; but in the background is the world of "Flavia and Her Artists," evoked as the dying singer and the brother of the great composer she has loved talk away her last afternoons in the Colorado summer, with the same chasm between the artist's devotion to beauty and what is ugly and small in his personal life. The fall in force from the scenes in the foreground to those in the background is always palpable. Only in the rendering of the Western elements is there an effect of moving authenticity or of depth.

In a very direct manner these tales are saying what Thomas Wolfe expressed more crudely as "you can't go home again." An image of "home" creates the tense and emotional climax of "A Wagner Matinée." As the music in Boston dies away and the reality of Nebraska replaces it, the aunt sobs: " 'I don't want to go . . . I don't want to go!' . . . For her, just outside the concert hall, lay the black pond with the cattle-tracked bluffs; the tall, unpainted house, with weather-curled boards, naked as a tower; the crook-backed ash seeedlings where the dishcloths hung to dry; the gaunt, moulting turkeys picking up refuse about the kitchen door."[3] In "A Death in the Desert" Katharine Gaylord's fate is summed up by her brother: ". . . She got to Chicago, and then to New York, and then to Europe, and got a taste for it all; and now she's dying here like a rat in a hole, out of her own world, and she can't fall back into ours." The burden of "The Sculptor's Funeral" is that even in death the artist cannot escape the harshness and hostility of his home surroundings where he is fated to be remembered as "queer" because he never conformed, and because he fled to unfamiliar worlds undreamed of by his family and friends. It is the town lawyer who pronounces the strange eulogy over the sculptor's coffin: "There was only one boy ever raised in this borderland between ruffianism and civilization who didn't come to grief, and you hated Harvey Merrick more for winning out than you hated all the other boys who got under the wheels." One couldn't go home even in death. Or, as Lucy Gayheart was to discover, to go home was to die.

Although different in setting and material, "Paul's Case" is of a piece with these tales. It has been the most widely read of Willa Cather's short stories; for many years it was the only one she would allow to be reprinted in anthologies or textbooks. A surprising number of the aspects in her experience of Pittsburgh are gathered into "Paul's Case." Paul is a student at the Pittsburgh high school; and in the early scenes the life of the school is given in classroom vignettes and in one long disciplinary incident in which the

3 This passage is quoted from the first edition. It underwent slight verbal alteration in the collected edition.

boy is under attack from principal and staff. The neighborhood where Paul lives has the petty-bourgeois dreariness
that Willa Cather had resented during her years of boarding-house living: the ugly dirty plumbing, the kitchen
odors, the unbuttoned laziness of Sunday afternoons, the
everlasting sameness from house to house and street to
street. Into this stagnant world there seeps one romantic
element, the legends of "the cash-boys who had become
famous." On every stoop there were tales of the prodigies
of effort by a Carnegie or a Frick, and of their costly
pleasures, their Mediterranean cruises, their Venetian pal-
aces. The practical deposit of these legends was not inspir-
iting to a boy like Paul: the whole duty of a boy was to
qualify by hard work, miserly economy, respectable living,
and the shunning of all distractions. One might almost as
well have lived in the small Western town of "The Sculptor's Funeral," in Red Cloud. From the routines of home
and school Paul's regular escape is to the symphonies and
pictures in Carnegie Hall; and for him the great "portal of
romance" is, as it was for Willa Cather, the stage entrance
to the downtown theater where a stock company plays.
The doors to the Schenley Hotel, where she had gone to
interview so many visitors when she wrote for the *Leader*,
make another such portal: Paul is drawn to them not only
because they are the approach to luxury but because the
singers and actors with whom he identifies himself are
always passing through them. Like Willa Cather and so
many others who lived in Pittsburgh, he felt the pull of
New York, the wish to exchange Carnegie Hall for the
Metropolitan Opera, the Schenley for the Waldorf, to feel
himself in the center of "the plot of all dramas, the text of
all romances, the nerve-stuff of all sensations."

The first half of the story describes Paul amid his circumstances in Pittsburgh, the second his yielding to the
pull of New York, stealing a thousand dollars from his
employers, buying everything one should have to mingle
with the millionaires, and after his few days at the Waldorf
carrying out the last phase of his plan by taking his life. In
the end Paul too can't go home again; he has burned his
bridges and has no wish to rebuild them. The Pittsburgh
scenes are vivid beyond anything in the series of sophisticated stories, with sharp strokes from experience both of
outer objects and of personal states, never multiplied in

excess of what the effects demand. New York is drawn in a contrasting manner, for which there is not a parallel in any of the other stories, as a dream city, snow-covered, with a beautiful thick impressionistic haziness that suits the setting for the dreamlike climax of Paul's life.

VII

The two strands of *The Troll Garden* belong to one experience. At the end of her decade in Pittsburgh Willa Cather stood at a crossroad: there was disillusionment in the garden and danger in the marketplace. The artist from the cornfields that reached to daybreak and the corrals that reached to sunset was still searching for a path upon which to set her feet. In the houses of the rich the trolls proved to be less magical and less creative than they seemed; in the goblin world the roots of success were tainted with the poison of evil and the threat of destruction. And there was that other world to which one might have to return like Katharine Gaylord, dying, or Harvey Merrick, dead, or even young Paul, frustrated and a suicide, a boy who "got under the wheels," the world of the Philistine of which Thea Kronborg discovered that "nothing that she would ever do . . . would seem important to them, and nothing they would ever do would seem important to her." The inner texture of these stories seems to reflect strong ambiguities of feeling: a continuing resentment of the West, a continuing fear of attaining success in the world into which Willa Cather had escaped and in which, temporarily, she had found a garden sanctuary. How to make peace with these two haunting worlds—this was the problem to which Willa Cather was to address herself, and the very book that stated the problem was instrumental in offering a solution.

S. S. McClure, publisher of the magazine that bore his name, came to Pittsburgh to meet the author of *The Troll Garden*. The stories had produced a marked impression on him. He dined at Judge McClung's and talked brilliantly all evening. Then he had a talk with Willa Cather. The upshot of it was that at the end of the school year she resigned from Allegheny High and moved to New York to enter upon a new career that mingled the experience of her journalistic days with her literary talents and ambitions. She became a member of the staff of *McClure's Magazine*. There had been the sudden, unexpected leap from Red Cloud to Pittsburgh ten years earlier; and now, as she neared her middle thirties, Willa Cather made the second leap—from an obscure classroom to a post on an important national magazine. S. S. McClure, with the magic of his talk and his capacity for eloquently pyramiding grandiose plans, had swept Willa Cather into the very path for which all the years of striving in the West and the bright hard years of Pittsburgh had prepared her. The inexperienced young girl who, tense and eager, had stepped from the prairies into the smoky Eastern city a decade before was now a mature woman of thirty-two; and though she could not have known it at this singularly triumphant moment, she was entering the final and most exacting phase of her long literary apprenticeship.

6

At *McClure's*

1906–1912

WILLA CATHER CAME to *McClure's Magazine* after
the worst upheaval in its never tranquil life. Ellery Sedgwick, who also came to it in 1906, speaks of the upheaval
as a "revolution," in which "the most brilliant staff ever
gathered by a New York periodical left Mr. McClure in a
body." The sort of revolution it was shows rather precisely
what it meant to work in S. S. McClure's dominion, as
Willa Cather was about to do for six years; and that the
secession at one time of Lincoln Steffens, Ida Tarbell, and
Ray Stannard Baker did not ruin the magazine, or even
endanger its strength, shows rather exactly what sort of
editor-in-chief S. S. McClure was, and why to the end of
her life Willa Cather admired him.

The magazine had been founded in the spring of 1893,
the *annus mirabilis* for intelligent popular monthlies. The
great monthly magazines of elder date such as the *Century*,
the model in format for *McClure's*, sold at thirty-five cents
a copy or more and were addressed to a relatively small
cultivated public. *McClure's*, and its two chief competitors, *Munsey's* and the *Cosmopolitan*, sold for a time at
ten cents a copy and sought twenty subscribers in towns
where the *Century* had one, and one in villages of the
Middle West where no one had ever heard of the *Century*
or the *Atlantic* or *Harper's*. The low price was possible
provided a large circulation was assured, because paper
had become cheaper and because the process of photoen-
graving had cut the cost of illustrations. How were the new
scores of thousands of subscribers to be won? Frank A.
Munsey described his formula years afterward: "I began to
analyze the magazines. They seemed made for anaemics,

and their editors editing for themselves and not for their subscribers. Living in an artificial literary world they got out publications which woefully lacked human interest. . . . I became convinced that both the prices and the magazines were wrong for a wide circulation. If a magazine should be published at ten cents and made light, bright, and timely, it might be a different story." S. S. McClure would never have accepted "light, bright, and timely" as a sufficient formula; he wished not only to win readers, but to improve them. He would, however, have endorsed with the greatest enthusiasm the stress Munsey laid on "human interest." With his own extraordinary indifference to the past, with his excited absorption in what was here and now, he would scarcely have understood how anything could have much "human interest" if it was not timely.

It was by its "human interest" that *McClure's* had its first great impact. The *Century* was running a sober, somewhat ponderous life of Napoleon; McClure persuaded Ida Tarbell, who was deeply read in the French eighteenth century and the Napoleonic period, to produce a much more humanly interesting life. From her serial on Napoleon she went on to another on Lincoln, enriched, according to another formula that helped the magazine to capture "human interest," by a profusion of pictures, some of them never before published. Among the features in the early years of *McClure's* was a new sort of interview in which one distinguished person was queried by another distinguished person on topics of a humanly interesting kind. S. S. McClure understood the importance for circulation of lively well-wrought fiction, especially serial fiction. In his syndicate, his main venture in publishing before he founded the magazine, he had negotiated with many of the most popular English writers, and he had paid them well. He was now able to draw on their goodwill, and to present in *McClure's* Stevenson's *The Ebb Tide* and *St. Ives, Rupert of Hentzau*—the sequel to Anthony Hope's *The Prisoner of Zenda*—and Kipling's *Captains Courageous*. Among the short stories in the early years of the magazine were some of Stephen Crane's and Conan Doyle's; the first of David Graham Phillips's short stories appeared in it.

"Human interest" was at the core of another specialty of the magazine with which its place in the history of American periodicals is now indissolubly linked. This was the "serious article," usually written by a member of the editorial staff. "Its method," one historian has said, "is to present, without sensationalism or exaggeration, facts skilfully marshalled and sternly compressed, and let them speak for themselves." Its substance was typically a report on an outstanding problem in American life, such as the corruptive forces in the government of a city or a state, or the effect on a community of some big business, or of some social evil. Lincoln Steffens, who was for many years the managing editor, desired above all else to "put news" into the magazine. He believed that a complicated news story lost much of its value, and more of its impact, when it was told in driblets in a daily, but that "a monthly could come along, tell the whole completed story all over again, and bring out the meaning of it all with comment." McClure had set Ida Tarbell to studying the Standard Oil Company some time before Steffens came on the magazine; and it is probable that he had a clearer idea of what a "serious article" should be than Steffens brought with him after years of work on newspapers. It was like S. S. McClure to know. Miss Tarbell was allowed to work at collecting and writing her material for three years before her first article appeared; her fifteen chapters consumed five years of her time; and McClure estimated that each article had cost him two thousand dollars. Circulation rose, and he was jubilant. "To secure the accuracy that alone makes such studies of value," he said, "I had to invent a new method of magazine journalism. The fundamental weakness of modern journalism was that the highly specialized activities of civilization were very generally reported by uninformed men, and what experts had to say was seldom interesting. I decided to pay my writers for their study rather than for their copy—to put them on a salary and let them master their subjects before they wrote about them." In "Ardessa," a story that appeared in the *Century* in May 1918, and is full of lighthearted reminiscences of *McClures's*, Willa Cather remarked: "The great men of the staff were all about her, as comtemplative as Buddhas, in their private offices, each meditating on the particular trust or form of vice confided to his care." In no other magazine was contemplation in private so normally linked with topics inherently practical.

Steffens soon appreciated that McClure's formula would

give the magazine the news value appropriate to a monthly publication. Not only would the story be told at once, the commentary on the story would have a solidity that could not be impeached. Although many of the "serious articles" were not complete in themselves, the new method in journalism was an immediate success: the combination in them of nearly expert knowledge of the problem under review with first-rate ability in journalistic writing, both brought to bear on a subject that every reader who thought at all would care about, deserved to succeed. It did succeed; it was much imitated; and whenever it is tried in more recent times the success is as certain as it was at the beginning of the century. What McClure was doing was simply deepening the idea that possessed Joseph Pulitzer, who wrote: "I should make a paper that the judges of the Supreme Court of the United States would read with enjoyment, but I would not make a paper that only the judges of the Supreme Court and their class would read. I would make this paper without lowering the tone in the slightest degree."

Steffens and Baker studied municipal and state and finally federal government. They brought out the ties between business and politics. They linked both with the world of crime. Yet they managed their material in such a fashion that the individuals they exposed did not appear to be ogres, but simply rather limited mortals with an extreme delight in the exercise of power, or in the accumulation of money. "Human interest" is very rich in almost all their exposures. Steffens was far too cynical to become a zealot; and from the observation of many businesses and many governments he drew the conclusion that whatever spots of deepest black might disfigure a politician he was preferable to the business mind in politics, or the humorless do-gooder. So able and so imitable a builder of circulation as the "serious article" was certain to spread across the country and to leave a mark on public opinion. That mark became permanent with the application of a phrase by a President of the United States. In 1905 the *Cosmopolitan* was bought by William Randolph Hearst and, at the instance of his managing editor, David Graham Phillips wrote a series called "The Treason of the Senate." The articles had that ferocious sincerity which Phillips applied to all his analyses and comments on contemporary life. The Senate was presented as a nest of conspirators against the welfare of the democracy, in the interests of big business. The effect was too much for Theodore Roosevelt. In the spring of 1906, without naming Phillips, and by leaving his indictment general, inviting the country to extend it to the entire tribe of "serious" journalistic critcs, he said:

> Expose the crime, and hunt down the criminal, but remember that even in the case of crime, if it is attacked in sensational, lurid, and untruthful fashion, the attack may do more damage to the public mind than the crime itself. . . . The men with the muckrakes are often indispensable to the well-being of society but only if they know how to stop raking the muck, and to look upward to the celestial crown above them, to the crown of worthy endeavor.

Men with the muckrakes, muckrakers, muckraking—these were the words that for years after the President used the phrase—drawn from *The Pilgrim's Progress*, that favorite book of Willa Cather's grandmothers and of Willa Cather's, too—people applied to the staff of *McClure's*, and to the specialty that was more than anything else the reason for the magazine's success and fame.

No one has praised McClure's powers as an editor so highly as men who found they could not remain on his staff. McClure was what a more modern generation would call an "idea man." "He was," says Steffens, "a flower that did not sit and wait for the bees to come and take his honey and leave their seeds. He flew forth to find and rob the bees." He knew where all the bees were; no one could doubt it; but all too often he would mistake another and perfectly useless insect for the bee he desired, and his staff had to dispose of the result. He would commission a series of articles from someone whose appeal lay in his having one idea or having had one experience of note; and when the articles arrived they would often be hopelessly past mending. Or he would appoint to his staff someone who could be put to no use. By the time manuscript or appointee arrived, McClure would be far away where he could not be reached, and even if he had been reached it would have done no good. He was no longer interested in what he had done; or rather, the interest had been overlaid by so many other and newer interests that he would not fix his mind on it. He was like the editor in "Ardessa," "who went in for everything, and got tired of everything; that was why he made a good editor." Someone else was required to deal with the outcome of McClure's reckless decision. When he was away from the office—and since he hated sitting still he was usually away—he was a source of trouble. But when he was there! Writing forty years afterward, Ellery Sedgwick recalls, "The blessed quiet of those days when McClure was abroad! The dove of peace descended upon the office and every man took up his own life. Never," he adds, "in American business was there a brighter genius than McClure's for disorganization." George Kibbe Turner, who came to the magazine in the same year as Ellery Sedgwick and Willa Cather, has described to me what the office was like when McClure arrived with an idea. The publisher's sanctum was at the rear of the suite. It would take McClure nearly half the morning to get to it, pausing at each desk and explaining, exhorting, excoriating; and it would take him the rest of the morning to get out as he repeated the process from the other end. Mark Sullivan reports McClure as saying after one such morning: "I get an idea. It comes to me in the night. I lie awake until morning. I rush to the office with it—and they throw cold water on it." No wonder they did; no wonder they spent much of their time circumventing him; no wonder that when a member of the staff was at work on an article or a story and the deadline was close, a room had to be taken for him (or for her) at some remote and unlikely hotel, and always, even if the hotel were in another city, there was the fear that somehow this man of genius would discover where the writer was. Since there was nothing McClure liked more than getting on a train, he would then unearth the absentee in person. "He could raise a rumpus," says Steffens in a tone almost of awe.

It was into the dominion of this remarkable person, from whom almost an entire staff had just fled, that Willa Cather came late in 1906. In September 1905 she came to New York at McClure's invitation, and remained for a week. Between them there was an immediate liking; and in the six years Willa Cather remained in his employ there was not a cloud on their relationship. She at once perceived that in McClure there was an element of wild genius: he was a great creator, and she thought of him much as she thought of the large-scale men who had opened the West. She responded to the warmth and enthusiasm with which he advocated all his ideas, with a kindred warmth and enthusiasm. Responding to his temperament did not mean that she accepted each idea; but when she disapproved, as she often did, she did not pour cold water on it. She could disapprove and yet not offend, not even discourage. In the campaign against corruption in business and politics, which went on unabated with a new corps of writers, she took scarcely any interest, and she did not pretend the interest she did not feel. McClure accepted her indifference, perhaps with regret, certainly with understanding.

During her first months in New York Willa Cather lived in an old studio building on the south side of Washington Square (Number 60), now torn down. In a story written long afterward, "Coming, Aphrodite!" she has captured the feel of that building, the dirt and must and paucity of baths, the young artists and musicians and writers who occupied most of the rooms, and the general air of a somewhat innocuous Bohemia. In that story she also records her delight in the beauty of the square, and the interest of the foreign populations near by. The main characters in "Coming, Aphrodite!" have dinner in "the back garden of a little French hotel on Ninth Street, long since passed away." This was the Griffou, where she lived for a short time. The inconvenience and drabness of her rooms in Greenwich Village were a sharp break from the ordered luxury of Judge McClung's house, but Willa Cather does not appear to have minded. To live among other young artists, and as they lived, was, for the present, more than enough.

It was her stories and perhaps also her poems that first interested S. S. McClure in Willa Cather; but her main task during her first two years on the magazine had no relation with either. Some months before the secession of talent, McClure was excited by the possibilities he saw in a manuscript that clearly had matter of extraordinary interest but just as clearly could not be used in anything like the form in which it had come in. This was *Mary Baker G. Eddy: The Story of Her Life and History of Christian Science*, by Georgine Milmine, the wife of a newspaperman in Rochester, New York. One of the first members of the staff to work over it was Mark Sullivan, who tells in *The Educa-tion of an American* of trips he took to remote villages in New Hampshire and other parts of New England to verify the astonishing facts of Mrs. Eddy's early life. The Mil-mine manuscript was packed with facts, some of them so startling that careful verification was necessary at whatever cost. After a while Mark Sullivan was taken off the scent, and others were put on. When the first installment was published, in January 1907, it was accompanied by a pic-ture that purported to present Mrs. Eddy in youth, but was in fact the likeness of one of her friends. The mistake was pointed out, and threatened to discredit the series. The chief responsibility for preparing the remainder of the long manuscript for publication was given to Willa Cather. The outcome was a series of thirteen articles (in addition to the first), appearing at intervals, the last of them in June 1908.

II

This was the outcome for *McClure's*; the important out-come for Willa Cather was quite different. It was the op-portunity to live for months at a time at the old Parker House in Boston, and then in an apartment on Chestnut Street—months broken, it is true, by trips to the neighbor-ing shoe towns and to a few places farther away. From the beginning Boston meant Ferris Greenslet, whose review of *April Twilights* had opened a cordial friendship, and who was soon to introduce this "fresh-faced, broad-browed plain-speaking young woman, standing her ground with a singular solidity," to Houghton Mifflin Company. It came to mean Mrs. James T. Fields and Sarah Orne Jewett.

It was not Ferris Greenslet but Mrs. Louis D. Brandeis who introduced Willa Cather to these women who were to leave so strong a mark on her life and art. From the beginning of their acquaintance Willa Cather admired and liked both the Brandeises. Louis Brandeis was among the few persons who seemed to her to have an intuitive under-standing of her art, so sure that she was safe in allowing it to influence her. She shared with the Brandeises many enthusiasms in literature and music, and she was pleased with their way of responding to life. Mrs. Brandeis, she thought, was an ideal wife for a great man, extremely handsome, extremely intelligent, extremely perceptive, very much at home in the world and yet very much superior to it.

Late in the winter of 1908 Mrs. Brandeis took Willa Cather to call at 148 Charles Street, the house where Mrs. James T. Fields had been living for over fifty years, the first twenty-five with her husband, who had died in 1881. He had been a publisher of the *Atlantic* as a member of the house of Ticknor and Fields, later Fields, Osgood & Co., a firm that had dealt generously with English authors in the bad days of piracy. The house on Charles Street had been the American home of Charles Dickens; in one of its upper rooms, scarcely changed since he had slept in it, Thackeray had written a part of *Henry Esmond*. Dr. Holmes had been a neighbor and had dropped in at all hours; another neighbor had been Thomas Bailey Aldrich, whose life Ferris Greenslet was writing while Willa Cather was in Boston. Longfellow and Lowell had come over from Cambridge on occasions great and small; and Emerson and Hawthorne had come in from Concord; Harriet Beecher Stowe had breakfasted there, and the young Henry James. James Fields had loved the theater from boyhood, and at his table the New England writers had met Edwin Booth and Joseph Jefferson, Charlotte Cushman and Christine Nilsson. Before and after his death Mrs. Fields, it has been said, came nearer than any other American to achieving a Parisian salon.

In her house Willa Cather felt at once, and was to feel increasingly, that the past continued alive. It seemed that the step of a great actor or writer of another day might again sound on the stairway that led to the long drawing-room on the second story, "that pleasant Charles Street parlor," as Whittier called it in his bucolic fashion. Here, beside the windows that overlooked the Charles River, Willa Cather was given her tea by a frail little woman who was almost eighty, but had kept the clear blue eyes and the bright lips of her youth, and who was not only, as her guest had expected, kind, inquisitive, gracious, and deeply distinguished, but above everything else gay. Her years in the company of the great she had always borne with ease; and now she bore with ease her memories.

The house in Charles Street was full not only of memories but of mementos. Thomas Gray's copy of the 1673 edition of Milton's *Poems on Several Occasions* was here, surely an acquisition of the later poet's extreme youth, for his name was signed on the title page in a large boyish hand no fewer than nine times. Here too was Charles Lamb's copy of *The Rape of the Lock*, a defective copy in which the missing pages had been replaced in Elia's meticulous calligraphy; and Byron's working copy of *Don Juan*, III, IV, V, given to James Fields by his Edinburgh crony Dr. John Brown; and a book given him by Tennyson, the poet's own volume of Keats, "a battered little copy in green cloth, with the comfortable aspect of having been abroad with some loving companion in a summer shower." The Fieldses had a cult of Keats. There was a drawing of him executed at Fields's desire by Severn, who had tended the poet's deathbed; there were many books concerning him that had been acquired with Leigh Hunt's library; and there was also the bust by Amy Whitney, which after Mrs. Fields died was to rest in Willa Cather's living-room. Mrs. Fields had once led Dr. Holmes to talk about it; he talked more as a doctor than as a connoisseur, and ventured to criticize the hair, adding that he knew a great deal about the nature of hair, and doubted that this was like Keats's though, since he supposed nothing was now known of Keats's hair, it might as well be one way as another. Rash words to use in this house. "I told him on the contrary," said Mrs. Fields, "I owned some of it; whereat I got it out." No wonder that in this house Willa Cather accused herself of a "Bœotian ignorance" and undertook a campaign to overcome it. If you wanted to know how Edwin Booth had delivered a passage in *Hamlet*, or what were the gestures of Turgenev's Pauline Viardot, in this house you could find out; but, Willa Cather found, you must not "go at" Mrs. Fields, you must involve your question in some general talk about acting.

All her life Willa Cather had wished for the atmosphere she found in Charles Street, an atmosphere where the arts and manners of a past time lingered with none of the desiccation of the classroom but with the fragrant natural life that can be maintained only by discriminating affection. She had found a little of it in Lincoln, with the Westermanns, the Canfields, and Dr. Tyndale; more in Pittsburgh, with the Andersons and George Seibel; but now she had it in the finest form in which it could be found in

America. She had always liked old women, felt easy with them, been kind to them, drawn them out; and now she was to have a high reward. Mrs. Fields liked her at once, as McClure had; and she was to return to this room many times during the seven years her hostess had to live, and also to stay with her more than once at Thunderbolt Hill, the cottage the family had owned at Manchester-on-the-Sea almost as long as they had owned the house in Charles Street.

Much as she was to gain from knowing Mrs. Fields, there was another person in that long green drawing-room at the time of her first call from whom she would draw a more precious benefit. This was the closest of Mrs. Fields's friends in the long decades of her widowhood, Sarah Orne Jewett.

Miss Jewett was to die a little more than a year after this first meeting, and Willa Cather was the last person to whom she gave her friendship. Between these two women, separated by a quarter century in age, and by all kinds of superficial circumstance, there were deep affinities quickly recognized. Both had grown up in small towns, and had seen these towns, which they loved, decline through the play of economic factors nothing could check. At South Berwick shipping and shipbuilding had almost disappeared in the years after the Civil War; at Red Cloud there had been arrest, and then decline, in the drought and depression of the 1890's. Both women had entered eagerly into the life of their towns and had been imaginatively stirred by the interplay between the townsfolk and the farm people. They had both ridden tomboyishly about the countryside, loving every tree in it; and had been taken on long rides to lonely farmhouses by the country doctor. Both had cherished intimacies with an older generation and a way of life that was vanishing before their eyes and giving place to something they considered to be cheap and nasty. "I was brought up with grandfathers and granduncles and aunts for my best playmates. They were not the wine one can get for so much the dozen now." The words are Miss Jewett's; they might have been Miss Cather's except that she would have begun the enumeration with grandmothers. Both had turned early to an apprenticeship to writing and had taken for a master Flaubert. That sentence of his that Miss Jewett had pinned to her desk and kept there—*Ce n'est pas de faire rire ni de faire pleurer, ni de vous mettre à fureur, mais d'agir à la façon de la nature, c'est à dire de faire rêver*—might have been pinned to Miss Cather's. No epigraph would be more illuminating for *Death Comes for the Archbishop* or *Shadows on the Rock*. Their literary enthusiasms were in general alike: the pilgrimage Sarah Jewett had made with Mrs. Fields to Tennyson came from just the same kind of devotion that had led Willa Cather to make her pilgrimage with Dorothy Canfield and Isabelle McClung to A. E. Housman's lodgings. For each the chosen poet was the perfect verbal artist, the pure lyrist.

The most important of the affinities between them was in a conception of literature, or at least of prose fiction, assumed by Sarah Orne Jewett in the long letter of advice she wrote in December 1908, the most important letter, beyond a question, that Willa Cather ever received. It is an instance of something very rare in the arts, advice of a fundamental kind, arriving at the right time, and exercising a strong if not an immediate influence. "You must find a quiet place," Miss Jewett wrote from Charles Street. "You must find your own quiet center of life and write from that. . . . To write and work on this level we must live on it—we must at least recognize it and defer to it at every step." One of the main reasons for the letter was Miss Jewett's dissatisfaction with the stories Willa Cather had been writing since she had gone to *McClure's*. To Miss Jewett these stories revealed no deepening of the author's inward life, no ripening of her talent. The failure to deepen and ripen was alarming, for Willa Cather was now thirty-five, and it was Miss Jewett's feeling that if the early years of an artist's activity were misdirected, some of the highest effects would be forever unattainable.

What were these stories? Were they repetitions of those in *The Troll Garden*? Or did they disclose some new qualities good or bad?

The first of them was "The Namesake," which appeared in *McClure's* in March 1907. Willa Cather had used the same title for a poem published in *Lippincott's* five years before, and that poem was addressed to the memory of her uncle William Lee Boak "of the Thirty-fifth Virginia," killed in the War between the States. The final feeling in the poem is pride in relationship. That feeling reappears in the story. The framework is simple, and introduces the kind of persons who had dominated most of the stories collected in *The Troll Garden*. A group of young American artists gather in the studio of Lyon Hartwell, in the boulevard Saint-Michel, the evening before one of them returns for good to the United States. Their thoughts are fixed for the time upon their country, and Hartwell, a great sculptor of the elder generation and a person of almost *farouche* reserve, explains how he was able to accomplish what the group considers his greatest statue, *The Color Sergeant*. His explanation is the story; the rest is machinery.

Fifteen years earlier he had gone home to his grandfather's house a few miles from Pittsburgh, "on the high banks of a river in Western Pennsylvania." Once the setting had been beautiful, but now it is ruined by the effects of an industrial civilization—air polluted, dreams discolored, vistas broken by coal shafts and oil derricks. What he saw had no value for Hartwell, a *déraciné*, brought up in Rome and Paris, obliged to stay amid the ugliness and grime because a relative was ill and his heart was kind. The only element that did achieve value was the group of objects that reminded him of the uncle and namesake he had never seen, killed, like Willa Cather's, in the War between the States. On one evening of concentrated apprehension the young artist broke through to a new level of awareness:

> For the first time I felt the pull of race and blood and kindred, and felt beating within me things that had not begun with me. It was as if the earth under my feet had grasped and rooted me, and were pouring its essence into me. I sat there until the dawn of morning, and all night long my life seemed to be pouring out of me and running into the ground.

Willa Cather is not yet ready to draw strength from her early environment, whether in Virginia or in Nebraska, to let herself mix with it: she must write of Pennsylvania, and the color sergeant must be a Union man and not a Confederate. She is developing an awareness of something, however, "that had not begun with me," of her family as a source not only of happiness and comfort, but of spiritual and artistic life. Her quest of that layer within herself from which her great fiction was primarily to come has taken a long step forward. But the story that records the step is not a success, either spiritually or artistically. Compared with the best of the stories in *The Troll Garden*, the rendering of the material in "The Namesake" is uneven and has patches of crudity. The picture of an evening among the American artists in Paris does not have the pressure of experience that gave a steady force to the picture of Paul in his luxurious room in the New York hotel or of the ill-assorted pair listening to Wagner at the Boston Symphony, to say nothing of the Western scenes in "A Death in the Desert." The evening in Paris is done not as Henry James might have done it, or even Edith Wharton, but as it might be done by someone who had read their works and assimilated something of their manners. Yet since the picture of this evening is subordinate, it does not make or mar the story which hangs on the realization of the feelings that came to Hartwell in his grandfather's house. In the rendering of these feelings the patches of crudity appear, melodramatic or sentimental, as in Hartwell's magnification of the simple drawing his namesake had executed in his dog-eared school text of Virgil. It may have been of passages like this that Sarah Orne Jewett was thinking when she warned Willa Cather that her recent stories fell short because they did not proceed from a quiet center, "her own quiet center of life." Even in the writings of her own twenties in the sketches of *Deephaven*, Miss Jewett had written from that. Her insight told her that Willa Cather, though it would take her much longer to do so, might attain to it.

Another story of this time, "Eleanor's House," which appeared in *McClure's* later in 1907, was, Willa Cather knew, a Jamesian experiment, almost, one might claim, a pastiche. All the personages are Americans who live abroad, so detached from their country that when something drives one from the countryside near Paris he goes to Normandy or the Riviera, or, a great decision, to Surrey. America does not exist. One of the personages is a typical Jamesian outsider—the clumsy girl from ordinary folk, with a heart of gold. The four others—Eleanor, who is dead, her husband, who has married the clumsy girl, and the Westerfields, a pair of Eleanor's understanding friends —are leisured, worried Jamesians, with nothing to interrupt their questionings of themselves and of one another. They talk with the Jamesian inflections and aposiopeses.

The mellow French settings are drawn with a good deal of the lightness and sensitiveness of stroke that James applied to landscape. The story is not, however, authentic James: the renunciations are somewhat unreal, the conflicts a little sullen. The pain that Eleanor's bereaved husband feels is healed too easily, and his state after escape from his grief is not an enlargement, but a reduction. The elaborate Jamesian form has no real affinity with the simple sequence of feeling. "Eleanor's House," like "The Namesake," does not proceed from a quiet center: it is a sketch in another's manner, not an organic development from the author's own fiber.

There were other stories published in 1907 and 1908, in *McClure's* and the *Century*, but none that had appeared by the end of 1908 would escape Miss Jewett's criticism: in a letter written at the end of November 1908 she expressed her dissatisfaction with the artifice in "On the Gull's Road," which was in *McClure's* for that month. "The lover is as well done as he could be," she wrote, "when a woman writes in a man's character." But she felt that there was some artifice in that, and she urged that it was "safer" to avoid becoming involved in what was, in her view, a "masquerade." She told Willa Cather she could almost "have done it as yourself—a woman could love her in the same protecting way—a woman could even care enough to wish to take her away from such a life, by some means or other. . . ." The problem raised by Miss Jewett—which indeed all writers face in their delineation of the opposite sex—was to be encountered again and to provide great difficulties for Willa Cather when she assigned the narrative of *My Ántonia* to Jim Burden. Miss Jewett felt that "On the Gull's Road" just missed being good, while offering the promise of the work Willa Cather could achieve, given the right circumstances. In later years Willa Cather disliked to be reminded of the short stories she had written during her years at *McClure's*; she was glad that she had the copyright and could prevent the republication of any among them. She compared her attitude to that of an apple-grower careful of his reputation: the fruit that was below standard must be left forgotten on the ground; only the sound apples should be collected. She was in the habit of saying almost exactly what Miss Jewett had said of them: she felt that these stories had the defects inseparable from creative work done in a hurry, when one was tired, and seeking relief from exacting work of another sort.

III

Soon after Willa Cather had finished her revision of the Milmine manuscript she sailed for Europe, in April 1908, taking the Mediterranean route, and enjoying a long and carefree vacation with Isabelle McClung. Their time was spent mostly in Italy and France. A few poems were written, but the journey was one of pleasure and absorption rather than of direct literary effect. On her return to New York she entered on her duties as managing editor of the magazine. Her salary was liberal, but she was determined to lay aside every dollar she could, withdraw at the first safe moment from any kind of office work, and depend for a living on what she could write. Her first years in Pittsburgh had been so hard and precarious that she never got over some fright about money. With Edith Lewis she took in September 1908 a small and rather uncomfortable apartment in Washington Place, just off the square where she had lived when she first came to New York. From the time they shared this apartment they were separated only when one or the other of them was traveling or called home by illness in the family. Besides the salary there was another great compensation for the heavier anxieties of the managing editor's post. S. S. McClure believed in travel not only for himself but for his staff, especially those who were charged with bringing in manuscripts and determining policy. He was convinced that the last place from which a magazine could be well edited was the editor's chair. He pressed Willa Cather to make trips to England, and in the spring and summer of 1909 she spent several months in and near London meeting a variety of striking people.

One of her encounters is described in a preface she wrote for a serial that began to run in *McClure's* in December 1909, David Soskice's *The Secrets of the Schlüsselburg: Chapters from the Secret History of Russia's Most Terrible Political Prison.* She was present when on the 23rd of June in that year the Russian colony in London gathered at South Place Institute, Finsbury, to welcome a political heroine, Vera Figner, who had spent twenty-two years, most of them in solitary confinement, in the Schlüsselburg prison, on a lonely island in the Neva. Prince Kropotkin and Soskice addressed the meeting in English, and Vera Figner spoke in Russian. It was characteristic of Willa Cather that in this hotly political company her deepest impression was of Vera Figner's voice, "one of marvelous resonance and power, beautifully modulated in spite of the fact that it was mute for so many years." Besides arranging for a long series of articles by Soskice, she was responsible at least in part, for a series of reminiscential pieces by Xavier Paoli, who had spent a quarter of a century as officer in charge of the security of royal visitors to France.

During the London visit she had other experiences nearer her usual habit than the meeting in South Place. William Archer, who became her guide to London, and was for many years her principal friend in England, took her to the funeral of George Meredith in May, and to the first London performance by the Abbey Players, where she sat with Lady Gregory in Yeats's box. *The Rising of the Moon* was the curtain-raiser, followed by *The Playboy of the Western World*. Synge's play was a puzzle to that audience, as to so many since, and at first Willa Cather shared the general feeling. At supper afterward Archer inquired about her judgment of the *Playboy*; she said, somewhat tentatively, that she had found it interesting but lacking in the dramatic, to which he replied that he thought anything that was interesting had its dramatic quality and its place in the theater. It was a remark she never forgot, and it was to have its effect when she began to loosen the conventional structure in her fiction. It told as Sarah Orne Jewett's theory and practice told, on the side of freedom. Archer, Yeats, and Lady Gregory all contributed to *McClure's*; so did another writer with whom Willa Cather formed a lasting friendship, Katherine Tynan. Archer introduced her to a number of stage people, and it was on memories of them that she drew in writing the London chapters of *Alexander's Bridge*. She had a strong sense of Anglo-American community; she was at ease in England, and in the years before the First World War she was reading at least as many English books as American. But none among her English literary friends ever had an influence on her work comparable to Sarah Orne Jewett's, and the visit was saddened by the news of Miss Jewett's death in June.

As managing editor Willa Cather continued to read a great variety of manuscripts; indeed, she read more than she had before. The impressions she formed were to have a strong effect on her own later practice of fiction. More than ninety per cent of what she read seemed to her incurably conventional: written according to formulas, written not for the sake of the subject but to display the cleverness of the author. The few manuscripts that were unconventional were almost all from writers so unpracticed that their crudities rendered what they wrote unpublishable. It seemed to her that a true writer would submit to his subject, and by submitting to it arrive at a form that was ideally suited to it, provided he had the command of his instrument, which might be assured him by an honest apprenticeship. She was probably aware during her years as managing editor that she had been an honest apprentice long enough, and that it was time to discover what she could achieve if she gave over experimenting and submitted to a subject from her early experience. Miss Jewett had said: "The thing that teases the mind over and over for years, and at last gets itself put down rightly on paper—whether little or great, it belongs to Literature." This was strangely like the words of Stephen Crane.

Shortly before she went to England she wrote a short piece that belongs to Literature. This is "The Enchanted Bluff," which appeared in *Harper's Monthly* in April 1909. Perhaps she went elsewhere to have it published because she appreciated how unlike her other writings of this time it was, how remote from formulas. One hopes that Sarah Orne Jewett saw it—her fatal stroke occurred before it was printed—for it was the first evidence that Willa Cather was working in the vein she advised. "The Enchanted Bluff" evokes one of the sandbars in the Republican River where she had spent so many of the intense hours of her youth. On the sandbar, camping overnight, are six boys: the narrator, unnamed and unspecified, but by implication male; the two Hasslers, sons of the local tailor and mighty takers of catfish; Percy Pound, the dime-novel fanatic; Tip Smith, the grocer's son and jester to the group; Arthur Adams, son of the town gambler and a wanderer in the fields and marshes. By way of the stars and memories of Coronado's legend, the talk turns to a bluff in the Southwest, the Mesa Encantada. Tip's uncle had seen it, and reported its aspect as mysterious, its history as terrifying. Before they turn in, the boys agree that, of all places, this is the one to which they would like to go. The group gathers again in skating weather and, reaching the sandbar, reiterates the wish. There is a short epilogue, written, it is said, twenty years after the gatherings at the sandbar. The narrator returns to the Nebraska town. No one has seen the enchanted bluff; the Hassler boys have settled into being the town tailors, though one did have a try at railroading and lost a foot; Percy Pound is a stockbroker in Kansas City, who will travel only where his car will take him; Arthur Adams died in the garden of the town's saloon; Tip Smith, careworn and henpecked, still intends to go and has imparted the story of the bluff to his son, who is as full of it as Tip used to be.

That is all. "The Enchanted Bluff" is just the recalling of persons and places and moments that have value, poured out in a quiet sensitive prose, and ending in suggestive indeterminacy. The persons and places and moments call for exactly the rendering given them: perhaps there is a brief obtrusion of the author in the epilogue, where the grip of the town and the region on the personages is emphasized with a bitterness that seems excessive, though it cannot be called irrelevant. Willa Cather had not yet made terms of peace with Nebraska. "The Enchanted Bluff" was never republished; but before the appearance of the next collection of Willa Cather's stories she had reworked this sketch into one of the most moving chapters in *My Ántonia*.

Under her direction *McClure's* prospered. During the first year of her responsibility the circulation increased by sixty thousand, and in the next the outcome was even more brilliant. In the issue for June 1910 McClure stated in the bold type he reserved for special announcements that within a twelvemonth three issues had gone out of print; the current issue was the largest June edition in the history of the magazine; and advertisers were guaranteed a continuation of the high circulation. The price of Willa Cather's success was nervous exhaustion. A remark she applied to Alexandra Bergson in *O Pioneers!* applied to her own work in the years at *McClure's*: "It was because she had so much personality to put into her enterprises and succeeded in putting it into them so completely, that her affairs prospered better than those of her neighbours." Willa Cather did not have Alexandra's stolid temperament. She could not meet a new person or one she did not know well without feeling stimulated; whether she was drawn to him or felt antipathetic, the encounter was intense. Elizabeth Shepley Sergeant, whose first meeting with Willa Cather concerned an article offered to the magazine, was astonished at the warmth of her reception; before she left the office she felt, as was true, that she had made a friend for life. Others felt Willa Cather's immediate hostility. After a morning of such encounters she would often retire to her apartment for the afternoon to read manuscripts and write letters in healing privacy. But such an escape was not enough. McClure understood, as he understood almost everything about Willa Cather. He would propose his grand nostrum of travel, and she was often glad to accept it. Every year she spent some weeks at Red Cloud; and sometimes she would visit her brother Roscoe, or go on a camping trip with him. In her own generation of the family Roscoe was now, as he always had been, the one with whom she was most intimate. He cared for what she wrote, and for the magazine; and she was eager to know how he responded. She was often in Pittsburgh, staying with Isabelle McClung, or in Boston staying with Mrs. Fields. Once she had the good fortune to find at the house in Charles Street another guest whose poetry she admired. Louise Imogen Guiney had written few poems in late years; but Willa Cather's interest led her to write again, and a number of her pieces appeared in *McClure's*. The meeting was less fortunate when Willa Cather, accompanied by George E. Woodberry, called on another of Mrs. Fields's friends, Amy Lowell. Miss Lowell's rudeness to Woodberry was so insultingly discourteous that Willa Cather formed an immediate dislike of her that nothing could relieve.

In New York also there were literary friendships, though none of them was at all decisive. There was a brief meeting with Mark Twain, and a morning spent at his bedside listening to his vivid talk. Edwin Arlington Robinson was living in the house of Mrs. Clara Potter Davidge near Washington Square; meeting him there and occasionally in the houses of other friends, Willa Cather was delighted with his intelligence, and more than a little puzzled by his reserve and the abruptness of his commentary on life and letters. For his poetry she cared less than for the man; it seemed to her unnecessarily enigmatic and somewhat clumsy. She was much more at ease with George Arliss and his wife, who had taken an appartment in the neighborhood. She always remembered conversations she had in the months when Arliss was studying the role of Disraeli; and she found the reminiscences of the drama, the theater, and the stage that the Arlisses could be persuaded to offer a perfect enchantment. Her interest in all that touched on acting and actors was as lively now as when she waited at the station in Red Cloud to watch a traveling company get off the train. The Arlisses often invited her to after-theater supper parties; and these were among the chief pleasures of her early years in New York. But it was not from her associates in Greenwich Village or from the staff at the magazine that her ideas and feelings about her art took shape, and it would be idle to list the people she saw or the places to which she went.

IV

In the intervals of her work, she completed by the fall of 1911 a short novel that she called *Alexander's Bridge*. Under the title *Alexander's Masquerade* it appeared in *McClure's* in three parts, from February to April of 1912.[1] It is a study in the split personality of Bartley Alexander, taking him when he is forty-three, eleven years after his marriage, and carrying him to his death a year later. All the other characters—Winifred, his wife, Hilda Burgoyne, his mistress, Lucius Wilson, his old teacher, Mainhall, his London friend, and the few minor persons who crop up in an episode—are in the novel only to furnish him with stimuli or to comment on his nature. The economy is somewhat rigidly perfect; not a chapter, not a scene, could be spared; hardly a word is excessive or distracting. There are moments when a fuller rendering of a mood, a more emphatic presentation of an interchange, would probably have deepened, and would certainly have clarified, the effect. The weight of Bartley Alexander's personality would

[1] The title *Alexander's Masquerade* was probably invented in the office of the magazine. As early as November 1911 the work is mentioned in the files of Houghton Mifflin Company as *Alexander's Bridge*. The English edition was titled *Alexander's Bridges*.

have borne a more massive presentation. If the book has fineness, it is also a little thin. One might say that Willa Cather was using some of the resources of Sarah Orne Jewett in approaching a subject that Miss Jewett would have thought beyond her bounds.

The stronger part of Alexander's personality, which is also the larger, is in keeping with his Western origins. If the state where he grew up is not named, he comes from Willa Cather's country. The Western touches are few but perhaps sufficient. Alexander grew up on a ranch, where he learned how to deal with "locoed" horses; as a boy he used to hunt jackrabbits; he liked to recall a campfire on a sandbar in the river that ran near his early home; he went to a Western university; and he had the bigness and hardness of physique that go with the pioneer hero. He was a "tamer of nature" as his forefathers had been; they subdued the land, he subdued the rivers of the continent with a dozen daring bridges. What Lucius Wilson has remembered is the force of the young Alexander, who had been "a powerfully equipped nature" and "simply the most tremendous response to stimuli" the professor had ever known.

In this strong nature Wilson had divined a flaw, which he could not find, much less name, but which might nevertheless bring complete ruin. In the first chapter, when he comes to stay with Alexander, he speaks of his misgivings, which had continued long after Alexander made a name. The greater the performance, and the greater the reputation, the more did Wilson expect that a big crack would appear "zigzagging from top to bottom" and leading to a crash of the whole man in dust and ruins. Wilson is free to mention his misgivings because they have at last been set to rest. He has observed Alexander in his Boston home overlooking the Charles River and (it would appear) around the corner from Mrs. Fields's house, and has found to his surprise that Alexander belongs in a setting of mellow traditional beauty. He has responded to the charm of Alexander's distinguished wife and felt her depth and strength, and has found that the relation between husband and wife is excellent. Either the flaw has worked out of the mature man or it was imaginary.

The mention of the vanished misgivings leads Alexander to a remark from which the action of the novel flows. He is unsatisfied with his life: it is not, he feels, a true expression of himself, but a building of himself into a social structure he does not care about, a swallowing of himself in a million details. "I sometimes wonder," he says gloomily, "what sort of chap I'd have been if I hadn't been this sort; I want to go and live out his potentialities, too." This is what he begins to do on a trip to London that follows close on Wilson's visit.

Hilda Burgoyne, an Irish actress whom he had not seen since he met Winifred, becomes his mistress; but what is significant is not his wish to make her this, but the wish it evolves from—to live out some of the potentialities that had gone unrealized in his marriage and his career. A long time elapses between the evening when he sees her act and the evening they are first alone together. The finest psychological probing in the novel is in the period between these two evenings. In long, introspective walks Alexander tries to pick his way from the cramping years of his middle life to his uncommitted childhood and youth. The process is extraordinarily like what Godfrey St. Peter was to undergo in *The Professor's House*. There was still, Alexander felt, "something unconquered in him, something besides the strong work-horse that his profession had made of him. . . . He remembered how, when he was a little boy and his father called him in the morning, he used to leap from his bed into the full consciousness of himself. That consciousness was Life itself." It was this consciousness Alexander was bent on recovering. To make sure that the reader will not for a moment suppose that what he feels for Hilda is a great love, Willa Cather gives the most emphatic signal in the novel. "He walked," she says, "shoulder to shoulder with a shadowy companion—not little Hilda Burgoyne, by any means, but someone vastly dearer to him than she had ever been—his own young self. . . . It was not until long afterward that Alexander learned that for him this youth was the most dangerous of companions."

The emergence of this second self was for a while delightful to Alexander. "This new feeling was so fresh, so unsatisfied and light of foot. It ran and was not wearied. . . . At this moment, it was tingling through him, exultant, and live as quicksilver." So it had been with Dr. Jekyll, whose second self was also much younger than his respectable nature, which might be described in the words Willa

Cather applied to Alexander's—"the strong work-horse that his profession had made of him." When Dr. Jekyll first assumed the personality of Edward Hyde, what he felt was what Alexander would wholly have understood: "There was something strange in my sensations, something indescribably new, and, from its very novelty, incredibly sweet. I felt younger, lighter, happier in body. . . . I stretched out my hands, exulting in the freshness of these sensations." The outcome for Alexander is what might be predicted in the light of our memory of what befell Dr. Jekyll. Although Stevenson was one of the authors Willa Cather most often reread, and his symbolic tale may have suggested, or clarified, the idea for *Alexander's Bridge*, between his work and hers there are immense differences. She keeps well within the round of realistic psychological portraiture, and the effect she seeks is far less violent and extreme than the horror of *Dr. Jekyll and Mr. Hyde*.

Yet the division in Alexander's nature ends in his destruction. The second self exerts a constantly increasing pressure on the first, twisting it out of shape and inhibiting its life. "Something had broken loose in him of which he knew nothing except that it was sullen and powerful, and that it wrung and tortured him." As it won control it would, Alexander knew, make him hateful even to Hilda, perhaps to Hilda above all. It is always—like Mr. Hyde—completely sterile: no new life can grow out of it; Alexander never so much as ponders a marriage with Hilda, or a new career apart from engineering. The growth of this new self began, he reflects just before his death, in "a mere folly, a masquerade"—the phrase from which the magazine title was taken—and quickly it escaped from his direction and reached over to ruin his severely patterned life. It threatens, but does not actually ruin, his marriage (if he had lived it would doubtless have ruined this), but it ruins his career.

The bridge he is building across the St. Lawrence during the year covered in the narrative is his first failure. In her account of the construction and collapse of this bridge Willa Cather follows closely the story of the Quebec bridge that was to span the river five miles from the city of Quebec. This bridge, though there was a subsidy from the government of Canada, was undertaken on a tight budget; the designing engineer knew he must use materials as sparingly as he could, just as Alexander yields to pressure from the contractors that he use less steel than he thought quite prudent. The principal designing engineer for the Quebec bridge, Theodore Cooper of New York, one of the great bridge engineers of his time, would not withdraw from the undertaking, just as Alexander would not, because the bridge offered the excitements of new problems in design to conquer and the promise of unrivaled fame. The most striking of the likenesses between Alexander and Theodore Cooper was that when signs of danger which they could have interpreted correctly began to appear, neither was on the scene. On August 27, 1907 the bending in some of the lower chords in an anchor arm of the bridge at Quebec, noticeable for some days, greatly increased. On August 28 ordinary workers began to be alarmed. The Royal Commission of three engineers appointed by the Canadian government to inquire into the disaster and assess blame gravely declared: "It was clear that on that day the greatest bridge in the world was being built without there being a single man within reach who by experience, knowledge and ability was competent to deal with the crisis." A warning sent by Alexander's assistant did not reach him in time, as he was at a tryst with Hilda. The series of warnings from Cooper's assistant had not clarified the situation for him, partly because the assistant was inadequately prepared for his responsibility, partly because Cooper, old and ailing, had never seen the bridge in all the years it was under construction. A final warning did stir Cooper into action; at one p.m. on August 29 he dispatched a telegram ordering the suspension of work; but in what seems to have been confusion of mind he sent it not to the office at the scene, but to the headquarters of the contracting company at Phoenixville, Pennsylvania, where it was decided that nothing should be done until the next day. At 5:37 p.m. the bridge collapsed, crushing or drowning almost a hundred workers. The Royal Commission declared that the blame for the collapse rested on Cooper, and the blame for the collapse of Alexander's bridge rests on him. Both men fail for the same essential reason: because they were no longer the men who had been commissioned to build a bridge, they are not what their employers, judging them by the past, assumed them to be. When Alexander at length receives the warning from his assistant, he hurries to the scene; but when he reaches the bridge, all he can do is make a vain attempt to draw the workmen off. He is carried to his death with them, one of them clutching him to the end, just as in *Lucy Gayheart* Sebastian drowned in the clutch of his accompanist, Mockford. The image Wilson had used to describe the flaw he divined in Alexander acquires a more literal truth than he had ever expected. From the moment Wilson has uttered it—spoken as it was of a builder of bridges—it broods over the novel. There are enough supporting references to ensure its being remembered by even a desultory reader.

In commending the manuscript to his associates at Houghton Mifflin, Ferris Greenslet wrote of its varied sorts of distinction, its "excellence of workmanship," its "perceptiveness," its "actuality"; but his heaviest stress fell on "the spiritual sense of life that informs it." Forty years afterward the phrase may seem a little vague, but it is a response to what is essential in the book. Only if it is read in the way Greenslet must have read it, as a study in the psychological processes of the protagonist, can it be understood. It has not often been read so. The objection that is taken to *Alexander's Bridge* is that its characters do not come to life, that they are not people as Ántonia Shimerda and Alexandra Bergson are people. Alexander is not a rounded person as these two women are; and certainly his wife and his mistress are not. There is no need why any of them should be. The subject is not Alexander, but the process through which he passes. That process is presented with a stern concentration and a cold accuracy that Willa Cather did not often use in rendering the central datum in a novel, although she was to use just these qualities again in *My Mortal Enemy*, and again to face deep critical misunderstanding. There also the subject was to be not a person but a destructive process within a person.

The severest critic of *Alexander's Bridge* was its own author in later years. She came to believe that it was not her sort of book, and in some degree it was not. She constantly disparaged it to her friends, and one who knew her very well and very long was surprised on rereading it after Willa Cather's death to find what power of psychological portraiture it has. In a preface that first appeared in the edition of 1922, and in an article of 1931, "My First Novels (There Were Two)," Willa Cather is forthright in her blame. She was right of course in saying that *Alexander's Bridge* was imitative, both in the choice of a milieu that was upper-class, sophisticated, cosmopolitan, and in the choice of a form that was bare and contrived. But the core of the novel is not touched by criticism of this kind. *Alexander's Bridge* gains nothing at all by the use of the superior milieu, and gains little by the contrived bare form; it would have gained something if the people in it were of the sort Willa Cather was profoundly at home with, people from the Western plains living on those plains, and if she had felt free to be discursive and lambent, as Sarah Orne Jewett had seen and as she was to be in the Nebraska novels. But the gains would not have been fundamental: the process in Alexander would have been the same if he had been a farmer on the Divide, with a hired girl for his wife and the daughter of a new settler for his mistress.

The reason for Willa Cather's aversion to her first published novel was a sudden turn in the direction of her life and writing that followed it. When she was writing it she was still uncertain of herself, and composition was a task, not the pleasure it was later to be. The usual way of describing what happened after it was written is to say that she left the editorial office of *McClure's*, went on a visit to the Southwest, a long one, gained a clear understanding of herself there, and wrote *O Pioneers!* So far as it goes the description is sound; substantially it is what Willa Cather has said in "My First Novels" and elsewhere. It is, however, a simplification. It ignores some things that are too important to be ignored. For instance it ignores "The Bohemian Girl." Before Willa Cather left the editorial office for good, she took a long leave and late in 1911 wrote this story, which appeared in *McClure's* in August 1912, only four months after *Alexander's Masquerade* had been concluded. Cameron Mackenzie, McClure's son-in-law, was managing the magazine at the time; he was so delighted with the story that he proposed to pay $750 for it; Willa Cather protested—would take only $500—but added, with a laugh, the next story might deserve $750.

In "The Bohemian Girl" Willa Cather for the first time wrote at length and appreciatively of life on the Divide. At length—the story runs over sixteen thousand words and is shorter than *My Mortal Enemy* only by four thousand—and appreciatively, with a smiling recognition of values not only different from those which had shaped her own life but inimical to these. Almost everything that is said of *O Pioneers!* in the article on her early novels is true of "The Bohemian Girl." This also is "a story about some Scandinavians and Bohemians" who had been neighbors of the Virginia colony in Webster County; it is in some degree a story "of the soil": it has the air of a "spontaneous" effusion; everything in it appears to have "taken its own place right or wrong." It is not quite so discursive as *O Pioneers!* nor does it give such an impression of the author's own pleasure in recalling her material.

Our guides to values in "The Bohemian Girl" are a man and a woman who were born on the Divide, but are conscious of not belonging and leave it for an entirely different form of life. Nils Ericson, the protagonist, is returning when the story opens, after an abscence of twelve years, roughly the length of time Willa Cather had spent in Pittsburgh and on the east coast. In the introductory picture of Nils what is stressed is assurance to the point of insolence; and the same quality is diffused through his dialogue in the early chapters. His silences and ironies and brief laughs are those of a person who has become invulnerable to the people with whom he has to do, and enjoys giving them the conviction that they have no hold upon him. Once they had had a strong hold upon him: he had been the atypical, disapproved, ridiculed child, the child who instinctively disliked the standards his family lived by, and was made to feel guilt for his deviation. What he had not been able to endure was the Ericson denial of life. This was embodied in his parents' house, "a grim square house with a tin roof" and the accompanying windbreak of mutilated poplars and straggle of small outbuildings, a landmark on the road that led from Red Cloud to the Cather farm. It was embodied also in the Ericson reduction of life to hard work done to get on in the world, and to a domestic routine marked by "mess, full of babies and washing and flies." As a child he had determined to get away; and he was no more than a boy when he did run off—as far as Bergen in Norway, where he made a new life for himself.

Our other guide is the Bohemian girl, Clara Vavrika, daughter of the tavern-keeper in a village to the north of the Scandinavian settlement (unnamed in the story, and very like Blue Hill), and bored wife of Nils's stolid and joyless brother Olaf. Olaf had always been the brother Nils cared for the least: "the one thing he had always felt in Olaf was a heavy stubbornness, like the unyielding stickiness of wet loam against the plow." No one could have been a more exasperating mate for Clara, mercurial, avid for pleasure, and finding it only in the desperate forms of baiting the Ericsons and "being witty" for herself alone. Nils persuades her in a series of carefully graduated talks that her one chance to live is to come back with him to Bergen. Her sense of desolation in living on the Divide has a parallel in a remark that Willa Cather made to her young friend Elizabeth Shepley Sergeant at about the time when she was writing "The Bohemian Girl," that her pleasure in revisiting Red Cloud was flawed by a feeling that a sudden death would overtake her somewhere on the prairie. That feeling would come on her obsessively and darken her life for days.

Clara's response to the Divide and its people is entirely hostile; only her father, whose fun-loving nature is irrepressible, escapes. Nils, however, makes discriminations interesting in themselves, and recurring in most of Willa Cather's later stories about the region. The most elaborate scene in the story is the supper at the raising of Olaf Ericson's barn, developed with the happy accumulation of detail that Flaubert allowed himself in the wedding chapter in *Madame Bovary*. All the neighborhood is there, and Nils cannot contain his appreciation of the grandmothers. He is amazed at how much they have done in their lives, and how much life they still have. Most of them have brown or blond hair still, and old Mrs. Oleson, a grandmother twelve times, has "yellow hair whose braids are as thick as her own wrists." Despite the mountains of food they have cooked, they delight in a feast; and even in the dancing they take a radiant vicarious pleasure. Even for his own mother, so dour, so unloving, so insensitive, he has a smiling appreciation: "a regular pile driver!" he says with enthusiasm. He does not have a particle of filial love for her; but for the "vigor and force" she has kept, his appreciation is unbounded. Clara is impatient at the praise of the grandmothers; they are her natural enemies; she detests them all. Nils's reply is an index to the author's feeling. "You won't," he says, "when you look back on them from Stockholm or Budapest. Freedom settles all that."

One must know the world, Willa Cather had been warned by Miss Jewett, before one can draw one's own part of it, which is an artist's natural subject. In Nils's response is the first strong evidence that the years in Pittsburgh, Boston, and New York, the travels in Europe, the association with artists and cultivated persons, were qualifying Willa Cather for the profound æsthetic realizations of Nebraska which she was now on the eve of making.

The appreciation of the older generation, the true pioneers, has no parallel in Nils's attitude toward his brothers. Clara remarks that "the second generation are a tame lot," and it is as tame, dull individual people they figure in "The Bohemian Girl." The good ones in this generation, the ones with a spark, like Clara and Nils, must leave, and the farms of the pioneers be occupied, as a cheerful old failure remarks, by the commonplace ones who "run over this here country like bindweed." What is remarkable, if one recalls the bitter early Western stories such as "The Sculptor's Funeral," is not that the appreciation has limits, but that it exists at all.

The degree of appreciation has a bearing on the unexpected and unsatisfactory close of the story. Nils had a special feeling for the youngest of his brothers, Eric, who had deviated from the family type in early childhood and always exhibits a delightful gentleness. At the end of the story, established now with Clara at Bergen, he sends Eric money for his passage. Eric begins the journey, but in western Iowa he changes his mind and returns to the farm after only one night of absence. If his return were rendered as a final proof of his gentleness and that alone, it would be satisfactory, and by contrast the hardness in Nils would be established as one of the conditions for his successful escape. But the end also involves a sudden and striking shift in the character of the mother: this woman, who has always acted and spoken as a hard-bitten feelingless nature, responds to the softness in Eric, and the final tableau is warm with a sentiment that not only confuses one about the meaning the story bears but also embarrasses by it unprepared demand on one's feelings. Only on the supposition that as she read over the story Willa Cather found it too severe in its estimate of the Divide and the people who live there can I account for the unlikely close, and it may have been because she was later aware of its weakness that she never republished "The Bohemian Girl." It has had many admirers, among her intimate friends and among her own family. The next book in which it might have been included was *Obscure Destinies*, twenty years in the future; and "The Bohemian Girl," vigorous and shapely as it is, would have needed more than superficial revision to take its place among the finest expressions of Will Cather's powers in short and intermediate narratives.

PART TWO

7

The Ancient People and the Pioneers

1913–1918

O PIONEERS!
THE SONG OF THE LARK
MY ÁNTONIA

IN THE SPRING of 1912, after resigning from *McClure's*, Willa Cather went to Winslow, a town in northeastern Arizona where her brother Douglass worked for the Santa Fe. Douglass, who never married and who delighted in the out-of-doors, was living in the most primitive simplicity, with a little group of railroadmen. Willa Cather was exhilarated by the rough life and interested in the character and idiom of her brother's associates. One of them suggested many of the traits that went into the personality of Ray Kennedy, the freight conductor in the early chapters of *The Song of the Lark*, who knew the Southwest "like the blisters on his own hands"; another was the model for the Englishman in Tom Outland's narrative in *The Professor's House*. This was the frontier, and Willa Cather felt that once more she was among pioneers, men who might have founded Red Cloud or put the first plows into the earth of the Divide. It was not merely exciting, it was reassuring in the West to find in men of her own age or younger than she, not the "tame lot" who had formed the second generation in Webster County, but the "greathearted adventurers" to whom only beginnings are stimulating. The vacation she had intended became a discovery—a discovery of the Southwest she had divined three years before in "The Enchanted Bluff." It was a discovery, and an enjoyment, of the land and the people.

She did not remain at Winslow. She took long pack-trips—riding was always a pleasure to her—and camped out for a week at a time. She crossed into New Mexico briefly. The colors and shapes of things were unlike anything she had seen before. How much she was affected by the joy the landscape of the Southwest gave her will appear in the record of later and even more important stays in the country. It was not only by the land that the Southwest charmed her; it was at least as much by the people, especially the Indians and the Mexicans, in whom she discovered survivals of Aztec beauty. The delight she had found in the company of some Latin Europeans in her trips abroad was renewed as she responded to the gaiety and vitality in some of these simple folk it was so easy to meet and, superficially at least, so easy to know. She felt in some of them a tragic and heroic quality, associated with the Aztec strain which gave to their other traits an intensity that was quite new to her. The picture of Johnny Tellamantez and his "Spanish" friends in *The Song of the Lark* caught a great deal of what she felt in her first encounter with Indians and Mexicans of the Southwest.

The most important of her discoveries was one that involved both persons and places, but the persons were dead. It came when she saw the ruins of the Cliff-Dwellers in Walnut Canyon, Arizona, the "Panther Canyon" of *The Song of the Lark*. In Nebraska there was no past unless one was geologically minded; everything that had not happened yesterday had happened the day before. In the villages of the Cliff-Dwellers Willa Cather found something that was not only extremely simple and extremely beautiful, but extremely old. The discovery was a lengthening of one's past as an American, especially if one were a Western American, an enlarging of one's frame of reference. The woman who was to inspire *The Song of the Lark* had never been in this canyon; but it is here that Willa Cather set the crucial phase in Thea Kronborg's history as an artist, and this is a proof of how very personal a work *The Song of the Lark* is. It is the one of her novels in which she is not recalling or resurrecting, but working in the impressions of the present or the immediate past.

During the months she stayed in the Southwest Willa Cather was unusually receptive. She had firmly closed the door on one career, which had brought her to great success. In 1906 she had left Pittsburgh a high-school teacher;

within two years she had become managing editor of a magazine that was successful to the point of the fabulous, and during the next four she had exercised, with an inspired skill, a measure of power and earned a comfortable living. It had required courage to close the door on so much so quickly gained. She had the courage, and she was determined to live for a while in the present, which poured in on her more powerfully and with less resistance than, perhaps, at any other time in her mature life. "I did no writing down there," she has said, "but I recovered from the conventional editorial point of view." What such a recovery meant she has told in her account of the growth in Thea Kronborg, the central person in *The Song of the Lark*—this also occurred on a first exposure to the Southwest.

All of her life she [Thea] had been hurrying and sputtering, as if she had been born behind time and had been trying to catch up. Now, she reflected . . . it was as if she were waiting for something to catch up with her. She had got to a place where she was out of the stream of meaningless activity and undirected effort.

Here she could lie for half a day undistracted, holding pleasant and incomplete conceptions in her mind—almost in her hands. They were scarcely clear enough to be called ideas. They had something to do with fragrance and colour and sound. . . . She had always been a little drudge, hurrying from one task to another—as if it mattered! And now her power to think seemed converted into a power of sustained sensation. . . . What was any art but an effort to make a sheath, a mould in which to imprison for a moment the shining, elusive element which is life itself . . . ? Her mind was like a ragbag into which she had been frantically thrusting whatever she could grab. And here she must throw this lumber away. The things that were really hers separated themselves from the rest. Her ideas were simplified, became sharper and clearer. She felt united and strong.

In a new state of mind, very like Thea Kronborg's, conscious of how she had grown as a person and eager to discover what the change might mean to her fiction, Willa Cather returned to the East by way of Red Cloud and the Divide, where she saw the wheat harvest and visited the Bohemian settlement, and Pittsburgh, where she stayed for some months with Isabelle McClung. At McClure's urgent wish, she kept a thread of connection with the magazine— she was to furnish two stories, and the business office as well as the proprietor hoped they would resemble "The Bohemian Girl." These stories were not written: instead Willa Cather went back to an old manuscript that became *O Pioneers!*

How much of *O Pioneers!* had been written before the stay in the Southwest is not precisely known. The mark of that country is on the fourth section of the book, "The White Mulberry Tree," and to a less extent on the third, "Winter Memories," in the allusions to Emil Bergson's happiness in Mexico, his response to the happiness and expressiveness of a Latin people so unlike the heavy, dour Scandinavian atmosphere in which he grew up. "The White Mulberry Tree" is known to have been written or perhaps expanded from earlier material after Willa Cather's return from the Southwest, and so, presumably, was at least a part of "Winter Memories." It was originally intended to be a self-contained story of middle length. The first section of *O Pioneers!*, "The Wild Land," must have been expanded at a relatively late stage in the composition of the novel. No other hypothesis will, I believe, account for a repeated error in the time schedule most unusual in an author who was meticulous in arranging this element in her fiction. So much for late additions. About the first state of the work there is a little precise knowledge. Some time after joining *McClure's* but before her journey to the Southwest, Willa Cather wrote a story shorter than "The Bohemian Girl" and called "Alexandra" after its heroine, who became the Alexandra Bergson of *O Pioneers!* It is probable that the early story was a study in a single character, with the other members of the Bergson family and their neighbors drawn only as stimuli for her and factors in her life. The shift in title from "Alexandra" to *O Pioneers!* —however much it may have been prompted by its similarity to the title of her first novel—pointed to a shift in interest: in the novel Alexandra remains the principal personage, but she is now presented as part of a study in the history of a family characteristic of a time and a place. All the additions that have been noticed build up the roles of other characters. In "The White Mulberry Tree" Alexandra is less important than Emil: in this section Willa Cather records his tragic love for Marie Shabata, which goes unperceived by Alexandra. The emphasis on Emil's Mexican adventures in this section and in "Winter Memories" adds to his importance. The changes that must have been made in the first section, whatever else they included, delayed the departure from the Divide of Carl Linstrum, who is in love with Alexandra, and assured him of more importance when he returns. Emil and Carl present a response to the Divide very unlike Alexandra's, but rendered with equal respect and almost equal sympathy.

The originality of "The Bohemian Girl" was in its material; in structure it was a conventional work. Nils Ericson returns home; he persuades Clara Vavrika to run off; they are happy in their new life. In *O Pioneers!* there is a conventional story parallel to this: Emil returns home; he wins Marie Shabata's love; they are killed by her husband. The unconventional element has its center in the portrayal of Alexandra. She too has her conventional story: Carl Linstrum returns to the Divide; he wins her love; they agree to go away for a while and then to live on the Bergson farm. But how small a part this story plays in the portrayal of Alexandra!

Her quality is impressed upon us by a very emphatic passage that closes an early chapter. With her brothers and Carl, she drives out to Crazy Ivar's, to ask this strange old seer how to protect her hogs from the cholera. Ivar, a delightful splotch of color in the grayness of the first section, bursts out: "I tell you, sister, the hogs of this country are put upon!" and bids her enclose a sorghum patch for hers and allow them plenty of clean water and clean feed. On the return of the party to the Bergson farm the boys go swimming after supper, and Alexandra sits on the kitchen doorstep. The chapter ends:

> It was a still, deep-breathing summer night, full of the smell of the hayfields. Sounds of laughter and splashing came up from the pasture, and when the moon rose rapidly above the bare rim of the prairie, the pond glittered like polished metal, and she could

see the flash of white bodies as the boys ran about the edge, or jumped into the water. Alexandra watched the shimmering pool dreamily, but eventually her eyes went back to the sorghum patch south of the barn, where she was planning to make her new pig corral.

Out of context the passage is comical, even farcical; but read in its place it has pathos, and a queer sort of austere heroism. Alexandra scarcely had a childhood; at twelve she was a help to her father's thinking about the land. She had no real youth, no religious elation, no romance, no personal life of any definable kind. "Her personal life, her own realization of herself, was almost a subconscious existence." When she has a falling out with her brothers Lou and Oscar late in the novel, Lou complains that Oscar offended their sister quite unnecessarily by blurting out that she was forty and beyond the age for falling in love. He comforts himself with the rationalization: "Of course, Alexandra ain't much like other women-folks. Maybe it won't make her sore. Maybe she'd as soon be forty as not!" To the misunderstanding of their sister is added this final failure in perception; Oscar is not capable of allowing her even those emotions which most persons, men and women, experience with the passage of their youth.

The pathetic quality in Alexandra requires to be stressed because, though it is essential to the emotional effect she has on a reader, it is overshadowed by her austere heroism. She was in her early twenties when her father died, and the responsibility for all decisions devolved on her: through a series of years harder than he had endured, she kept the land he had broken, imposing her will on her brothers, and forcing on their stupid routine-loving natures modes of farming suited to the soil. It was in the land that her impersonal nature expressed itself. The large house she had built for herself is a disappointment; but "you feel that, properly, Alexandra's house is the big out-of-doors." By the kind of feeling she has for the land she rises far out of the circle of strong, austere, vital Scandinavian women in "The Bohemian Girl." It is something to her that the land she lives on was first settled by her father; and something too that it was land she could work with and subdue; but

at the heart of her feeling for the land is a poetic appreciation that no character that preceded her in Willa Cather's
fiction had even adumbrated. Early in the book, when she
returns to the Divide from a few days spent on the farms
in the valley, appreciation fairly flows through her frame.
"For the first time, perhaps, since that land emerged from
the waters of geologic ages, a human face was set toward it
with love and yearning. It seemed beautiful to her, rich and
strong and glorious. Her eyes drank in the breadth of it,
until her tears blinded her. Then the Genius of the Divide,
the great, free spirit which breathes across it, must have
bent lower than it ever bent to a human will before." Much
later, after she has subdued the land, making it yield a
succession of rich crops, its power to enchant her is not so
strong. "I even think," she admits to Carl Linstrum, "I
liked the old country better. This is all very splendid in its
way, but there was something about this country when it
was a wild old beast that has haunted me all these years.
Now, when I come back to all this milk and honey, I feel
like the old German song, *'Wo bist du, wo bist du, mein
gelibtest Land?'*" The austerity and strength of the woman
are in unison with the austerity and strength of the land—
"the wild land" as it is called in the title of the first section;
and it is in the unison that the poetic force of the novel has
its center. Sometimes one wonders why Alexandra was
never driven, like old Chapdelaine in Louis Hémon's novel,
to give up the acres she had tamed and begin again in a
new frontier. Her regret for the passing of the first phase in
the development of Nebraska, the phase of hardship, heroism, and imagination, was to be echoed more and more
deeply in the novels to come.

Alexandra rises above the Scandinavian women in the
earlier fiction by her appreciation of forms of life and
character unlike her own, and in some ways at odds with
her own. Clara Vavrika was right in feeling that the old
women Nils admired were her natural enemies; and Nils
admitted that in order to appreciate them he had to begin
by assuring his freedom from any pressure they could exercise. Alexandra has none of the Scandinavian intolerance
that is so strong in her brothers Lou and Oscar. Marie
Shabata delights her; she is happy attending the services at
the Catholic church in the French settlement; and, most

striking, perhaps, of all, she draws from knowing how life goes on in other places a wider and more satisfying sense of its significance. "If the world were no wider than my cornfields, if there were not something besides this, I wouldn't feel that it was much worth while to work." She does not believe that Carl Linstrum made a mistake in leaving the Divide, in being an artisan in big Eastern cities, in wanting to seek his fortune and much else in the Klondike. She appreciates in him a sensitive nature, somewhat uncertain of its powers, and determined, above all, on freedom. The perfect test of her liberal judgment of the world outside, which she has never seen and does not wish to see, is in her attitude toward the one brother she really cares for, Emil, almost twenty years younger and rather her son than her brother. She is delighted that Emil wishes to live away from the Divide and beyond its values: "Out of her father's children there was one who was fit to cope with the world, who had not been tied to the plough, and who had a personality apart from the soil. And that, she reflected, was what she had worked for. She felt well satisfied with her life."

Alexandra is a large woman. No man on the Divide, we are told, could have carried her gleaming white body very far. It is a case of a large frame, large nature. Never for an instant does she seem in the least unreal; yet when the novel ends she is a personality of more than life-size. Her last act is the final proof of the extraordinary largeness of her nature. Emil has been killed by Frank Shabata, and Frank has begun a ten-year prison term. Alexandra visits him to say she will not rest till he has been pardoned. Unalterable fact, once more: "Being what he was, she felt, Frank could not have acted otherwise"; and jail is bad for him, will destroy him.

The style and the structure in *O Pioneers!* are what they should be if the substance of the book is to have the fullest effect. There is nothing of the tightness of organization, the cold clearness of style, that were so right for the story of Bartley Alexander. The structure of *O Pioneers!* has a happy looseness and the style an easy strength that belong in a story where the great values are the land, the large nature of Alexandra, and the warm love of Emil. At last Willa Cather was writing as a person writes when he is doing what he came into the world to do.

II

Early in 1913, before Ferris Greenslet was telling the others at Houghton Mifflin that *O Pioneers!* "ought to . . . definitely establish the author as a novelist of the first rank," Willa Cather and Edith Lewis took an apartment at 5 Bank Street, in Greenwich Village. Here they lived from 1912 to 1927, when the house was torn down to give place to a more modern apartment building. These were Willa Cather's best working years. The apartment, its furnishings, and its atmosphere are described by Miss Lewis in this note:

> 5 Bank Street was a wide, brick, five-story house which had been built by a rich brewer as a wedding-present to his son, and had later been made, with very few changes, into an apartment house. A wide staircase ran up through the middle of the house, dividing it into two apartments on each floor. The one we rented was on the second floor above the street. It had seven rather large rooms, with high ceilings, and all the rooms had big windows, facing east, south, and west. The three front rooms we used as one large living-room. It was heated (as was the dining-room) by a coal grate, under a white marble mantelpiece; there was no central heating-system in the house. We bought little copper-lined gas stoves to heat the two bedrooms. The house was lighted by gas, instead of electricity, and in cold weather the gas sometimes froze.
>
> We were delighted with the spaciousness and fine proportions of this apartment, so different from the boxlike place we had on Washington Place. We did not mind certain discomforts, such as having to make our own coal fires and carry coal for them, and having the gas freeze occasionally. The house was very solidly built, with thick walls which shut out the cold in winter and the heat in summer. . . . We got very little noise from our neighbors. Overhead, a German family lived. Their place was thickly carpeted, and the only sound we heard from them was the daughter's practising of the piano in

the mornings. She never practised but the one thing
—Beethoven's *Appassionata*; but after a while Willa
Cather came to like this practising—she said it was
like a signal to work, and she associated it with her
working hours. . . .

We had very little furniture when we moved into
5 Bank Street, but at auction rooms on University
Place we bought mahogany chests and a round mahogany dining-room table for a few dollars. Among
our possessions were a number of large oriental rugs;
and we got some comfortable chairs. An Italian carpenter built us low open book-shelves for our books.
Willa Cather found a large etching, by Couture, of
George Sand, and had it hung over the fireplace in
the living-room—not because she particularly admired George Sand, but because she liked the etching. She had brought back a number of photographs
from Italy—copies of Tintorettos, Giorgione, Ti-
tians, etc.—and these she now had framed and
hung. She also discovered some fine Piranesis at a
little print shop which was selling out its wares—
she was very much pleased by this find, I remember,
and considered them a great treasure.

After we had made the apartment fairly comfortable, we gave no more thought to acquiring
new things, or getting better ones than those we had.
What money we had we preferred to spend on flowers, music, and entertaining our friends.

It is in the setting of the apartment in Bank Street that
most of Willa Cather's friends have cared to remember her.
The spaciousness of the living-rooms, the generous coal-
fire, the warm colors in the rugs, the large, comfortable
chairs, all belonged to her way of life and her outlook on
it. There was nothing mannered or fancy or constricting
about her home—or about her. During the early years in
Bank Street the apartment was often full of her friends.
She was not so pressed for time as she had been; and the
fatigue that often settled on her in later years was still a
rare visitation. For a while she was at home to her friends
on Friday afternoons: people from Nebraska and Pittsburgh, people she had met at *McClure's*, stage people,

musicians, writers. The spirit of these highly informal at-
homes is captured in another note of Miss Lewis's:

> These Friday afternoons became very popular—
> so popular, in fact, that eventually she had to give
> them up; instead of half-a-dozen or so of her friends
> dropping in for tea, more and more people came,
> sometimes bringing strangers with them; and it be-
> came at last too much of a responsibility. But those
> informal gatherings . . . were very pleasant while
> they lasted. Every one talked as if there were not
> nearly enough time for all they had to say. Often a
> small group of Willa Cather's more intimate friends
> would stay on after the others had drifted away,
> lingering until eight o'clock or later, and driving the
> cook, Josephine, to despair; and the talk was then
> always at its best.

During her first year in Bank Street Willa Cather did a
final service for S. S. McClure. Writing came hard to him;
yet he was determined to publish an autobiography. He
would talk to her at length of the main episodes in his life;
she would listen, taking no notes; then when he had gone
she would set down the gist of what he had said, so far as
possible in his own words and units of thought. He was, as
Kipling said, "one of the few with whom three and a half
words serve for a sentence." She allowed the special Mc-
Clure words and ideas to recur much as they would have
recurred in his own speech; but she supplied the connective
tissue and the perspective that were beyond McClure's
powers. Technically *My Autobiography*—which ran in *Mc-
Clure's* from October 1913 to May 1914, and appeared as
a book in the latter year—belongs to the canon of Willa
Cather's writings, but she was right in her opinion that in
every sense that matters it was McClure's. McClure was so
pleased with the outcome of their collaboration that long
afterward he would plead directly and indirectly for her
help in getting his ideas about government on paper. She
was sorry that she could not accede, but the years of indis-
criminate writing were over; now she could write only
what came to her as irresistible impulsion.

Her part in the autobiography is only one of many evidences of the friendly relations she kept with the magazine after she had resigned. For the issue of October 1913 she prepared an article: "Training for the Ballet—Making American Dancers," an account of the Metropolitan School of Ballet Dancing, founded by Dippel and Gatti-Casazza to furnish dancers for the Metropolitan Opera. Her sympathies were warmly with the classical ballet as it was understood in this school. A remark on Isadora Duncan is in the vein of the sharper critical writing she had done in the years at Lincoln and Pittsburgh: "This kind of interpretative dance is for those who like it. I agree with the New York reporter who in summing up Miss Duncan's dancing of *The Rubaiyat* said that on the whole he preferred Omar's lines to Miss Duncan's." In February 1914, in "New Types of Acting: the Character Actor Displaces the Star," she sets George Arliss at the head of recent actors in America; and in an estimate of Alexander Carr and Barney Bernard in *Potash and Perlmutter* she deviates to express her deep discontent with New York City. The life of the city is dominated by the desires of people intent on getting on in the world, and gorging on the material things that are the rewards for having got on. "This city roars and rumbles and hoots and jangles because Potash and Perlmutter are on their way to something." One has to wear the kinds of clothes that have been "designed to enhance the charms of their wives"; and most apartment houses were garish jerrybuilt monsters because they were built by Potash and Perlmutter to be lived in by Potash and Perlmutter. The discontent with New York City was to grow until it became a problem with Willa Cather whether its pervasive horrors were outweighed by its special delights —ballet and theater, music and galleries.

Another article, which appeared in the issue of December 1913, led to a new friendship, which was to determine the subject of Willa Cather's next novel, *The Song of the Lark*. To write this article, "Three American Singers," she was obliged to interview Louise Homer, Geraldine Farrar, and Olive Fremstad, all of them familiar to her as singers from her years of opera-going. Much as she admired Louise Homer's even competence as a woman and an artist, and Geraldine Farrar's charm and vitality, it was only by Olive Fremstad that her imagination was captured. Miss

Lewis has recorded the peculiar facts of the first meeting with Fremstad:

> Fremstad had given her a late afternoon appointment at her apartment near Riverside Drive. Willa Cather was to interview her there, pick up a hasty supper somewhere, and join Isabelle McClung (who was visiting us) and me at the Metropolitan Opera House, for we had tickets for *Tales of Hoffmann* that evening. But when she arrived, just before the curtain went up, she told us, to our great disappointment, that the interview had not come off.
>
> She had gone to Fremstad's apartment—waited— Fremstad was away on a motor ride, and there was some delay about getting back. Finally she came in, very tired, and began at once to apologize; but she could scarcely speak—her voice was just a husky whisper. She was pale, drawn—"Why, she looked forty years old!" Willa Cather told us. She begged Fremstad not to try to talk—said she would come back for the interview another time, and left.
>
> This was all she had time to tell us before the opera began.
>
> The second act of *Tales of Hoffmann* is of course the Venetian scene. The intermission seemed very long, and the audience got very restless. Finally the manager came out before the curtain. The soprano, he announced, had been taken ill, and would be unable to appear; but Mme. Olive Fremstad had kindly consented to sing in her place. Then the curtain went up—and there, before our astonished eyes, was Fremstad—whom Willa Cather had left only an hour before—now a vision of dazzling youth and beauty. She sang that night in a voice so opulent, so effortless, that it seemed as if she were dreaming the music, not singing it.
>
> "But it's impossible," Willa Cather kept saying. "It's impossible."

The experience of that evening was to give Willa Cather one of the most dramatic chapters in the later part of *The Song of the Lark*, with Thea Kronborg taking the role of

Sieglinde in *Die Walküre* at the beginning of the second act.

The interview came soon afterward and led to many other meetings. Fremstad was often at the apartment in Bank Street for dinner, and Willa Cather at her apartment for tea. In the summer of 1914 Willa Cather visited her at Bridgeport in Maine.

In Fremstad Willa Cather found an artist of a kind that had always given her deep pleasure, and a woman who might have been Alexandra Bergson's sister. Fremstad was born in Sweden and brought to America as a small child. The family settled at St. Peter in Minnesota—it might as well have been Red Cloud—where her father combined the practice of medicine with a stormy religious life and a passion for music. Fremstad's childhood was hard: she was driven hard and punished hard. "She grew up," as Willa Cather said, "in a new crude country where there was neither artistic stimulus nor discriminating taste. She was poor, and always had to earn her own living"—she had to give piano lessons, at her father's demand, when she was twelve—"and pay for her music lessons out of her earnings. She fought her own way towards the intellectual centers of the world." In her early twenties she was studying in Germany, and had just turned thirty when Willa Cather heard her soon after she began to sing at the Metropolitan Opera. "The most thrilling to us of all the new stars that came up over the horizon," Miss Lewis has said, "was Olive Fremstad. We heard her nearly every time she sang." Her singing, which was usually in Wagnerian roles, was so profound an experience for Willa Cather because so much brain work lay behind the voice, and the brain work had been carried on within a personality of austere strength and fierce originality. In her originality there was nothing of the petty sort; Fremstad was sparing in gesture, she disdained stage business, she never cared to enrich a commonplace conception of a part with superficial embellishments. She evolved her conception of a part from the depths of her nature, passed what her nature told her through her brain, and made her voice and all else serve the conception. "With Madame Fremstad," Willa Cather wrote, "one feels that the idea is always more living than the emotion; perhaps it would be nearer the truth to say that the idea is so intensely experienced that it becomes emotion." The qualities that Willa Cather found in Fremstad are qualities one might hope to find in a great artist who came from the frontier; in her singing were the force and originality of the pioneers, translated into the terms of disciplined art. In Fremstad she saw realized what she was soon to realize in her own art. In *The Song of the Lark* it was not difficult for her to combine what she felt about Fremstad with what she felt about herself: in Thea Kronborg both are projected.

Some others who knew Fremstad in her great years, and shortly afterward when her voice was ruined, found her to be unperceptive and overbearing. Undoubtedly she could be rough with those who crossed her even in trifles; and with triflers she was habitually merciless. Like S. S. McClure she knew how to raise a rumpus, and like him she did not always have just reasons for doing so. She was often, perhaps she was usually, withdrawn and cold. To Willa Cather none of this mattered. She believed, she always had believed, that the artist is not amenable to the standards by which other folk may rightly be judged. For mastery of an art, she thought, a fearful tax is levied on the entire personality of the artist. Artistic achievement means a constant bleeding of a person's strength. Imaginative understanding of the artistic process should bring, she thought, a deep compassion for what the personality of the artist undergoes, if not homage for his acceptance of his destiny. In *The Song of the Lark* Willa Cather brought together the imaginative understanding, the deep compassion, and the homage. It is no wonder that after reading the novel Fremstad flung her arms about Willa Cather, exclaiming that she could not tell where Thea left off and she began.

The writing of *The Song of the Lark* was begun in the winter of 1913–14. Willa Cather was able to work at it without much regard to where she happened to be. In the spring of 1914 she was in Pittsburgh staying with Isabelle McClung, and happy about the progress of the manuscript. She paid short visits to Maine, staying with Fremstad and with Mary Jewett, the surviving sister of Sarah Orne Jewett. In midsummer she was in Nebraska: the outbreak of war in Europe found her on a farm, and her memory of the way the news was received there and in Red Cloud gave her some of the most moving pages in *One of Ours*. After a stay with Roscoe Cather in Wyoming, she went again to the Southwest, but even in the Sangre de Cristo country the reports from France made her inattentive and restless. In the late fall she was again staying with Isabelle McClung, enjoying the company of her youngest brother, Jack, a student at the Carnegie Institute, and writing so successfully that she could not bear to leave until almost midwinter 1915. The interruptions to which she was subject in writing *The Song of the Lark*, and the stimulating, disturbing variety of experiences and associations among which composition went on, account in part for the special qualities, good and bad, in that novel.

She was happy writing it, and it came quickly. Although it is by a great deal the longest of her novels, extending almost to two hundred thousand words, it was finished in little more than a year. Among her books it has the most conventional structure, a typical massive *Entwicklungsroman* in the tradition of *Clayhanger* and the early Dreiser. In retrospect it seems curious that the novel in which Willa Cather is most explicitly engaged with artists and the artistic process is the least artistic of her works. In later years she was deeply dissatisfied with the artistry of *The Song of the Lark*. She had said of Fremstad that she "rejects a hundred means of expression for every one she uses"; and she was sorry that in her novel she had not shown the same austerity. For the reissue of 1932 she revised *The Song of the Lark* as no other of her novels has been revised. Nearly a tenth of the text was cut away, the longer excisions coming in the later parts. The conversations Thea Kronborg's friends hold about her are so cut down that one feels the author's impatience with her earlier impulse to drive an idea deep into presumably inattentive heads. Now and then Thea's own account of her processes, whether in dialogue or unspoken reflection, meets the same fate. Sometimes what is removed is an expansive comment by the author, which may shine like a jewel but does not cast any light on the essential subjects of the book. It was when I looked in vain through one of the lately printed copies of the novel for an agreeable phrase about Denver that I became aware of the excisions. What inspired them is plain in a sentence from William Heinemann's letter rejecting the book which Willa Cather quotes in "My First Novels—There Were Two." She had known Heinemann when she was collecting material in London for *McClure's*; and he had taken both *Alexander's Bridge* and *O Pioneers!* About *The Song of the Lark* he wrote: "As for myself, I always find the friendly confidential tone of writing of this sort distressingly familiar, even when the subject matter is very fine." Certainly in revision the novel is less confidential, less familiar; it is also less explicit. But even in the revised form Willa Cather was critical in later years about *The Song of the Lark*.

In "The Bohemian Girl" and in *O Pioneers!* she had written of the Western countryside and farm people, not of towns and townsfolk. At the beginning of "The Bohemian Girl" Nils Ericson, on leaving the train, avoids the town and sets off across country—at Red Cloud it would be easy to do so, for the town is a mile from the station. Until he and Clara go to the train on their way to Europe, everything happens on the Divide or at her father's saloon near by. Townsfolk do not appear in that story; nor do they in *O Pioneers!* That novel opens with a great winter scene in town, but the cold has swept the townsfolk from the streets and kept them from visiting the stores. Only the farm people are about, and the storekeepers, who remain unindividualized and even unnamed. To little Emil Bergson, whose kitten has been put out of doors and has climbed a pole, "this village was a very strange and perplexing place where people had fine clothes and hard hearts." His sense of the town as something marginal and alien to his life remains with us through the book. But in *The Song of the Lark* the town is everything until Thea goes east. Farm people do not appear; and the countryside, which might as well be uninhabited, is only the few miles around town.

There was an excellent reason for placing Thea in a town rather than on the Divide, the same reason for making her a minister's daughter. She must have the maximum of exposure to the Philistines; she must suffer "the fear of the tongue, that terror of little towns." On a Western farm she would not have been exposed to anyone beyond her family; the disapproval of the neighbors would not have been something to reckon with. Willa Cather does set Thea in a disapproving family; her sister and all her brothers except the baby, Thor, have a natural enmity toward her. But this is not the enmity that counts for most, since during almost all the time she is in Moonstone the idea that anyone in her family might be hostile does not occur to her as even possible. Only in her last summer she "suddenly realized" that her sister "had always disliked her." In accounting for this dislike, and her brothers', she merges the family in the town. "She had done them the honour . . . to believe that though they had no particular endowments, *they were of her kind*, and not of the Moonstone kind. Now they had all grown up and become persons. They faced each other as individuals, and she saw that Anna and Gus and Charley were among the people whom she had always recognized as her natural enemies." That phrase "her natural enemies" occurs more than once in the novel: it is used of the principal of the high school who in addition to lethargy and stupidity has the deeper sin of diagramming poems in the manner of Professor Sherman. It is used of Mrs. "Livery" Johnson, who intrigued to give her protégé, "the angel child of the Baptists," a mean victory over Thea at a concert. None of her natural enemies, whether inside the Kronborg family or outside, is strongly individualized: there is no one in the novel like the Ivy Peters of *A Lost Lady* or the Wick Cutter of *My Ántonia*. It would have been easy to add to the portrait of Dr. Archie's mean and petty wife some jealousy of her husband's romantic and innocent attachment to Thea. Mrs. Archie does not care about it, she remains only mean and petty, and so do the rest of Thea's natural enemies. Among them there is a lukewarm malice that never comes to a boil, and is never exhausted. By contrast, Thea's friends are highly colored individuals: the heartbroken, decaying music teacher Wunsch, Johnny Tellamantez, Dr. Archie, the railwayman Ray Kennedy, Thea's queer maiden aunt, and—the most complex of the portraits in this group—her mother.

To anyone who has seen Red Cloud and taken his bearings there, the topography of Moonstone will seem familiar. Moonstone has been set, however, in Colorado, some distance to the west of Denver. It lies not among farmlands but in the desert: it is a "frail, brightly painted desert town . . . shaded by the light-reflecting, wind-loving trees of the desert." The desert is constantly emphasized: the beauty in the countryside is a desert beauty. Moonstone is also a town with a Mexican settlement—something Red Cloud did not have—and toward the Mexicans, so graceful, with such a feeling for beautiful turns of speech, so dependent on music and dancing, Thea is strongly attracted. By the combination of a desert landscape and a Mexican colony we are prepared for Thea's being immediately at home in Arizona.

A desert setting is important to another effect. Like *O Pioneers!* this novel opens in January, but with what a difference! *O Pioneers!* begins when a "mist of fine snowflakes was curling and eddying about the cluster of low drab buildings huddled on the grey prairie, under a grey sky." The sidewalks were "grey with trampled snow"; the countryside with "its sombre wastes" had an "uninterrupted mournfulness." In *The Song of the Lark*, when Dr. Archie steps out of his office into the January night, "overhead the stars shone gloriously. It was impossible not to notice them. The air was so clear that the white sand hills to the east of Moonstone gleamed softly." Brilliance of light pervades the novel. In the picture of Chicago the stress comes on brightness: when Thea stepped out of the Auditorium, after hearing the *New World* Symphony for the first time, "the sun was setting in a clear, windy sky, that flamed with red as if there were a great fire somewhere on the edge of the city"; and what is most vividly represented in the street scenes is simply the brilliance of the shop windows at Christmas. Thea's life in Arizona "was simple and full of light, like the days themselves"—"she had loved the sun, and the brilliant solitudes of sand and sun" as "the earliest sources of gladness that she could remember," and now the sun filled her being, for months on end. Even in the seedy hotel in Union Square which is her first lodging in New York her room is "flooded by thin, clear sunshine." But it is the final part of the novel, the rendering of Thea's triumph, that brings to its height the effect of light to which we became accustomed in the early desert scenes. This section opens in Denver, which, "under a thrilling green-blue sky, is masked in snow and glittering with sunlight." The blaze of the sun on the Capitol is so dazzling that the outlines of the building are lost in light. On the peaks of the mountains "the fiery sunshine is gathered up as by a burning-glass." When the scene shifts to New York, the sun continues to shine, the snow is bright in Central Park, and when dusk comes the lamps banish any possibility of gloom. In the last scene, when, after singing Sieglinde, Thea left the Metropolitan, she stepped into the same kind of sunset that had met her years before when she left the Auditorium in Chicago. A more subdued brightness streams through the epilogue, in which Thea's queer old maiden aunt, the only Kronborg left in Moonstone, shows how happy she is in the reflected glory of a great name.

The white and gold colors of the sunlight playing on sand and snow are matched in the appearance of Thea herself. Her beauty has a much finer correspondence with the play of sunlight. It is not a constant thing, like the sensuous fairness of Lena Lingard in *My Ántonia*, or like the steady blond beauty of Alexandra Bergson. It comes and goes as her feelings shift. Just as the canyons in Arizona are like "a grey ghost, an empty, shivering uncertainty" when the sun does not shine, Thea's face is heavy and lifeless when she is balked or worn.

The use of light, repeated and varied with an artistry more resourceful than analysis can mirror, is never painfully obtrusive. Its principal value is not intellectual but emotional: without quite knowing why a sympathetic reader is suffused with warmth as he moves through the story, and long afterward when most of the events have been forgotten and most of the characters have grown dim, a mention of *The Song of the Lark*, a sight of the faded blue cover on the bookshelf of a friend, is enough to bring back a radiant feeling that no other writing by Willa Cather can evoke. The spirit of the book is too strong for the massive structure to crush.

III

In the summer of 1915, with the manuscript of the novel already at Houghton Mifflin, Willa Cather returned to the Southwest for a third long stay. For years she had wished to visit the Mesa Verde in Colorado. On this trip, accompanied by Edith Lewis, she traveled by rail to Mancos, twenty miles or so from the Mesa, and engaged there a team and driver to take them to it. Miss Lewis describes the visit to the Mesa Verde in this striking narrative:

Willa Cather had heard that one of the Wetherill family, a brother of the Dick Wetherill who first "discovered" the Mesa Verde, was still living in

Mancos, and on the evening before we started for the Mesa she went to call on him; and from him she heard the whole story of how Dick Wetherill swam the Mancos river and rode into the Mesa after lost cattle, and how he came upon the cliff dwellings that had been hidden there for centuries.

We spent a week on the Mesa Verde. Very few people visited the place then—we were, I think, the only guests for the greater part of that week—and the forest ranger and guide, a young man named Jeep, who ran the government camp for tourists, was able to spend a great deal of his time taking us around to the different cliff dwellings. I recall that we spent a whole day in Cliff Palace, the cliff dwelling with a tower, described in the *Tom Outland* part of *The Professor's House*, cooking our lunch there and drinking from the spring behind the cliff houses.

The day before we were to go back to Mancos, Jeep had planned to take us to a cliff dwelling called the Tower House, which had not then been excavated. But just as we were about to start on this excursion, a large party of tourists arrived; and Jeep announced that he would not be able to go with us. He said that, instead, he would send us with his brother-in-law, a young man named Richnor. We were disappointed, for Jeep was a splendid guide, familiar with every foot of the Mesa, and we knew nothing about Richnor. However, as Jeep made this announcement in Richnor's presence, we could hardly decline, and we started off with him.

To get to the Tower House, one had to walk through the woods to the rim of Soda Canyon, climb down to the bottom of this canyon, and follow along it for some distance. The Tower House was up the other wall of the canyon.

Richnor got us to the Tower House all right, but by a very rough trail—in climbing down to the bottom of Soda Canyon, we had in many places to hang from a tree or rock and then drop several feet to the next rock; we could not have returned by this trail without ropes. Richnor said he would take us back by another trail, further down the canyon. But by five or six o'clock that evening, after we had done a good many miles of walking, he was still unable to find this trail, and had to admit that he did not know how we were to get back. (The sides of the canyon were everywhere precipitous, and for several hundred feet beneath the rim the bare rock generally overhung.)

We had by then come to a place where another canyon, Cliff Canyon, opened at right angles from Soda Canyon. Richnor told us he thought, but was not sure, that about four miles up Cliff Canyon there was an archaeologist's camp (Dr. Fewkes' camp), and suggested that we try for it. But Willa Cather sensibly told him he had better go up Cliff Canyon and find out whether the camp was really there; we would wait, in the meantime, at the intersection of the two canyons.

The four or five hours that we spent waiting there were, I think, for Willa Cather the most rewarding of our whole trip to the Mesa Verde. There was a large flat rock at the mouth of Cliff Canyon, and we settled ourselves comfortably on this rock—with the idea, I believe, that we should be able to see any rattlesnakes if they came racing up. We were tired, but not worried, for we knew that we should eventually be found. We did not talk, but watched the long summer twilight come on, and the full moon rise up over the rim of the canyon. The place was very beautiful.

We were sitting there in the moonlight, when we heard shouts from up Cliff Canyon, and presently two men came in sight. They were two of the diggers from Dr. Fewkes' camp, whom Richnor had sent down to get us. He himself was so exhausted by the time he reached the camp that he was unable to come back.

Soda Canyon has a wide, grassy bottom—one simply walks along it—but Cliff Canyon is a very difficult canyon to climb—just a mass of broken rocks all the way, some of them as big as a house. We could never have got through without the help of the two diggers, who were both splendid men—kind, chivalrous, resourceful, and full of high spirits and encouragement. . . . Their names were Clint

Scarf and Audrey Grey Pearl. Each of them took us
by the hand and steadied us over the rocks. (At one
place we had to lie down and be pulled through a
sort of tunnel in the rocks.) . . .

About four miles up the canyon one could reach
the top of the cliffs by mounting part way on the
lopped-off branches of a huge pine tree, which was
laid along the side of the cliff like a ladder. We got
to Fewkes' camp at about two in the morning. Our
diggers then went out into the pasture, caught a
couple of horses, hitched them to a wagon, and
drove us back to our own camp. At eight o'clock
that same morning our team and driver arrived to
take us back to Mancos.

Much of what befell Willa Cather on that day and night,
and something of the spirit in which she took it, were to go
into "Tom Outland's Story." After the visit of 1915 Willa
Cather never saw the Mesa Verde; but her feeling toward
the Cliff-Dwellers, her sense of the contrast between their
way of building and living and the modern American way,
were to shape *The Professor's House*. These were to be
long delayed effects; never again did she convert the present or the immediate past into fiction as she had done in
The Song of the Lark.

From Mancos Willa Cather and Edith Lewis traveled
southward to Taos, at that time a very isolated place, approached only by team over a long distance of rough road.
There was no American hotel, only an adobe hotel, run by
a Mexican woman, which Willa Cather found comfortable
if primitive. She stayed at Taos for a month or so, exploring the country either on horseback or behind a team she
drove herself. She was always glad she had seen the Southwest before the invasion of automobiles, when one still had
to be on the alert for every landmark and had time to note
all the contours of the land and all the detail.

In the summer of 1916, accompanied again by Edith
Lewis, Willa Cather returned to Taos, for a longer stay.
She also spent some time at Santa Fe, explored Frijoles
Canyon and the Espanola Valley, and at Santa Cruz talked
with a Belgian priest, Father Haltermann, who knew the
history of the French and Spanish missionaries in the
Southwest. The impressions were now accumulating for the

greatest of her novels, but many years were to pass before they fell into place and she could write the first word of *Death Comes for the Archbishop*.

On the way back to New York after each of these two summers Willa Cather stayed for some weeks in Red Cloud. One day in 1916 she drove out to a farm on the Divide and saw, surrounded by many children, Anna Pavelka, a Bohemian woman whom she had known well, very well, when they were girls. It seemed to her that this woman's story ran very close to the central stream of life in Red Cloud and on the Divide, that she stood for the triumph of what was vigorous, sound, and beautiful in a region where these qualities so often seemed to suffer repression or defeat. Before she returned to New York, Willa Cather had begun to write this story in *My Ántonia*.

She always showed impatience at the complaint that *My Ántonia* is not precisely a novel. Why should it be? She had never said it was. In this book she was gathering her memories of some persons and places very dear to her, and as she was a writer of stories, the memories had taken a narrative form. Besides, in the very curious preface she had given notice of what the book would be like. This introduction, like so many of her writings, opens on a scene in a train to the west of Chicago. She is talking, she says, with Jim Burden, whom she had known when she was a girl, and who is now the legal counsel for a Western railway. They both live in New York, but she rarely sees him, for she dislikes his wife. Mrs. Burden, who is not aboard the train, is given a full page: she is a superficial, spoiled, restless woman, who has her own money and lives her own life. The failure of Jim Burden's marriage has not injured his character: he remains what he always was, romantic in disposition, in love with the Western country, as impressionable as a boy. They talk of the early days in Nebraska, and find they "kept returning to a central figure, a Bohemian girl, whom we had known long ago and whom both of us admired. More than any other person we remembered, this girl seemed to mean to us the country, the conditions, the whole adventure of our childhood." Willa Cather says she had the feeling that Jim Burden could tell the story of Ántonia better than she could: "he had had opportunities that I, as a little girl who watched her come and go, had not." It was agreed that both would record their memories of Ántonia; but when in the course of the next winter Jim Burden called at her apartment with his manuscript complete, she had not gone beyond a few straggling notes. Jim was taken aback at the mention of notes for what was to be not a created fiction but a record of fact and impression. "I didn't arrange or rearrange," he says, "I simply wrote down what of herself and myself and other people Ántonia's name recalls to me. I suppose it hasn't any form. It hasn't any title either." Then across the cover of the manuscript he wrote "Ántonia," prefixing in a moment "another word, making it 'My Ántonia.'" When she read his memoir she was so pleased, Willa Cather says, that she did not write hers, and it is his she presents.

This is the substance of the preface in the early editions. Willa Cather was never happy about it; she had found it unlike the rest of the book, a labor to write. For the reissue of 1926 she revised it in important ways. The agreement that both she and Jim would record their memories of Ántonia is removed; and instead of Jim's undertaking to write because of his talk with her, he has been at work on his manuscript long before the meeting in the train. By these changes the effect is, I believe, improved. Jim's concern with Ántonia seems more profound when the decision to record his memories stems not from a meeting with a professional writer but from his own inward impulse. The agreement had, besides, the defect of starting in the reader's mind a question that could do the book no good—whether in fact it would not have been better told by another woman, the query Miss Jewett had raised about "On the Gull's Road." Most of the satirical account of Mrs. Burden was removed, though enough was left to establish the failure of Jim's marriage. The excision at this point is also a gain: for the earlier text left one wondering whether Jim was not ignominiously weak in continuing to lend himself to the purposes of such a creature. Unless Jim can satisfy the reader that his impressions and judgments about women are sound, his value as an appreciative recorder of Ántonia is threatened. What was important in the original preface remains: that the book is to be taken as the work of an unprofessional writer; of a man who had left the Divide, Red Cloud, the West, but kept his attachment to all three; of a man whose personal life in later years has been frustrated and who has judged the phase to which Ántonia belonged to have been the high water-mark of the whole.

It could do the book no good, I suggest, for the reader to ponder whether it might not have been better told by a woman. The new preface does not raise the question; but readers are likely to raise it for themselves before the book ends. A young man who feels that a young woman is the most important thing in his life might be expected to fall in love with her. Jim is curious about Ántonia, interested in her, charmed by her, but he does not fall in love with her; nor when in later years he visits her at her farm (as Willa Cather visited the original of the character), does he have any feeling that he ought to have married her, though he does say that when he was a young boy he had been unconsciously in love with her. At the very center of his relation with Ántonia there is an emptiness where the strongest emotion might have been expected to gather. A comment on *My Ántonia* that Willa Cather made in an interview she gave in Lincoln a few years after the book came out shows that in her use of Jim as narrator she had been trying to achieve two effects that were not really compatible: Jim was to be fascinated by Ántonia as only a man could be, and yet he was to remain a detached observer, appreciative but inactive, rather than take a part in her life.

Jim's failure to take a part in Ántonia's life is made conspicuous by one of the main social themes in the book. In *O Pioneers* as in "The Bohemian Girl," people of old American stock had no roles; apart from the Scandinavians and Bohemians the only other racial group to appear (in "The White Mulberry Tree" section of *O Pioneers!*) was the French. In *The Song of the Lark* individuals of old American stock had important roles even in the early Western chapters, but they appeared as individuals; there was no study of a family of old American stock, nothing to approach the account, so tenderly discerning, of the old German couple with whom Wunsch, the music teacher, lived. In *My Ántonia* Willa Cather is deeply concerned with the relations between the families of old American stock and the families of the immigrants from Europe. The reader is constantly required to make comparisons, and to perceive superiorities in the immigrants. At no point are the comparisons more pointed, the superiorities more conspicuous, than when the Scandinavian girls like Lena Lingard and the Bohemians like Ántonia are set beside the girls of old American stock who have grown up not on the Divide but within the rigid code of the leading families in town. For the young man in one of those families who has marriage in his mind, the choice is between life and death. Sylvester Lovett, the son of a local bank president, appears in the book for a moment to make his choice. He has danced with Lena Lingard, taken her driving, and shown the world that he is infatuated; but marry her he will not, he chooses a well-to-do widow much older than himself. Jim Burden had hoped that Lovett would marry Lena; if he had done so, Jim thinks the "foreign girls" would all have taken higher places in the town's scale of values. When Lovett did not, Jim burned to find some way of manifesting his contempt for the white-handed high-collared young man.

Jim too had his chance to marry Lena and did not take it. Lena is the most beautiful, the most innocently sensuous of all the women in Willa Cather's works. The portrait of Lena has a merciful softness as if the novelist's critical power were deliberately withheld except for an occasional touch of humorous realism. Lena is never a rival for the central place in the book—she has not Ántonia's force or her insight, she is never so much alive. At times she is a foil: her fairness against Ántonia's sparkling nervous dark beauty, her slowness and quietness against Ántonia's vivacity. It is easy to understand how in her rosy semi-naked beauty she became so constant a figure in Jim's adolescent dreams. Despite her richness in what a younger generation than Willa Cather's calls "sex appeal," her hold on Jim never becomes firm. She and Jim were attracted to each other early in the book; but it is only after he has gone to Lincoln as an undergraduate and Lena as a dressmaker that he singles her out. In his own town he did not have the daring. Just as Sylvester Lovett had found her a girl who could really dance, Jim finds her a girl who can really respond to the theater. Their relation is one of the most beautiful elements in the book, with the charm of an idyll (it is intertwined with his study of the *Georgics*), of a sharing of youth rather than a relation between two personalities. Jim is no better than the Sylvester Lovett he had so despised. When his favorite instructor warns him he should part from his "beautiful Norwegian," who is "quite irresponsible," he does so without even an appearance of struggle. I seem to hear the creaking of the novelist's machinery as the idyll ends and Jim retreats so easily into the status of a detached observer. What is excellent in *My Ántonia* does not depend on a masculine narrator. It inheres in the material itself and in the appreciation of it, which might have been just as sensitive, just as various, if Willa Cather had presented this story omnisciently—as Miss Jewett counseled earlier—as she had presented Alexandra Bergson's, or if she had made herself a part of the structure.

The beauty of the book was at once apprehended by W. C. Brownell in a letter (still unpublished) to one of Willa Cather's associates at *McClure's,* Viola Roseboro'.

> I feel somehow [he wrote] as if the proper epithets to characterize the book were something "up," almost physically floating above the material, as it were. I don't mind being incoherent, if I convey my notion in the least by my flounderings. Arnold, on Homer, talks about Homer not (like a Dutch painter) "sinking with his subject." This has that air. But would it be too much to say it *lifts* the subject somehow—not, of course, by treating it idealistically, since it is one of the most notable instances I know of the contrary—but by a sort of continuous and sustained respect for the material: a sort of "what God hath made call thou not common" implication, putting Nature for God, of course. . . . At first I thought it was casual and episodical (though *so* well written, so simple, so obviously saying all it felt and with such ease) and though large minded and as unmeretricious as salt itself, still rather a desultory document of Western civilization. But ere long it differentiated itself imperceptibly and subtly into a picture crowded with real people, made somehow real, given souls, by—well, by what? I don't know. I don't remember any art more essentially elusive.

Where so penetrating a critic as Brownell was aware of floundering, and pronounced an author's art "essentially elusive," one hesitates to offer clarifications. I believe that something can be said of the means that have given this book its effect of "almost physically floating above the material." The elements that weigh a book down scarcely exist here. In *My Ántonia* there is no massive central trunk such as the development of Thea Kronborg, phase by phase, provided for *The Song of the Lark*. In *My Ántonia*, instead, there is a gallery of pictures. For a while, as happened to Brownell, the pictures seem to be hung in a casual and episodical fashion; before long they affect one as illuminating one another and contributing to a general tone. They have been painted and arranged so that one may apprehend the values in that old Nebraska world, gone forever before the book was written.

The epigraph and the comment upon it taken together are a sufficient clue to the method of the book. The epigraph, from the third *Georgic*, runs: *"Optima dies . . . prima fugit."* Jim was preparing this part of the poem and translating this passage as "the best days are the first to flee," when Lena Lingard made her first visit to him at Lincoln. When she had gone, "it came over me, as it had never done before, the relation between girls like those [Lena, Ántonia, and their friends] and the poetry of Virgil. If there were no girls like them in the world, there would be no poetry." His old dream of Lena returned to him awake, and "it floated before me on the page like a picture, and underneath it stood the mournful line: *'Optima dies . . . prima fugit.'* "

Everything in the book is there to convey a feeling, not to tell a story, not to establish a social philosophy, not even to animate a group of characters. The feeling attaches to persons, places, moments: if one were to pin it in a phrase it might be called a mournful appreciation of "the precious, the incommunicable past"—those are the last words in the book. Earlier Jim Burden has voiced the feeling in the remark: "Some memories are realities, and are better than anything that can ever happen to one again."

This feeling attaches itself above all to Ántonia. She is the person whose inner strength enables her to live the enviable life. At the foot of Willa Cather's scale, as usual, are people who live in the town or on the Divide and make nothing of the opportunity. These are the narrow money-minded people like Wick Cutter and Ántonia's brother

Ambrosch. Then come the people who must go away to achieve a life. They are much more important to the book; Jim Burden and Lena Lingard are among them. Their lives will not bear comparison with Ántonia's. Jim has become wealthy and "important"; but he is childless and has no attachments to any person or any place except what he preserves of the Nebraska past. Lena has been successful— and her friend Tiny Soderball, another girl from the Divide, has had almost unbelievable success; but their lives in San Francisco are solitary and rootless. Ántonia has remained on the Divide; she had found a good husband, who has fragrant memories of Prague and Vienna, of music and song; she has a dozen children, all of them delightful; the farm is big and fertile; and Ántonia has given it some of the amenities that would have pleased her fastidious father—orchards and hedges and a grape arbor. She had worked herself and worn herself to accomplish her life, but if she was "battered" she was not "diminished." In middle life, when she makes her last appearance, her hair is grizzled and most of her teeth have gone; but she "was still there in the full vigour of her personality." Looking at her, one feels that is how one should have lived—if one could.

My Ántonia marks a new phase in the long process of Willa Cather's reconciliation with Nebraska. In this book she values not only the land and the pioneers, but aspects in the life of the town which have taken on an affecting charm in the long retrospect. The simplest experiences become charming by the play of a strong retrospective emotion: the casual warmhearted fun in the Harlings' kitchen, the dances in the park on summer Saturday evenings, the lonely walks at night under the cottonwoods to the edge of town. What was harsh, narrow, and malignant in the town, so strong an undertone in *The Song of the Lark*, has lost its menace; the face of Wick Cutter's wife is the "very colour and shape of anger," but she can do no real harm.

In the reconciliation with Nebraska the Southwest continued to have a role. The last summer before he went to the university Jim spent a long day by the river with Ántonia, Lena, and two other Scandinavian girls; in this episode Willa Cather reworks "The Enchanted Bluff" with deeper meanings and happier implications. In "The Enchanted Bluff" the wish of all the boys is to go away, and the failure of their lives is in not going away, or not going far

enough. Now in *My Ántonia* the story of Coronado is told
again. On a sword dug up by a farmer breaking sod near
by, the parish priest found the name of a Spanish maker
and an abbreviation that stood for the city of Cordova.
Jim and the girls wonder about the motives for the long
northward journey and how the country looked when the
Spaniards first saw it. "Why had Coronado never gone
back to Spain, to his riches and his castles and his king? I
couldn't tell them. I only knew the school-books said he
'died in the wilderness, of a broken heart.' " As they wondered, the sun was setting; the "edge of the red disk rested
on the high fields against the horizon," and "a great black
figure suddenly appeared on the face of the sun." This was
a plow left standing on an upland farm. "Magnified across
the distance by the horizontal light, it stood out against the
sun, was exactly contained within the circle of the disk; the
handles, the tongue, the share—black against the molten
red. There it was, heroic in size, a picture writing on the
sun." The mention of Coronado, the feeling of a Spanish
past in which inexplicable adventure had ended in heartbreak and disaster, has woven an enchantment about the
region. It is no longer a place to leave, it is a place to live
in—if one has, like Ántonia, the stuff of which the heroic
Spaniards were made.

8

The World Broke in Two

1919–1923

THE THREE NOVELS about the West, published within six years, had pre-empted most of Willa Cather's imaginative activity; but writing them had not dulled her awareness of what was interesting in the lives of the people she knew or heard about in New York. Most of these were artists or devotees of the arts; and among them, from the time of her getting to know Olive Fremstad, the opera singers had most to say to her imagination. She did not care to write about them at length, but when she was free for a while from the weight of a novel, she found herself writing short stories about them. There was "The Diamond Mine," which came out in *McClure's* in October 1916, when she was beginning *My Ántonia*; "A Gold Slipper," which came out in *Harper's* in the following January; and "Scandal," another episode in the life of the same singer, which came out in the *Century* in August 1919.

In these stories the center of interest is not where it had been in most of the earlier treatments of artists—in the greatness, growth, or decline of a talent or in the destructive force of Philistinism. Such grave matters usually do come in, but they receive only a secondary emphasis. What now has most interest for Willa Cather is the kind of relationships artists have with those who are not artists but are brought into contact with them. At the core of "Scandal" is a shabby trick played on the singer Kitty Ayrshire by a garment-manufacturer whose hobby is pretending to intimate relations with women who are highly successful in the arts. The trick hurts her personal reputation, but it does not hurt her; and in retrospect she can afford to smile at it. In "A Gold Slipper" the core is ever slighter: Kitty has a forthright talk in the course of the one meeting she will ever have with a pillar of the coal industry and the First Presbyterian Church in Pittsburgh; his scorn for artists cannot make her even momentarily uncomfortable, and there is nothing he could do to jeopardize either her talent or her personal life. The effect in "The Diamond Mine" is a little graver. The theme of an artist's suffering exploitation by her family, sounded briefly in "A Gold Slipper," runs through this story; it is disheartening to think that there are people like Cressida Garnet's sisters and brother, as it is disheartening to think that there are people like the coal-man and the garment-maker; but the artists are too strong to be injured. In Pittsburgh, before she had an intimate knowledge of serious arists, Willa Cather had felt that the failure of an artist's family and friends to understand him was a horrible disaster, disabling to the artist's personal life, if not fatal to his talent. She had said so in "The Sculptor's Funeral." She had misread the artistic nature: now that she knew Olive Fremstad and George Arliss and had observed for some years at first hand many artists practicing their craft on many levels and in varied fields, she was aware of the toughness of fiber in an artist. She knew that his talent could not be ruined or his life embittered just because clever scoundrels exploited him, or stupid people wrote him down for a fool.

In another story of these years, "Coming, Aphrodite!" Willa Cather pits one kind of artist against another—an original painter against a conventional opera singer whom he loves. His disappointment with her, her failure to perceive his distinction do not really matter. His painting is not lamed by his experience, nor does it seem to change the independent curve of his life.

Early in 1920 Willa Cather decided to bring out a second collection of short stories. It was fifteen years since *The Troll Garden* was published, and it had long been our of print. For the new book she would keep four of its seven tales, submit some of them to much revision, and add the four recent tales about artists. From this decision came *Youth and the Bright Medusa*, the first of her books to be published by Alfred A. Knopf. She had been happy when *Alexander's Bridge* was accepted by the Houghton Mifflin Company; she knew that this house was one of the few in the country with a history and standards; and she had found in Ferris Greenslet a sympathetic counselor as well as a firm friend. His report on *My Ántonia*, the last of her books to appear with a Houghton Mifflin imprint, was everything an author could wish. "Of all the remarkable portraits of women that Miss Cather has done," he wrote to his colleagues, "no other is so poetic and appealing. . . . This is undoubtedly Miss Cather's best book so far. It is a very distinguished piece of work and with a human quality that will, I think, make it a permanent success." He had been entirely right at every point; the portrait of Ántonia was the most poetic and the most appealing in her writings; the book was her "best . . . so far" (and when she wrote a better, Ferris Greenslet was prompt to say so); it did have permanent success both popular and critical. But if Ferris Greenslet's attitude toward her work was generous as well as perceptive, he had not been able, Willa Cather believed, to persuade the rest of the directorate to accept it. The company did not get behind her books, she thought, did not give them sufficient play. She was especially displeased with what she thought a torpid interest in making *My Ántonia* known and getting it into the bookstores. Besides, she was not happy about the format of her novels. A company that had been giving soberly beautiful covers and pages to Irving Babbitt (to name but one other author) had given a crowded page to *The Song of the Lark* and an awkward drab cover to *My Ántonia*. The parting came without acrimony, and Ferris Greenslet was a close friend as long as Willa Cather lived.

In *Alfred A. Knopf, Quarter Century*, Willa Cather has related her first conversations with the man who was to publish all her books in the last twenty-seven years of her life. She went to see him because she had liked his lists and the format of his books. During her first call she picked up some samples of blue paper from his desk; he had gone to the Metropolitan Museum of Art "to find exactly the right shade among the Chinese blues" for a volume of translations from Chinese poetry. She liked the way he talked about the works he had published and wished to publish. She liked his independence, and the blend of "a fiery tem-

perament" with "a rather severe taste." In their second talk
she formally asked him to become her publisher, and entered on a relationship that was as happy as the world
knows it to have been successful. Miss Lewis notes:

> Next to writing her novels, Willia Cather's choice of
> Alfred Knopf as a publisher influenced her career,
> I think, more than any action she ever took. It was
> not so much that with him she was able in a few
> years to achieve financial security . . . as that he gave
> her great encouragement and absolute liberty to
> write exactly as she chose—protected her in every
> way he could from outside pressures and interrup-
> tions—and made evident, not only to her but to the
> world in general, his great admiration and belief in
> her. Life was simply no longer a battle—she no
> longer had to feel apologetic or on the defensive.
> She was always very modest about her work, but
> she was a person of great pride. Her pride was no
> longer threatened.

II

When she first talked with Alfred A. Knopf in the spring of
1920, Willa Cather mentioned the novel she was writing—
One of Ours, then tentatively named *Claude*. That book
had its inception when she learned, in May 1918, of the
death in battle at Cantigny of a young cousin who had
grown up in Webster County and about whom she had
cared a great deal. G. P. Cather, Jr., who had served in the
navy and in the national guard before the war, had shown
unusual skill with big guns, and became a lieutenant almost
as soon as he enlisted. He was extremely happy in the
armed services and was believed to have great promise by
his superior officers, one of whom was Theodore Roosevelt,
Jr. But it did not require a personal loss to make Willa
Cather feel the impact of the war. For a year before her
cousin was killed, soldiers from Red Cloud and Lincoln and
Pittsburgh, friends, students, friends of friends, had come
in groups to see her, often when they were on the last leave
before embarkation. One of her students in the Pittsburgh
years, Albert Donovan, had an army post in New York

which drew him into touch with great numbers of soldiers, and he was always encouraged to bring to call on her those he thought would care to come.

After her cousin the soldier who interested her most was a young violinist, whom she saw only four times, David Hochstein. She met him first in the winter of 1916 when he played in a quintet at an informal musical party in a New York hotel. In his playing and in the man himself she found poetic insight and a mixture of reticence and sincerity that delighted her. Hochstein was a relative of the anarchist Emma Goldman, and an admirer of the civilization of Germany, where he had received much of his training in music. She did not meet him again until after the United States had declared war, and he was in much doubt about its issues and outcome, and about the course he should himself pursue. He entered the army, and when Willa Cather saw him next he was in the depression that the first months of military training so often bring. Some months later she saw him for the last time, and marveled at the change in him: he was now delighted with the kind of men he had to do with and the special terms on which they lived. In the autumn of 1918 he was killed in the Argonne. Willa Cather was allowed to see some of his letters to his mother, as she also saw some of her cousin's letters home, and was moved by the intellectual and emotional maturity in both. How had a Nebraska farm-boy, with little education and slight experience of life, and how had a New York musician of solitary and pessimistic temper, changed so much and so quickly? How could war and the army and France produce such effects? These were the questions that led to the writing of *One of Ours*. Willa Cather was mystified when Sinclair Lewis, in a review, remarked: "The whole introduction of the great war is doubtful; it is a matter to be debated." One might question the authenticity of the war scenes, and argue about the conception of war and the army, but there is no doubt whatever that the war was an intrinsic part of her original conception.

One of Ours was written slowly. In August 1918 Willa Cather visited Red Cloud, and in the early fall she stayed with her brother Roscoe in Wyoming. The novel was in her mind before she went west, and as soon as she returned to New York she started to write. She was at work on it during the whole of 1919. In the autumn of that year she made a long stay at Jaffrey, New Hampshire, which she had found a good place for work when she was reading the proofs of *My Ántonia*. She came down with influenza and was treated by a local doctor who had served as medical officer of a troopship when a severe epidemic of the disease broke out. From his diary she drew much of the material for the fourth part of the novel, "The Voyage of the *Anchises*." By the spring of 1920 two thirds of the novel existed. To write the remainder, which is laid in France, Willa Cather felt that she must live in that country for a time. In June, accompanied by Edith Lewis, she went to Paris by way of Cherbourg, and for almost two months lived at the Hôtel du Quai Voltaire, with windows opening on the Seine. She used no introductions, seldom crossed over to the Right Bank except to hear opera, and acquired impressions of the older Paris that went into *Shadows on the Rock* as well as into the pages she was preparing to write. There are no Paris scenes in *One of Ours*, but from her absorption in the past of the city she drew what she felt she had needed: a feeling of the meaning of French civilization and culture as a whole. She visited the battlefields with Isabelle McClung and Jan Hambourg, moving for two weeks through a countryside still pitted and scarred by war, and visiting the grave of her cousin. Almost as soon as she had returned from this trip she was eager to go home—she was ready to write the rest of the novel. It did not come quickly, and the proofs did not begin to arrive until the summer of 1921. She read a part of them during her first stay at Grand Manan, an island in the Bay of Fundy, where before long she was to find her summer home. *One of Ours* appeared in the autumn of 1922, four years after she had begun writing it.

Of her earlier novels only *The Song of the Lark* has any resemblance to *One of Ours*. Each is a novel of development, with a large number of carefully detailed phases, beginning on the Western plains, ending far away when the development has been completed, with an epilogue to show what the development meant to someone who remained in the original setting. In the Western part of each novel the developing character lives in a crisscross of alliances and enmities. Thea Kronborg's youth, roughly contemporary with Willa Cather's, came in the pioneer phase of her society; in Claude Wheeler's the next phase has succeeded, prosperous, mechanized, prosaic. In the second decade of the century the pioneers are still living on their farms and in the town; but except for Claude's own family they do not often appear, and when they do, as when old Troilus Oberlies is charged with disloyalty, they have a force and a color somewhat out of scale with the rest of the cast. One reason why the dramatis personæ seem dull in comparison with those of the earlier novels is that the immigrants have no important parts, nor do their children. There are no Scandinavians, and there is only one Bohemian, a pleasant thoughtful boy, of no force or imagination. The world in which Claude grew up needed to be a dull world; what Willa Cather wished to show was how a boy who had an exceptional nature, but no exceptional gift or strength of will, was undergoing a slow strangulation of intellect and feeling until the war provided an escape from Nebraska. The dullness was necessary, but even when one rereads the early parts of *One of Ours*, aware of what the theme requires, interest often flags.

The forces that are hostile to Claude's nature are best rendered in his brother Bayliss Wheeler, a new type in Willa Cather's fiction, and a preliminary sketch for Ivy Peters in her next novel, *A Lost Lady*. Because Bayliss was undersized, his father had been ready to see him leave the farm and set up a business in town. His interests were to make money, having made it to save it, and to make life disagreeable for anyone who had other interests. He suspected all forms of pleasure that did not relate to money-getting and was prone to suspect all other forms of activity. When he hears that one of Claude's friends in Lincoln plans to become a professor, he asks dryly: "What's the matter with him? Does he have poor health?" There is no active cruelty in Bayliss, no vicious scheming; he remains dull and petty, on the scale of the cast; it is Willa Cather's triumph that he nevertheless seems formidable. It does not seem silly that on his last leave, as he is turning over in his mind what his experience in the army and in France has taught him, Claude should say: "No battlefield or shattered country he had seen was as ugly as this world would be if men like his brother Bayliss controlled it altogether. . . . He knew the future of the world was safe; the careful planners would never be able to put it into a strait-jacket—cunning and prudence would never have it to themselves."

About Claude's younger brother Ralph there is nothing sinister; but he represents another trait in the generation that followed the pioneers which alarmed Willa Cather, the cult of machinery. In "Coming Aphrodite!" at the end of the preliminary picture of the beauty of Washington Square in the years before the First World War, she wrote: "Looking up the Avenue through the Arch, one could see the young poplars with their bright, sticky leaves, and the Brevoort glistening in its spring coat of paint, and shining horses and carriages—occasionally an automobile, mis-shapen and sullen, like an ugly threat in a stream of things that were bright and beautiful and alive." Ralph Wheeler yearned after every machine he saw or read of; no sooner had his mother and old Mahailey, her general helper, found out how to operate a washing machine or a churn than he produced another, more complicated and more vexatious. The cellar was full of machines that had been superseded or had never been useful. Claude reflects that Ralph spent more money on unnecessary machinery than his friend in Lincoln, Julius Erlich, would use for his grad-uate study in Germany. The Erlichs, he reflected, might be poor, but they knew how to live, spending "their money on themselves, instead of on machines to do the work and machines to entertain people. Machines . . . could not make pleasure, whatever else they could do. They could not make agreeable people, either."

The machine is a recurrent symbol of disaster in the Nebraska part of the novel. One day when Claude is at work with a mule team, a gasoline motor-truck frightens them, and Claude's face is driven against a barbed-wire fence. Erysipelas follows, and, what is much worse, during his recovery the visits of Enid Royce lead him to marry her. His marriage to this loveless bigoted girl is the worst of his misfortunes. Its failure is symbolized in her creeping about the countryside for hundreds of miles in her black electric spreading leaflets for the cause of prohibition while Claude picks up a lonely meal and broods through a lonely evening.

In the last part of the novel machinery loses its evil sense. One of Claude's friends, Sergeant Hicks, who had intended after he got home to open a garage with his pal Able, plans to have his sign read "Hicks and Able" though Able has been killed. Machinery serving a humane man, with vistas of experience and some imagination, is a very different force from machinery at the Wheelers' or the Royces'. For Ralph Wheeler and Enid Royce, it is part of a way of living. How deeply mistaken Willa Cather felt this way of living to be was made plain in her essay "Nebraska," written a few years after *One of Ours*. "The generation now in the driver's seat," she said, "hates to make anything, wants to live and die in an automobile, scudding past those acres where the old men used to follow the long corn-rows up and down. They want to buy everything ready-made: clothes, food, education, music, pleasure." An old lady who grew up in Red Cloud with Willa Cather remarked to me that boys and girls no longer went walking or on horseback to swim in the Republican and loll on its sandbars; they drove forty or fifty miles to an artificial pool. The generation after Ralph's and Enid's, as Willa Cather was to notice, prolonged their attitudes.

It was those attitudes, the glorification of money-getting and the cult of the machine, that Willa Cather wished to produce for the reader of *One of Ours*, not elaborate individual characterizations of people such as Ralph and Bayliss and Enid. The characters ruled by money and machinery must merge into the gray world, and do. None of them actively harms Claude, or has any wish to harm him. Seeing around him so many people sure of these miserable values, and scarcely anyone to deny them, is what does the harm. Claude asks himself the most dangerous question that can arise in a person of exceptional nature who is without an exceptional gift or exceptional strength of will: Am I mistaken, weak, queer?

In the choice and rendering of Claude's sympathizers Willa Cather again needed to avoid creating persons of great comprehension or vitality, who would have vigorous roles in Claude's story. There could be no Wunsch, no Dr. Archie. If there were, Claude would not be so full of self-distrust as he needs to be, and the world would not be gray enough. The rendering of Enid's father, Jason Royce, is an instance of Willa Cather's skill. Jason is a pioneer, the first miller of the county, a strong, heavy man, with a gentle heart. He had seen something exceptional in Claude long before the novel opens, and envied his unperceptive father; when the water-power in the mill was replaced by an engine he had felt that little Claude Wheeler was the only person who would regret the change. But Jason has been broken by his wife and daughters; he does not have the strength to say the right things, much as he wants to, in his one great scene—when he tries to avert the disaster of Claude's marriage. Gladys Farmer is rendered with equal skill. If her full strength had been let loose on the novel, there would have been an end to grayness. She is an exceptional nature—as much so as Claude—and she discerns and admires his way of being exceptional. They could easily have fallen in love, and were indeed on the way to doing so before the novel opens; then the lines of communication between them were cut. She appeared to encourage Bayliss as a suitor, and Claude was so outraged that he avoided her and the thought of her is "a sore spot in his mind." Not until he is in uniform and back on his last home leave is there a clearing up of the difficulty that has kept him apart from Gladys Farmer.

Within his own family Claude has sympathizers, much more active in the story than Jason Royce and Gladys Farmer. His mother is a portrait of great pathos. A sensitive, affectionate, and somewhat cultivated woman, she has been dominated so roughly by her husband that her frail spirit and her wandering step are the index to her inability to do for Claude anything at all like what Mr. Kronborg did for Thea. She understands much of what makes life hard for her son, but cannot be a confidante because she is so rooted in a narrow religious code that she translates anything he says into terms with no reality for him. Mahailey, her servant, is the one character in the novel who might have stepped from the pages of *My Ántonia* or *O Pioneers!* The affections and instincts that have faded in all the other characters who have much to do or say in the novel have kept their full strength in Mahailey. But she is simple-minded like the Margie Anderson in the household of Willa Cather's parents from whom she was drawn; and if she has a queer wisdom of her own, much like Crazy Ivar's in *O Pioneers!* which lets her glimpse what is wrong in Claude's circumstances, her efforts to bring them right are as ineffective as his mother's.

The early parts of *One of Ours* are the product of Willa Cather's close observation of Red Cloud and the Divide during the long visits she paid nearly every year. It had become plain to her that the day of Ántonia was over: now one had to go away to grow, there was no other choice. The world she had known in the eighties and nineties was ceasing to exist; everything in it that had encouraged her own growth was dead or dying, and what had opposed her growth was now victorious. In *One of Ours* she turned from the pleasure of recalling memories that were full of life and charm to the comparatively dreary task of rendering a world as humdrum as that of *Madame Bovary*.

But with that humdrum world she proposed to contrast the belated growth of Claude Wheeler once he came into circumstances that would give him his great unforeseen second chance. These were, in ascending importance, the army, the war, and France.

Of the three, as a woman, Willa Cather has least to say about the army. Nothing in her earlier stories since the historical romance about Lord Fairfax's castle was so remote from her experience as the representation of Claude's life in the army. Much as she learned from the young soldiers who came to see her, she left Claude's sense of what he drew from associations within the army a suggestion rather than a realized picture. It was an opportunity for forming friendships, as with the violinist Gerhardt, that would in peace have been impossible. It was a coming together for reasons more satisfying than making money, or getting the upper hand. The effect of war on a soldier is also suggested rather than worked out. Taking part in it was responding to an idea or a feeling, and was therefore outside the range of the life Claude had known in Nebraska. "History had condescended to such as he . . . the feeling of purpose, of fateful purpose, was strong in his breast."

With the impact of France on Claude, Willa Cather could work more freely. One understands her need to return to that country and immerse herself in its life and its history before she wrote the last part of the novel: here was a factor she could master. What Claude takes from France comes to him from places and persons. He is like Niel Herbert in *A Lost Lady*, who "had no curiosity about what men had thought; but about what they had felt and lived he had a great deal." For Claude, France is the Church of Saint-Ouen at Rouen, with its arches, windows, and chimes; the glades in the forests, green beyond a Nebraskan's imagination; the devotion of the people to their flowers and their cooking; the language that "couldn't be

mumbled, that had to be spoken with energy and fire or
not at all"; the bright sympathetic understanding of French
women; above all, the interweaving with the lives of individuals of something lasting and strong that sustains them.
"Life," he reflected, "was so short that it meant nothing at
all unless it were continually reinforced by something that
endured; unless the shadows of individual existence came
and went against a background that held together." Otherwise it was what he had known in Nebraska: "buying and
selling, building and pulling down," it was Bayliss Wheeler,
who put the proceeds of his buying and selling into the one
place near by that had tradition and beauty, and proposed
to "tear down that old trap and put up something modern."

The army, the war, and France combined to give
Claude the youth he had never had. When he has had it, he
may die. Indeed, Willa Cather insists it was best he should.
When he was killed in the fall of 1918, it was "believing
his own country better than it is, and France better than
any country can ever be." The beliefs would have perished
had he seen the postwar world. In the last pages of the
novel, speaking briefly in her own person, Willa Cather
says:

> "One by one the heroes of that war, the men of
> dazzling soldiership, leave prematurely the world
> they have come back to. Airmen whose deeds were
> tales of wonder, officers whose names made the
> blood of youth beat faster, survivors of incredible
> dangers—one by one they quietly die by their own
> hand. Some do it in obscure lodging-houses, some
> in their offices, where they seemed to be carrying on
> their business like other men. Some slip over a
> vessel's side and disappear into the sea."

This passage needs to be set beside her remark in the
prefatory note to *Not Under Forty*: "the world broke in
two in 1922 or thereabout." By the time she had finished
One of Ours she was beginning to feel that estrangement
from modern American life that was to grow more acute as
she got older.

In a lecture at Omaha, in October 1921, she pointed to
tendencies in Nebraska that were contrary to life itself and
would surely suffocate art. Democracy was more and more

applied as a regime of sameness, in which the Bohemian housewife must be encouraged to give up her ancestral recipes for roast goose and draw food from an array of tins, and her children were to be denied instruction in their rich and beautiful tongue so that they might speak English like all the rest of Nebraska, and nothing else. The new god was the short cut, dependent on the machine. "We have music by machines, we travel by machines—the American people are so submerged in them that sometimes I think they can only be made to laugh and cry by machinery." In art there were no short cuts and, besides, a dead level of sameness would be the end of art. To an interviewer in New York not long afterward she was more explicit about how the failure in American life would lead to a deterioration in American art.

"The Frenchman," she said,

> doesn't talk nonsense about art, about self-expression; he is too greatly occupied with building the things that make his home. His house, his garden, his vineyards, these are the things that fill his mind. He creates something beautiful, something lasting. And what happens? When a French painter wants to paint a picture, he makes a copy of a garden, a home, a village. The art in them inspires his brush. And twenty, thirty, forty years later you'll come to see the original of that picture, and you'll find it changed only by the mellowness of time.
>
> Restlessness such as ours, success such as ours, do not make for beauty. Other things must come first; good cookery, cottages that are homes, not playthings; gardens, repose. These are first rate things, and out of first rate stuff art is made. It is possible that machinery has finished us as far as this is concerned. Nobody stays at home any more; nobody makes anything beautiful any more.

That art depended on the artist's being able to find beauty and individuality in the world about him was not a conclusion to which she had come by reasoning: her own art was characteristically a flow of memories. The theme of a novel or a shorter story was hers as the outcome of much living and feeling. For the rest she depended on what she had observed and divined. If there had been no people within her experience in whom personal life flowed richly, she felt that as an artist she might as well have lived in an igloo. Sometimes, as she looked about her in the years after the First World War, she wondered if there would be much lost if she did elect the igloo.

Her friends noticed the pessimism that was so strangely unlike the exuberance of her youth and her first years in New York. In conversation she avoided self-analysis—she detested it in others as well as forbidding it to herself. The seriousness with which she was examining the world and herself in 1922 appears more sharply in an act than in anything she said. On December 27, in the company of her parents, she was confirmed in the Episcopal Church by the Bishop of Western Nebraska, her old friend Dr. Beecher. She had set her foot on the way that led to *Death Comes for the Archbishop* and *Shadows on the Rock*; and in the books that intervened she touched more and more closely on religious issues.

III

One of Ours brought to Willa Cather a Pulitzer prize and her first great popular success, happy omens both for her association with her new publisher. When the prize was announced she had finished the next of her novels, *A Lost Lady*. That book, so apparently effortless, so deceptively simple, had cost her more labor and involved her in more frustration than anything she had attempted before. Miss Lewis describes the chief problem it presented and the various approaches Willa Cather tried:

> Although *A Lost Lady* has been regarded by many critics as the most perfect in form of all her novels, Willa Cather had, at the start, more trouble with it than with any of the others. As a rule she was unhesitating in her attack on a new piece of work. She did not try first one way and then another, but took at once, with sureness and great momentum, the road she wished to follow. Her difficulty in the case of *A Lost Lady* arose largely, I think, from the fact that *Mrs. Forrester* was more a direct por-

trait than any of her other characters except *Án-tonia*; and although Mrs. Garber, from whom *Mrs. Forrester* was drawn, and her husband, Governor Garber, were both dead, some of their relatives were alive and might be (and, indeed, were) offended. Probably because of this, she at first set the scene of her story in Colorado, and wrote it at some length in this setting. But she found it would not work. Her memories of Mrs. Garber, and of the Garber place were among the strongest, most enduring impressions of her childhood; a whole ambiance of thought and feeling surrounded them, and she could not transfer them to an artificial climate. So she started the story anew, writing of things just as she remembered them.

But she still was not wholly satisfied with the construction of the story. As nearly as I can recall, her dissatisfaction arose from the difficulty of maintaining what she felt to be the right balance in the presentation, which is sometimes direct, but more often done through the boy *Niel*. When she had written perhaps one-third of the story, she decided to change and write it all in the first person, and she recommenced it a second time, and wrote several chapters in this manner.

That June [of 1922] she had accepted an invitation to give two or three talks before the English classes at Breadloaf, Vermont. . . . She took the two versions of *A Lost Lady*, so far as she had written them, along with her, and in the week or so that she spent at Breadloaf she went over them; and came then to the conclusion that her first method was right. She discarded the chapters she had written in the first person, and from that time on wrote the story without any break or hesitation.

Even without the personal reason, one can see why to maintain a balance in presenting the lost lady Mrs. Forrester was a problem, why Willa Cather needed the intelligent, appreciative young Niel Herbert (who is simply Jim Burden from *My Ántonia* renamed, even to being from the South), and why she could not trust the whole story to Niel. He could not know how fully Mrs. Forester was lost, living in the little Nebraska town of Sweet Water, and he could not know how fully she was a lady according to the code of the society in which she was a figure. For that society is not in Sweet Water; no one else in Sweet Water belongs to it, though Niel's bachelor uncle, Judge Pomeroy, hangs precariously on its edge. It is the society of the "railroad aristocracy," about which Willa Cather begins to speak in the first sentence of the novel when she qualifies the Forresters' house as "well known from Omaha to Denver for its hospitality and for a certain charm of atmosphere." Later we are told that railroad presidents leave their private cars on the siding and scramble up the hill in their eagerness to be with the Forresters; and that among the guests at one party was Marshall Field—he is not reported as saying anything, but the fabulous name is enough. For the effect Willa Cather wants, the reader must believe from the beginning of the novel that in this society Mrs. Forrester is accepted, missed, sought out. Willa Cather takes this society with completely serious respect; it was always her view that the men who put through the railroads and organized the settlement of the land were pioneers just as truly as any farmer on the Divide; in both kinds of pioneers she found the imagination and daring and warmth of life that she constantly looked for. When a former president of the Missouri Pacific praised *The Song of the Lark*, she felt a contentment more instinctive and complete than any purely literary critic could give her. We are to feel that Mrs. Forrester is receiving an award of merit in the respect, interest, and gallantry of the railway pioneers.

Her story lies in her decline from being a member of their world to being a member of the village world of Sweet Water. It can be apprehended best by someone who has a place in that village world and from it at first looks up to Mrs. Forrester as to a visitor from another planet. This is the position of Niel Herbert, and when the author appears more directly, she often takes this same position, which was her own as a girl contemplating the life of Governor Garber and his wife. The stages in Mrs. Forrester's decline are few and strongly marked: Captain Forrester, who is twenty-five years older than his wife, has a stroke; she takes a lover in the society of the railroad aristocracy; the captain loses most of his money in the panic of the nineties; illness and poverty mean that the Forresters must stay at Sweet Water the year round; the captain has another stroke; Mrs. Forrester loses her lover; she drinks more and more heavily; the captain dies leaving her little more than the house; she falls into the hands of Ivy Peters. To pass from the society of the railway aristocracy to that of village roughs was quite within Mrs. Forrester's range, provided that she was never without the desire and devotion of some strong male.

She is the central variable in the novel; and the strongest reason why *A Lost Lady* has the very texture of life is the number of variables in it, and the force with which they act upon one another. The changes in the woman are matched, or almost, by the changes in the village. Sweet Water also has disappointed expectations; some of the best villagers leave; others are elbowed aside; and in the new order Ivy Peters is the type figure—a Bayliss Wheeler with an addition of malignant cruelty and sensuality. Mrs. Forrester had kept aloof from the village in its earlier and better days; she comes to terms with the new order. Ivy Peters is her lawyer, her confidential man, and, it is strongly implied, her lover. The shift in Mrs. Forrester and the shift in the village come to us mainly through another variable, Niel Herbert, to whom a few years, a little experience, and some travel gradually bring new shades of comprehension and reservation. His disillusionment with Mrs. Forrester and with the village—in which the author shares —adds to the force of the downward movement in the novel.

That downward movement, becoming stronger and stronger, distinguished *A Lost Lady* from the other Western novels. The best days may have been the first to flee in *O Pioneers!* as well as in *My Ántonia*, but the downward movement in those works did not affect the central person. Ántonia's own days were of the best up to her last appearance, and it is implied that only death could injure them; the phase that is about to begin for Alexandra Bergson as *O Pioneers!* ends will be in keeping with her early appreciations and victories and will have a gentler poetry of its own. In *One of Ours* the glory had departed before the story opens, and the novel has an eddying movement until, with the great chance for escape and expression that the war provides, the movement turns sharply upward. *A Lost*

Lady, written for the most part in that very year, 1922, in which Willa Cather fixed the breakup of the world, records the passing of a woman and a village from the regime of a Captain Forrester to that of an Ivy Peters. As Niel got ready in the last chapter to leave Sweet Water he "felt that he was going away for ever and was making the final break with everything that had been dear to him in his boyhood. The people, the very country itself, were changing so fast that there would be nothing to come back to." Niel did not trouble to say good-by to Mrs. Forrester; even more quickly than the village she had ceased to be as he had known her in the first days, which were the best. Carl Linstrum could come back to Alexandra Bergson after twelve years of wandering and find her essentially unaltered; after twenty years Jim Burden could come back to Ántonia and find her essentially unaltered; such as it was, the world in which Claude Wheeler grew up survived his death and could have been revisited by his spirit; but the woman and the village that Niel Herbert admired were as if they had never been. In the first three novels of the West Willa Cather had evoked the great decades; in *One of Ours* she had recorded the tame decades that followed; in *A Lost Lady* she had shown how the great decades gave place to the tame ones. Her record of Nebraska in fiction stood complete. If she were to write again of Nebraska, it would be only after she had learned from life to look deeper into the meanings of her memories. For the present the subject was exhausted.

The lifelike texture of *A Lost Lady* depends also on the avoidance of what is rigid and massive in structure or in style. Helen McAfee recalls that some time after the appearance of *The Song of the Lark* Willa Cather declared she would never write a novel of that detailed sort again, that she would aim at a more concentrated effect. In *One of Ours* she did write the detailed sort of novel, for the last time; it was in *A Lost Lady*, even more than in *My Ántonia*, that she showed what she could achieve by concentration. Ántonia, Jim Burden reflected toward the end of her story,

> had always been one to leave images in the mind that did not fade—that grew stronger with time. In my memory there was a succession of such pictures,

fixed there like the old woodcuts of one's first primer: Ántonia kicking her bare legs against the sides of my pony when we came home in triumph with our snake; Ántonia in her black shawl and fur cap, as she stood by her father's grave in the snowstorm; Ántonia coming in with her work-team along the evening sky-line. She lent herself to immemorial human attitudes which we recognize by instinct as universal and true.

Mrs. Forrester also left images that did not fade, and grew stronger with time; and in *A Lost Lady* these images stand out more boldly than the sequence of images concerning Ántonia. The images that give us Mrs. Forrester are more highly colored, and sometimes more richly phrased; but what is best about them is the amount of vitality they have, the movement, the intensity. When Willa Cather needs to tell us just what it was that Mrs. Forrester drew from her affair with that early lover who moved in the railroad aristocracy, she concentrates her meaning in an image, to which a half chapter leads. With her lover Mrs. Forrester goes out driving one winter afternoon on the pretext of getting some cedar boughs. The pair leave the cutter and carry their buffalo robes deep into the wood; after hours have passed, a village boy sees them return to the cutter. The lover goes back into the wood to get the forgotten boughs, and little Adolph Blum, lying behind a log, so near to Mrs. Forrester he could almost have touched her, finds that "when the strokes of the hatchet rang out from the ravine, he could see her eyelids flutter . . . soft shivers went through her body."

Intensity and economy of this kind were to mark the highly experimental books to which Willa Cather turned next, *My Mortal Enemy* and *The Professor's House.*

9

Religion
and the Artist

1924–1927

THE PROFESSOR'S HOUSE
MY MORTAL ENEMY
DEATH COMES FOR THE ARCHBISHOP

IN THE SUMMER of 1923, *A Lost Lady* completed, Willa Cather left for a long stay in France. She went almost at once to Ville-d'Avray, where Jan and Isabelle Hambourg had arranged a study for her in the house they had bought since her previous visit to France, when she was absorbing impressions for *One of Ours*. Miss Lewis writes: "The Hambourgs had hoped that she would make Ville-d'Avray her permanent home. But although the little study was charming, and all the surroundings were attractive, and the Hambourgs themselves devoted and solicitous, she found herself unable to work at Ville-d'Avray. She felt indeed that she would never be able to work there."

One outcome of this summer was the portrait by Léon Bakst, which hangs in the Public Library at Omaha. When funds had been subscribed, the first striking recognition Willa Cather had from people in her own state, she was asked to choose a painter. On the advice of friends she chose Bakst, though such a portrait was far from the usual round of his work. It was an unfortunate choice, though Willa Cather was immediately delighted with the man and enjoyed the talks she had with him and his friends during the twenty sittings. At one of these Nijinsky appeared. After he had been introduced and had kissed her hand, he withdrew to a corner and stood with his face to the wall. He believed himself to be a horse. It was plain to Willa

Cather that Bakst, who was supporting a number of White Russians, was in great need of money, and she could not bring herself to cancel the commission. At each sitting she felt the portrait become more mistaken—stiff, dark, dead, lifeless—and she could tell from Bakst's desperation that he knew better than she how bad it was. She felt that she was behaving unworthily to the kind admirers in Omaha, but she could not say the word that would have extricated her from the false position. No expression of complaint, reproach, or even regret ever came from Omaha, and she was deeply touched by the magnanimous silence. After the sittings were over she escaped to Aix-les-Bains, where she stayed for several weeks of the early fall. It was here that the idea of *The Professor's House* began to take shape, and on her return to the apartment in Bank Street in November, she began at once to write that novel.

The Professor's House, at which she worked steadily through 1924, in Bank Street and, during the summer, at Grand Manan, is among the most revealing of her novels. Toward the end of the book Professor St. Peter reflects on what Tom Outland was spared in escaping by an early death "the trap of worldly success." "What change," the professor wonders, "would have come in his blue eye, in his fine long hand with the back-springing thumb, which had never handled things that were not the symbols of ideas? A hand like that, had he lived, must have been put to other uses. His fellow-scientists, his wife, the town and State, would have required many duties of it. It would have had to write thousands of useless letters, frame thousands of false excuses. It would have had to 'manage' a great deal of money." No writer of her time was more successful than Willa Cather in keeping freedom and anonymity. She never became an official personage, and the crucial decisions were taken in the years of her first popular success, from 1923 to 1927. She declined to join societies, no matter who asked her, no matter what their aim; she declined to recommend books, and wrote a review so rarely that she could decently avoid pressures to be nice and helpful. Instead of working for charities she gave as if from a bottomless purse to old friends fallen on hard times, or institutions in Webster County. If a letter appeared useless, she did not write it; and instead of a false excuse she preferred a frank explanation, which usually saved her from repetition of a request she could not grant or an invitation she could not accept. Her royalties mounted substantially with the popular success of *One of Ours* and she handled all money matters herself; anything, she felt, was better than living like the singer in "Coming, Aphrodite!" who used to drive down to Wall Street and review her holdings in the light of the latest oscillations of the market. Miss Lewis writes:

> The struggle to preserve the integrity of her life as an artist, its necessary detachment and freedom, cost her something—cost a considerable expenditure of nervous energy, for it meant a steady exertion of her will against the will of the public. But it was not disdain for the tributes people wished to pay her, or a feeling of superiority or indifference, that caused her to withdraw more and more from the world. It was self-preservation.

Into Professor St. Peter Willa Cather poured her grief at the decline of so many of the values she cherished. The postwar students at the small Midwestern college where he has taught since before the end of the last century are now, he thinks, a common lot. The young professors are utilitarian, political, self-interested. The programs have suffered by the pressure of the will of the state legislature and the community, for whom the ideal in higher education is a trade school passing under the name of college. The war which had taken the life of Tom Outland had, "in one great catastrophe, swept away all youth and all palms, and almost Time itself."[1]

The novel is a revelation of an attitude in Willa Cather more desolate by far than any fear of the price that worldly success tries to impose, or a disapproval of new forces in American life. There is a startling comment on its meaning in Alexander Porterfield's essay on Willa Cather, perhaps the most considered English estimate of her fiction. Mr. Porterfield says: "Briefly, it is the story of a scholarly professor at a Middle Western University passing through that critical, uneasy period between middle and old age—at least, it should be taken as a study of such,

---

[1] This sentence was deleted from the collected edition.

otherwise its meaning is difficult to perceive exactly." *The Professor's House* is a study of the passing, prematurely, from middle to old age, and St. Peter, at fifty-two, is exactly at the age the author reached in the year of the novel's appearance. But it is disquieting to find a critic shutting the door on his perception that there is in a book more than he can comprehend, and deciding that his comprehension is the measure of its meaning.

It is by a scrutiny of the approach to houses that the deepest meaning in the novel will disclose itself, and by the same token clarify the beautiful relation among the three parts in which it is arranged. At the outset Willa Cather presents St. Peter living between two houses. There is the expensive conventional house that he has built because his wife wanted it and into which he has moved with reluctance, with indeed a positive distaste that greatly surprises him; and there is the old rented frame house, ugly, inconvenient, run down, in which he has lived for thirty years—for the whole of his adult life, the whole of his career, the whole of his marriage. He finds that he can write, and think, only in its attic study, encumbered with the forms on which a dressmaker has fitted clothes for his wife and daughters ever since he was a young husband. It is oil-lit and stove-heated; it has almost every disadvantage a room can have; but it has been the home of his mind and spirit. It is very easy to mark the two houses as symbols of no apparent depth, nor do they acquire in the first part of the novel any depth beyond the practice of a Sinclair Lewis or a James T. Farrell.

The obviously surprising element in the structure of *The Professor's House* is its second part, a long story inserted after the fashion of Cervantes or Smollett, and giving, as Willa Cather has said, an effect similar to those Dutch pictures of an interior where a square window offers a contrasting vista of a gray sea or the masts of ships. The length, vitality, and power of the intercalated tale are surprising, and not only at a first reading. The substance in this middle part of the novel is the crucial episode in the life of Tom Outland. Once and once only in the thirty years of his teaching St. Peter encountered a mind and personality of the first order, a student from whom he learned, and whose impress is strong upon the many-volumed history of Spanish exploration in America which brought St. Peter his fame, gave him his full mental and personal growth, and as a by-product provided the new house, built with literary prize money. When the novel opens, Tom is dead.

That crucial episode in Tom's life was the discovery of a Cliff-Dweller village in a New Mexican canyon. The discovery gave a new dimension to American life for Tom Outland. "I had read of filial piety in the Latin poets," he says, "and I knew that was what I felt for this place." Here was beauty, the beauty of pure and noble design, unspoiled by clutter or ornament, undistracted by cosiness, uncontradicted by the ugliness of machinery or industry. An expert to whom Tom showed some of the pottery was struck by its likeness to the decorative art of early Crete. The effect Willa Cather produces in her account of the Cliff-Dwellers, so much more vivid, so much more austere, than in the parallel passages in *The Song of the Lark*, is very near the evocation of the Greek town in the "Ode on a Grecian Urn." "It was as still as sculpture—and something like that. . . . The tower was the fine thing that held all the jumble of houses together and made them mean something. . . . That village sat looking down into the cañon with the calmness of eternity. The falling snow-flakes, sprinkling the piñons, gave it a special kind of solemnity . . . preserved in the dry air and almost perpetual sunlight like a fly in amber, guarded by the cliffs and the river and the desert." The houses of the Cliff-Dwellers are never overtly contrasted with those in the Middle Western college town where the first and third parts of the novel are laid; and in the modern town the emphasis falls on individual buildings, in the ancient village, significantly, on the architectural as well as the social unity of the whole.

A light but telling touch will show how firmly the novel has been stitched together. Between his discovery of the village in the canyon and his death a few years later, Tom made physics his principal study. He devised and patented a bulkheaded vacuum, which after his death became the nucleus of a great improvement in aircraft. He had willed everything to his fiancée, one of the professor's daughters, but with not a particle of the professor in her make-up. With some of the immense fortune the invention brought, she and her entrepreneur husband, a born front-office man, built a country house and called it Outland. The professor's new house is a wrong house, but wrong only by its acceptance of prevailing convention. Outland is much more deeply a wrong house. Although it stood on a high site, it held no reminiscence of the village in the canyon—it was a Norwegian manor-house set down in the sultry Middle West, without a vestige of American feeling. We are spared a sight of its interior, but are told what is to furnish it—the loot of the antique shops of Europe imported by way of a Spanish-American port in a dodge to avoid customs duties. This is the worst of all the houses in the novel, but there are a number of wrong modern houses—for instance, that in which the head of the physics department lived, "in the most depressing and unnecessary ugliness"—and none has any affinity with the village of the Cliff-Dwellers. With the kind of past it stands for, the ugly insensitive present seems to have no conceivable bond.

But in the third and final part of the novel the bond is suddenly revealed. The first and second parts, which have seemed so boldly unrelated, are brought into a profound unity. In the first part it was plain that the professor did not wish to live in his new house, and did not wish to enter into the sere phase of his life correlative with it. At the beginning of the third part it becomes plain that he cannot indefinitely continue to make the old attic study the theater of his life, that he cannot go on prolonging or attempting to prolong his prime, the phase of his life correlative with that. The personality of his prime—the personality that had expressed itself powerfully and in the main happily in his teaching, his scholarship, his love for his wife, his domesticity—is now quickly receding, and nothing new is flowing in. What begins to dominate St. Peter is something akin to the Cliff-Dwellers, something primitive that had ruled him long ago when he was a boy on a pioneer farm in the rough Solomon Valley in western Kansas. To this primitive being not many things are real. What counts above all is nature, seen as a web of life and finally of death.

The binding passage is in terms of houses:

[The Professor] . . . really didn't see what he was going to do about the matter of domicile. He couldn't make himself believe that he was ever going to live in the new house again. He didn't belong there. He remembered some lines of a translation from the Norse he used to read long ago in one of his mother's few books, a little two-volume Ticknor and Fields edition of Longfellow, in blue and gold, that used to lie on the parolur table:

> *For thee a house was built*
> *Ere thou wast born;*
> *For thee a mould was made*
> *Ere thou of woman camest.*[2]

Lying on his old couch, he could almost believe himself in that house already. The sagging springs were like the sham upholstery that is put in coffins. Just the equivocal American way of dealing with serious facts, he reflected. Why pretend that it is possible to soften that last hard bed?

He could remember a time when the loneliness of death had terrified him, when the idea of it was insupportable. He used to feel that if his wife could but lie in the same coffin with him, his body would not be so insensible that the nearness of hers would not give it comfort. But now he thought of eternal solitude with gratefulness; as a release from every obligation, from every form of effort. It was the Truth.

All that had seemed a hanging back from the future—the clinging to the old attic study, the absorption in Tom Outland's quality and the civilization of the Cliff-Dwellers, the ways of the missionary fathers, the revival of interest in the occupations of childhood and its pleasures—was something very unlike what it had seemed. It was profound,

---

[2] Miss Cather was quoting from memory the opening of Longfellow's translation of the Anglo-Saxon "Grave":
> *For thee was a house built*
> *Ere thou wast born,*
> *For thee was a mould meant*
> *Ere thou of mother camest.*

unconscious preparation for death, for the last house of the professor.

Willa Cather had begun on the surface with a record of mediocrities, of the airless prosaic world of a small college town—how airless, how prosaic, only those who have lived in one know; and with the disenchantment a distinguished spirit felt in the narrowing utilitarianism of the postwar years. The mediocrities and the utilitarians do not have everything their own way. For all his shortcomings on the surface, the head of the physics department is as sound in essence as one of Willa Cather's pioneers. Even through the first part of the novel the aura about Tom Outland's name is an assurance of other values, not as yet defined. St. Peter himself cannot be hemmed in by what is here and now: the descendant of a Napoleonic soldier, he has the look and many of the tastes of a Latin, and on him is the mark of his preoccupation with the Mediterranean culture and the Spanish explorers. Yet he and those who belong with him do not dominate this first part of the novel; they belong to a minority not only weak numerically but edging to extinction. In the second part the balance is reversed: the mediocrities and utilitarians—in the main civil servants, remembered with contempt and pity from Willa Cather's stays in Washington a quarter century earlier— are few and feeble; and against them is set something that is quite overwhelming—the life the Cliff-Dwellers lived, and the understanding of that life by the sensitive and civilized Belgian priest Father Duchene, to whom Tom turned for interpretation; and, in the foreground throughout, Tom's own ever growing understanding of the Cliff-Dwellers and everything else.

The profound surprise for the reader is in the strange, short third part. Between the life of the Middle Western college town and the life of the Cliff-Dwellers' village the common quality is simply that both end in death. Guided by the feeling that they both end in death, we know how to measure them. What aspect of beauty, of dignity, even of interest would the ruins of the college town hold for Macaulay's New Zealander if he were to pause on this continent on his way to sketch the ruins of St. Paul's?

Not by any answers it proposes, but by the problems it elaborates, and by the atmosphere in which they are enveloped, *The Professor's House* is a religious novel. The parallels in Willa Cather's earlier fiction for the depth of self-scrutiny and the anxiety about alternatives in St. Peter all have to do with the rendering of artists, with the development of Thea Kronborg's talent or that of the sculptor from Kansas in *The Troll Garden*. In the one specimen of St. Peter's lecture we are permitted to overhear, the link between art and religion is forged in our presence:

> As long as every man and woman who crowded into the cathedrals on Easter Sunday was a principal in a gorgeous drama with God, glittering angels on one side and the shadows of evil coming and going on the other, life was a rich thing. The king and the beggar had the same chance at miracles and great temptations and revelations. And that's what makes men happy, believing in the mystery and importance of their own little individual lives. It makes us happy to surround our creature needs and bodily instincts with as much pomp and circumstance as possible. Art and religion (they are the same thing, in the end, of course) have given man the only happiness he has ever had.

The shift is not a weakening in Willa Cather's belief in the primacy of art, but a bracketing of religion with art. The same bracketing occurs when Father Duchene sums up the distinction between the Cliff-Dwellers and other tribes of the region. On their mesa he feels, with reverence, humanity "lifted itself out of mere brutality," and the agencies by which it did so were art (as expressed in the ancient people's "distinct feeling for design," whether in the shaping of a water-pot or the grouping of the village) and religion (as expressed in their "manifold ceremonies and observances"). Less explicitly, Tom Outland makes the same response: for him the mesa, which was at first a stimulus to "adventure," assumed a beauty like that of sculpture, and finally aroused "a religious emotion." So it is with the novel as a whole; one passes from a record of happenings to the achievement of startling and satisfying form, and then to the suggestion of essential feeling abou^ final issues.

II

The Professor's House was published in September 1925. Willa Cather had spent the early months of that year in Bank Street, writing *My Mortal Enemy,* the first part of which is mainly laid near by, in an apartment overlooking Madison Square and in hotels and restaurants in the lower Fifth Avenue district. The New York of this story is the city of the early 1900's, the New York of "Paul's Case," with a sensuous richness and metropolitan glamour it had held for Willa Cather in the years when she came on from Pittsburgh for brief visits packed with going to the opera and the theater and dining out. Myra Driscoll Henshawe, the protagonist, is a study of a woman, older by a full generation, whom Willa Cather had known well through connections in Lincoln, and who had died before the First World War, but whose life and nature could be understood only by one whose religious sense had become acute. Although the story was awkwardly short for a book, Willa Cather believed that it should appear by itself, that it was in fact a book. She had misgivings about the judgment Alfred A. Knopf would pass. Twenty years later she still spoke with enthusiasm of his quick response to *My Mortal Enemy.* He made no difficulty about publishing it as it was, and his opinion was speedily ratified by the sales, which required five printings before the end of 1926, and by the closeness with which the critics discussed a psychological portrait that was felt to be sharp and original, if at points a little mystifying.

All that Willa Cather cared to do with Myra, all that she needed to do, could be done quickly, by showing her at two points—as a mature worldly woman and ten years later face to face with death. Her childhood and youth could be sketched in sparing strokes in a retrospect. The first picture abounds in the poetry of worldliness. It is d̲   ̲ n for us by a young provincial girl, agog at the refine-
   ̲ f Myra's dress, the distinction of her speech, her
      ̲ manner, the devotion of her husband, the charm
         ̲ rtment, the interest of her friends, among them
            ̲ oung poetess, and Madame Modjeska herself,
               ̲ ather had once met and who is an enriching

thread through the story. But the worldliness is not a complete armor. At moments when there is not enough money —she had given up a fortune to marry as she wished—or when her husband's devotion, extreme as it is, comes short of what she requires, Myra becomes another being, malevolent and rough. In the first picture there is just enough of this other being to render the future ominous.

The second picture is drawn by the same person, but in the interval of ten years she has ceased to be provincial; she has as much insight and sympathy as are compatible with being twenty-five; but she is as much puzzled by Myra's new phase as when in her middle teens she had come under the spell of her worldliness. The distance between the subject and the portrayer has, if anything, increased. Myra has lost almost all that had given to her life the appearance and atmosphere of enviable achievement. Not only is she incurably ill (she is shown in the last four months of her life); she has drifted out of the orbit of her friends—Modjeska is dead; the money is gone; the New York apartment has given place to a miserable room in a jerrybuilt hotel on the west coast. What remains to her is simply her husband's devotion; and the growth of her other self has turned her against this and against him. He has become, she says, her mortal enemy, the idol that drew her away from the course of life that was natural to her.

Myra's feeling about her husband is bound up with the revival in her of a self that, like St. Peter's early self, found no expression in the values of her prime. It was a rough self that had nothing to do with artistic friends or charming apartments or gentle husbands; it was the product of her Irish forebears, and of the fierce willful uncle who brought her up. But within the roughness was an intense religious feeling. As death approaches, Myra feels that her marriage to "a German freethinker" has separated her from religion, and she returns "ardently to the faith of her childhood." Her thoughts run on profound religious values. The young priest who attends her exclaims, to our amazement, "I wonder whether some of the saints of the early Church weren't a good deal like her." His remark amazes because Myra has none of the kindness, charity, or humility that we conventionally associate with a religious spirit; but it also illuminates—for it becomes plain to us that this worldly woman has passed out of worldliness into preoccupation with primary realities. Her final mood is much like St. Peter's: she cares for light and silence and solitude, the sweep of the wind, the sight and smell of broad waters. It is her triumph that when she comes to die she has all these circumstances—and unlike St. Peter she has a crucifix.

My Mortal Enemy is a pure instance of what in an article for the *New Republic*, written in 1922, Willa Cather had called "the novel *démeublé*," the novel stripped of its superfluous furnishings. It is the boldest experiment she had made in leaving out, in the subordination of secondary characters, the abbreviation of incidents, the reduction of settings to where "they seemed to exist, not so much in the author's mind, as in the emotional penumbra of the characters themselves." Nothing distracts from the rendering of Myra, least of all the style, fluid and transparent beyond anything Willa Cather had accomplished. Economy and concentration do not lead to slightness: Bartley Alexander had been drawn rather as a theater in which two selves conflicted, but Myra Henshawe is a full personality, subject to development as well as to conflict, and she is as completely realized as Mrs. Forrester herself. Of all Willa Cather's writings this is the one on which Sarah Orne Jewett's judgment would have been most rewarding.

III

In the summer of 1925, accompanied by Edith Lewis, Willa Cather stayed for months in New Mexico, making Santa Fe her center. The essential story of the Southwest, she had come to believe, was neither that of its ancient Indian civilizations nor that of the Spanish explorers and martyrs: it was that of the French missionaries in the nineteenth century. About these remarkable men she had heard from Father Haltermann in her first visit to the region. He was now an invalid, after his service in the war; she had seen him but once and she was unable to see him again; but he had produced an impression. From old traders and Mexicans she had met during her many visits she had heard so much of the first Archbishop, Lamy, that she "never passed the life-size bronze of him which stands under a locust tree before the Cathedral in Santa Fé without wishing that I could learn more about a pioneer churchman" whose career had been so extraordinary, and whose countenance expressed, in every reproduction, "something fearless and fine and very, very well-bred—something that spoke of race."

While she was in Santa Fe in 1925 she came on an obscure book, printed at Pueblo, Colorado, seventeen years before, Father W. J. Howlett's *Life of the Right Reverend Joseph P. Machebeuf, Pioneer Priest of Ohio, Pioneer Priest of New Mexico, Pioneer Priest of Colorado, Vicar Apostolic of Colorado and Utah, and First Bishop of Denver.* When Willa Cather opened the biography of Bishop Machebeuf her interest was already fixed in the personality and experience of his friend Jean Lamy. How much she may have known about Machebeuf before she read Father Howlett's book cannot be said for sure—probably it was very little. The record of his life, and especially the long intimate letters to his sister and brother in Auvergne, made a strong appeal to her feelings, for he was the ideal of a missionary bishop, the very man to spread a faith and found its institutions on the frontier. All the interest and respect Bishop Beecher had aroused in her went to strengthen and brighten her response to Bishop Machebeuf. He would have been in his element breasting the winds on the Divide, raising a church for the Bohemians near Blue Hill, trading secrets of cookery with Ántonia, begging a horse from Captain Forrester. He was a man of the people—his father was a baker—impulsive, cordial, violent, enduring. He is drawn in the figure of Father Vaillant, very much in the manner of the secondary characters in the Nebraska novels, with emphatic lights and shades, massively, with no suggestion of mystery or hagiography.

A character with such vitality, when given the second place throughout an extended narrative, is likely to seize the first just as Mercutio threatened to overshadow Romeo. Nothing in *Death Comes for the Archbishop* is more masterly than the novelist's instinct of how fully and warmly Father Vaillant could be rendered without jeopardy to the primary position of the Archbishop. In the prologue there is no mention of Father Vaillant, and in the first two chapters of the first part the Archbishop comes to grips with the Southwest alone. The record of the journey to Santa Fe in Father Howlett's book gave the two priests equal prominence; but in the novel it is only in the later chapters of the first part, after they are installed at Santa Fe, that the two friends appear together. How much could be safely risked is best shown in the first chapter of the second book, where Father Vaillant appears by himself, in the vigorous episodes at Manuel Lujon's ranch, where the priest marries, baptizes, cooks his lamb *saignant*, begs the two beautiful white mules, and by all he says as well as does fixes his nature for us forever. Throughout the third and fourth books Willa Cather again refuses him a role, and by the beginning of the fifth, when he returns to the scene, the Archbishop's less definite, less expansive character has by subtle and gradual means made itself the center of the narrative. It was not necessary, though it was a gain for the climax and the symmetry of the book, that Willa Cather shift the chronology of her materials and have the Archbishop outlive his friend and go to his funeral.

The vitality of Father Vaillant is not the only hazard to the effect the Archbishop is to produce. The obvious opportunity for a dramatic conflict between the Archbishop and his circumstances is refused: the sensitive, aristocratic, scholarly man at once accepts and finally loves the wild country of his diocese, the rough people, the alien traditions. His troubles with the native clergy—all the Spaniards had been required to leave in 1821, thirty years before the Archbishop came, and all who remained were natives of the region or of Mexico—do not disturb his inner peace, and his victory over those who oppose him appears easy and inevitable—much easier than Lamy's victory was in historical fact. No conflict of exciting force enters the Archbishop's life. Most of the recorded events occur in the late afternoon, usually toward sunset, and as one succeeds another the record seems as serene and gently mechancholy as the cadences in which it is conveyed.

The appeal the Archbishop made to Willa Cather hung on the absence of such inner conflict as Professor St. Peter sustained. The Archbishop is the great example in her fiction of a personality extraordinarily fine and cultivated finding on the Western plains the ideal circumstances for his life. Torn herself, during so many decades, between the appeal of the Divide and her home in Red Cloud and the appeal of the cities of the east coast, with their opera, concerts, and galleries, she experienced an intense if somewhat sad pleasure in contemplating a life that was not torn but was a seamless unity.

The narrative is in essence, however, something much more than a presentation of the two French priests and of the traditions and qualities they embody. They would not wholly suit Willa Cather's purpose—their story would not be the story of the Southwest—if in any way they came short in appreciation of the region—its aspect, its people, its past. Here Indian villages, the exploits of the Spanish adventurers as well as of the missionaries, the coming of a new layer of high civilization with the French priests, and the small but true contribution of the best of the great-hearted Anglo-Saxon adventurers—men like Kit Carson—are set before us as on a frieze. The composition of this frieze, in the grouping of its figures and their portrayal against a living background, is the most beautiful achievement of Willa Cather's imagination. In it at last her craftsmanship and her vision were in relation, and that relation was complete. The length of her unconscious preparation to write it had served her well indeed.

Willa Cather had always understood that a person's relation to a place might be as valuable to him, and as decisive in his growth or retardation, as any relation he might have with other persons. What happens in one place could not happen in just the same way in any other. Thea Kronborg could not have taken from Moonstone or from Chicago what the villages of the Cliff-Dwellers gave her. But in the earlier novels the landscape did not impinge upon the reader with the vitality that distinguishes it in *Death Comes for the Archbishop*.

The Archbishop, from the first of his appearances, is "sensitive to the shapes of things." We see him as he rides alone through a waste area of New Mexico, a mass of uniform conical red sandhills on which conical junipers are symmetrically spotted; the "geometrical nightmare" oppresses his spirits and he shuts his eyes; when he opens them, the first thing he sees is a unique juniper—"living vegetation could not present more faithfully the form of the Cross." The sight of that juniper is a turning-point for him. Color matters to the Archbishop as much as shape.

One day years after his arrival in the southwest, following by accident an unfamiliar road on his way to Santa Fe, he found among many green hills one that was yellow—"a strong golden ochre much like the gold of the sunlight." This, he knew at once, was his cathedral. Better no other church than the simple little adobe he found when he came to Santa Fe—better than a red brick horror such as he had known in his days in the diocese of Cincinnati. The vicar was quite unmoved when he was shown the yellow stone; he had always assumed that when there was a cathedral at Santa Fe, it would be a large pile of red brick, and he did not see that it mattered.

Much to his own surprise, Archbishop Latour decides against returning to his native Auvergne to pass the years of his retirement and preparation for death. The ties of his family, the promise of fine architecture on every side, and of the scholarly associations of which through his long years in Santa Fe he had been deprived, were less powerful than the atmosphere of New Mexico. When he wakens in the early morning at Santa Fe, the Southwestern air communicates to him a conviction of eternal youth, of energy, of ever possible spiritual growth. A response of this kind might have been a part of *My Ántonia* or of *The Song of the Lark*, but at the time when she wrote those novels Willa Cather could not have found such language as she uses in conveying the quality of the atmosphere at Santa Fe. "His first consciousness was a sense of the light dry wind blowing in through the windows, with the fragrance of hot sun and sagebrush and sweet clover; a wind that made one's body feel light and one's heart cry, 'To-day, to-day,' like a child's. . . . Something soft and wild and free, something that whispered to the ear on the pillow, lightened the heart, softly, softly picked the lock, slid the bolts, and released the prisoned spirit of man into the wind, into the blue and gold, into the morning, into the morning!" Her craftsmanship in language, her sense of a true economy, her command of rhythms individual without being eccentric, had never before reached such a delicate sureness. It is the language that makes the impressions of the New Mexican landscape superior to any presentation of setting in the earlier books. She had borne the memories of this landscape in her mind for a long time; at last she had the words to convey them in simple, perfect strength.

The same sure delicacy marks her manipulation of character and incident, a richer material than she had ever before worked in, more varied, more intense, and at times more heroic. The deliberate and often pondered movement in the earlier narratives is now replaced by a movement wonderfully quick and light, beautifully appropriate to the atmosphere. It is always through the Archbishop's eyes that we catch the splendor of Southwestern sunsets, the spirit shining through the faces of Mexican, Indian, and American types, the somber beauty of the old Spanish churches, but it is the vicar who is our guide to the appreciation of human qualities. The Archbishop knew that he had difficulty in responding to people, that he was impeded by a reserve and an inadaptability only rarely to be overcome. He admired, and in a pious sense he envied, the warmth in his friend, to whom every encounter with a person, even with a convicted murderer, was an opportunity. No matter what parish the vicar was given, no matter whom he met on his travels, he delighted in the humanity of everyone, and everyone delighted in his—"he added a glow to whatever human society he was dropped into." The Indians and Mexicans he met in the new diocese seemed to him the purest Christians he had known, souls like those in the primitive age of the Church. Guiding them was, he felt, "work for the heart, for a particular sympathy, and none of the new priests" from his own Auvergne understood "those poor natures" as he did. To the Archbishop he bursts out: "I am *their* man." He responds to them both as groups and as individuals, always prizing in each not what is unlike others but the binding quality of humanity.

The Archbishop's appreciation was reserved for rare individuals such as Kit Carson. He had long wished to meet the scout, and when he did, he "felt a quick glow of pleasure in looking at the man. As he stood there in his buckskin clothes one felt in him standards, loyalties, a code which is not easily put into words, but which is instantly felt when two men who live by it come together by chance." The Archbishop had the same sense of immediate and instinctive unity with the Navajo chief Eusabio, who had the face of a Roman general in the time of the Republic, the authority of a natural force and fineness; it was through his intimacy with Eusabio that the Archbishop had so strong a compassion for the Navajos, long hunted for the bounty the Mexican government had set, under American rule driven from the region of their gods beyond the boundaries their gods had forbidden them to cross. The vicar would have loved them for themselves. A rare extremity of misfortune borne with courage by a very simple person would move the Archbishop as much as Kit Carson's splendid integrity and daring or Eusabio's austere intensity. In the chapter called "December Night"—Willa Cather liked it so much she allowed it to be republished as a Christmas book in 1933—the Archbishop responded to the devotion of an old Mexican woman living as a slave among people who despised her, a woman who could not read and could scarcely think, as the deepest experience of religion he had ever beheld. What led the Archbishop to feel with such strength was not the individuality of old Sada but the height to which religion rose in her. The complementary natures of the two clerics allow a record of all that called for appreciation in the people of the Southwest: at the center is the Archbishop's response to whatever is distinguished and exalted, surrounding it is the vicar's quick infectious pleasure in all that is human.

In the structure of the book what might have become solid masses, comparable with long reaches in the earlier novels, is broken up by brief tales inset with an apparent casualness that recalls the ingenious narrative manner of Cervantes or Smollett. Willa Cather had done this many times before; one has only to recall the story of the Russian wedding and the chase of the wolf pack interpolated early in *My Ántonia*; but in the earlier novels this material seemed sometimes to intrude and delay the march of the story; it was not a part of its organic structure. Willa Cather could not resist piling anecdote on story, and fable on anecdote; her largest experiment of this kind is the perfect placing of the *nouvelle* of Tom Outland into the novel of *The Professor's House*. By the time she wrote *Death Comes for the Archbishop* she had mastered the art of the inset. It is the manner appropriate to the older and better kind of hagiography, simple, concrete, unemphatic, concentrated. The material lends itself at every turn to the narrative within the narrative—tales of miracles and old Church happenings, miniature stories, such as the anecdote of the Mexican youth devoted to the rooster he had bred for cockfighting or the touching miracle of the neophyte to whom the Mother of God appears, clad in blue and gold, and leaves a painted picture of herself on his *tilma*, the mantle worn only by the very poor. The tale of the bold and evil friar who ruled on the crag at Ácoma is among the perfect short narratives, suggestive, swimming in the atmosphere of the time and the place, without a touch of false exaggeration or falser complexity. At every turn in the story the setting is alive, almost overpoweringly sensible: the friar and his clerical guests at dinner and the servant whom he kills say next to nothing, but we catch them in their characterizing attitudes and know them as human beings. The height in Willa Cather's success is in the pages that follow the death and evoke a silence and immobility as thick and ominous as Conrad with his more lavish methods could suggest. With the simplest of means, which are also the most difficult, she has accomplished a triumph.

In its simplest terms, *Death Comes for the Archbishop* is a chronicle of two missionaries and of the Southwest in which they carry out their appointed tasks; their response to the new land and their memories of the old; their relations to people and things each in his own way as well as to the past, and this interspersed by relevant anecdote and recollection, an accretion of story and tale which is the making of folklore, history, literature. In the pages in which landscape and character merge in vivid pictorial narrative there is much more than the *tableau vivant*, the effect of a Puvis de Chavannes mural, for the muralist painted with a purposeful thinness and an exaggerated two-dimensionalism whereas Miss Cather is able to use color in its richest and fullest tones and depth and perspective. There is a quality of feeling conveyed by material and language which, as Rebecca West discerned when the book was first published, translates the work into the realm of the senses so that on every page there are for the reader not only the tones but the overtones: the mesas and the cloud-mesas, the contrasts between the Southwest and Auvergne, the constant balancing of pioneer life and of civilization beyond the seas and the ever present sense of a beneficent and also ominous nature—the crash of thunder in the canyons, the sinister deep hum, like the buzzing of bees, of an underground river heard through a fissure in the rock. And there is food: the savory smell of the *potage*, the rich swimming gravy which brings into play the drama at Ácoma, the *gigot d'agneau saignant* carved by Father Vaillant, "a delicate stream of pink juice" following the knife. All the senses seem to have been in Willa Cather's pen as she wrote the book.

There is another side to the book which Willa Cather herself described—"a conjunction of the general and the particular." She did not address herself at any point to the larger problem of the paternal Church courting dominion and prosperity in the New World as well as carrying out the propagation of the faith; what Willa Cather was trying to tell was the story of man's capacity to establish dominion over the immutable, as the farmers had done in Nebraska. The Rock was here "the utmost expression of human need." Man too could learn to be as hard and as steadfast as rock. In the rock, however, was rigidity, while in man there was suppleness of spirit and the endless realm of feeling. In no portion of *Death Comes for the Archbishop* is this conjunction of general and particular better exemplified than in the chapter in which the austere Bishop is confronted with the sensual, carnal priest: Bishop Latour represents the triumph of discipline and religion and the mind over things temporal; Padre Martínez accepts the appetites and lust as a reality with which he will not argue, yet he is exemplary and passionate in his religious devotions. The dramatic power of the book is never higher than in the description of Latour's visit to Taos and the home of the insurgent Mexican padre; the place is in disorder; the signs of worldliness and of carnality are everywhere; "the place seemed overrun by serving-women, young and old— and by large yellow cats with full soft fur, of a special breed, apparently." During their meal the talk gravitates to celibacy, and Martínez, who has defiantly introduced Latour to his son, attacks it: it may be well for the French clergy, he argues, but not for the Mexican. Had not St. Augustine himself written it was better not to go against nature? "Celibate priests lose their perceptions," Martínez says. "No priest can experience repentance and forgiveness of sin unless he himself falls into sin." A priest must not make of religion mere "dead logic." When Latour sharply demurs and warns Martínez that he intends to have the priests in his diocese keep their vows, Martínez responds: "We have a living Church here, not a dead arm of the European Church. Our religion grew out of the soil, and has its own roots."

Bishop Latour goes to bed troubled. He does not "like the air of this house . . . the clatter of dish-washing and the giggling of women across the *patio*" keep him awake, and on the floor he thinks he sees a mouse, only to discover it is a little "bunch of woman's hair that had been indolently tossed into a corner when some slovenly female toilet was made in this room."

Yet the same Padre Martínez, so rebellious, disorderly, and carnal, presides the next morning in a beautifully ordered church, clean and in good repair, and the Bishop "had never heard the Mass more impressively sung than by Father Martínez." His baritone emerges "from some deep well of emotional power" and "nothing in the service was slighted, every phrase and gesture had its full value." He discovers too that Martínez knows his country and finds him deeply versed not only in the Church Fathers but in the Latin and Spanish classics. Willa Cather traces the contrasting sides of this worldly scoundrel and libertine, yet devout and religiously inspired priest with such skill that Latour's decision not to change "the curious situation" comes as no surprise. "It is not expedient to interfere," he explains to Father Vaillant. "The church is strong, the people are devout. No matter what the conduct of the priest has been, he has built up a strong organization, and his people are devotedly loyal to him. . . . For the present I shall be blind to what I do not like there."

When Father Vaillant protests that Martínez's life is an open scandal, the Bishop replies: "I do not wish to lose the parish of Taos in order to punish its priest." What Bishop Latour has seen in his wisdom is that the passion Martínez gives to living is also given to the Church; and that the Church must recognize realities and mold them patiently to ultimate ends. Latour knows the Church's time will come. "Padre Martínez is getting too old to play the part of Don Juan much longer," he observes. And he knows also that if ultimately Martínez is to be replaced, it will have to be by a Spanish, not a French priest.

To the writing of this chapter, with its heightened drama

—the confrontation of two churchmen, the sensuous with the austere, the ebullient priest of the New World with the disciplined priest of the Old—Willa Cather brought not a heavy load of scholarship and reading, as Rebecca West seemed to think, but broad sympathies with men and an understanding of the problems civilized persons encounter in the wilderness; one who had made the jump from Virginia to Nebraska in childhood, and from Nebraska eastward as a young woman, could understand the contrast between Auvergne and New Mexico. Willa Cather suggested that writing the book was "like a happy vacation from life, a return to childhood, to early memories." This sense of the past permeates the work from beginning to end.

In their appreciation of the past, Latour responds to the historical record, Vaillant to the interwoven strand of legend and miracle. Early in the narrative the contrast in interest is amusingly underlined. The Archbishop, who has returned from a long journey, is awakened on the first morning by a bell that the vicar has had hung. He dismisses the experience as a dream, a reminder of the mornings when he had awakened to the Angelus sounding at St. John Lateran, but with a suggestion also, that puzzles him, of something Oriental. The vicar tells him that the bell is Spanish, with the date 1356 inscribed; that after its shipment to the New World it was brought by cart—the largest bell in North America!—the thousands of difficult miles from Mexico City, that it hung for over a hundred years in the Church of San Miguel at Santa Fe, and then lay for another hundred in a cellar. For the Archbishop the history of Spain in America is in that bell: a century of eclipse and ruin after an age of hardy achievement guided by a religious feeling that overrode all practical obstacles and expressed for the New World that affinity of religion with art and beauty which had grown up in the Old. The Archbishop broods, to the vicar's discomfort, on the Oriental suggestion in the bell's tone—it must come of Moorish workmanship or a Moorish formula, the infidels from Africa having taught the Spaniards to work finely in metals, as the Spaniards taught the Navajos. The vicar, for whom such musing is too thin-spun, too disengaged from faith, responds with a plea that the Archbishop receive a simple native priest who has just come back, edified, from the shrine of Our Lady of Guadalupe, burning to tell of the miracles wrought there since Mary's first appearance in the New World, in 1531. "Doctrine is well enough for the wise," he adds, "but the miracle is something we can hold in our hands and love."

10

The Rock

1928–1931

THE ORIGIN OF *Shadows on the Rock* was very unlike
that of *Death Comes for the Archbishop*. The narrative of
the Southwest was undertaken thirteen years after Willa
Cather's first strong response to the country and the people; it drew on one of the most lasting enthusiasms of her
life. For the narrative of French Canada there was no such
background of slowly accumulating knowledge and feeling.

What associations with Canada she had had before she
resolved to write *Shadows on the Rock* were unrelated to
the French elements in its life and history. In the early
years of their marriage Isabelle and Jan Hambourg lived in
Toronto, and Willa Cather was often with them for short
visits; but Toronto is as alien from French Canada as
Pittsburgh itself. To Isabelle Hambourg, indeed, it seemed
another Pittsburgh, another city ruled by the values of
business and the social conventions of an incurious and
intolerant upper middle class, where the only friends worth
making were musicians and artists and an occasional exile
from a more cultivated world.

In the summer of 1922 Willa Cather took an old cottage
on the island of Grand Manan in the Bay of Fundy, off the
coast of New Brunswick. The bright warm days and cool
nights, the natural beauty of the place, the great remove
from all harassments, were ideal accompaniments to writing. After another stay on the island she had a cottage built
in the autumn of 1925. It still stands, unoccupied since her
death, on a sloping hillside about fifty yards from the edge
of the cliffs, in the middle of an open meadow, and with a

semicircle of spruce and birch woods not far off. In the large undivided attic, with a vista of cliffs and sea, she did her writing, and much of *Shadows on the Rock* was written on Grand Manan. The pleasure this place gave Willa Cather has been described by Miss Lewis:

> The outdoor surroundings were unsurpassably lovely. The weather had a perpetual enchantment; it was always changing, and all the changes were interesting and beautiful. There was a kind of gentleness and innocence in the natural character of the Island; wild flowers grew everywhere in the clean grass, the streams that rushed in waterfalls over the cliffs were pure and uncontaminated, the wild creatures that lived in the woods never harmed anybody; even the slender, emerald-green snakes one occasionally met on the paths seemed friendly and sociable—did not glide away as one approached. The wild snow-shoe hares that came close to the cottage to nibble at the clover would creep under the very chair one was sitting in. Birds often built their nests four or five feet from the ground in the little spruce trees. Sometimes, at dawn or dusk one encountered a deer or fawn.
>
> There was solitude without loneliness. One could walk for miles along the cliffs without meeting anyone or seeing any mark of human life; but there was always activity on the water. Small craft of all kinds went to and fro, setting out lines, visiting the herring weirs, carrying lumber. Indians from the reservation at Point Pleasant sometimes paddled over to the Island in their canoes—looking down from the cliffs one would see a string of them rounding a point.

The "solitude without loneliness" of which Miss Lewis speaks was exemplified in the sense Willa Cather had of being securely hemmed in from the world, embraced in the soft damp intensity of isolation by the great all-engulfing fogs that settled around this pinpoint on the North Atlantic, sometimes for days. And on some days there was no sound but that of the beating rain, the roaring waters, and the British buoy whose bell melodiously seemed to call from a great distance.

The aspect of the island, and of its life, had much the same kind of charm that Sarah Orne Jewett had felt along the Maine coast, not many miles to the south. The people on the island, apart from the summer visitors, who came chiefly from the United States and the English cities of Canada, were maritime Canadians, akin to the people Miss Jewett knew in the Maine villages.

Willa Cather had been in Canada much more than most American writers before she wrote *Shadows on the Rock,* but there had been nothing in her Canadian associations to give her an awareness, let alone a feeling, of what was remarkable in the French region of that divided country.

Far more important as preparation was her long and admiring preoccupation with the literature, arts, and history of France. At the University of Nebraska she had found August Hjalmar Edgren a teacher of romance languages and a philologian of international reputation, and it was in part by the insight he communicated that even as a girl she could pierce beyond the techniques of the nineteenth-century novelists she read so constantly to some sense of the European life and feeling that enabled men to achieve techniques so subtle and so fine. Dorothy Canfield, who had passed much of her childhood in Paris, and her mother, who felt Paris to be a second home, gave her a yet more intimate sense of what it meant to be French. In 1902, when she had visited France for the first time, Willa Cather's enthusiasm was stirred not only at Rouen, sacred to her because of Flaubert and Maupassant, or Barbizon, but most of all in the south, especially at Avignon, where she came under the spell of a France that was older than any of her literary or artistic cults, the France from which the *ancien régime* in Canada derived. The story she was writing in the last years of her life was to express what Avignon, the Avignon of the popes, had meant to her over a period of forty years. In the summer of 1920 on the left bank of the Seine and on the Île Saint-Louis she was exploring streets and churches not very different in aspect from the time when the footsteps of Count Frontenac or Monseigneur Laval might have resounded in them.

Memories and feelings from her experiences in France and with French things stirred suddenly when in the summer of 1928, going to Grand Manan by a roundabout way, she first saw the city of Quebec. As she was soon to write, "These heavy grey buildings, monasteries and churches, steep-pitched and dormered, with spires and slated roofs, were roughly Norman Gothic in effect. They were made by people from the north of France who knew no other way of building. The settlement looked like something cut off from one of the ruder towns of Normandy or Brittany, and brought over." Willa Cather had an extraordinary power of obliterating from a historic scene its modern encrustations. She had done so at Avignon, and at Paris, more recently at Santa Fe; she did so again at Quebec. Edith Lewis, who accompanied her, fell ill the evening of their arrival at the Château Frontenac Hotel and was ordered to bed for ten days. Willa Cather walked about the city and its environs; Miss Lewis remembers the excitement with which she described her successive discoveries—the convent of the Ursulines, the great Laval seminary, the Church of Notre Dame in the lower town, the old marketplace. In the evenings they read histories from the hotel library, especially the chronicles of Parkman.

For Willa Cather, Parkman had always been the best of American historians, and it was through his eyes that she began to see the life of Quebec in the seventeenth century. The fifth part of his history opens:

> The events in this book group themselves in the main about a single figure, that of Count Frontenac, the most remarkable man who ever represented the crown of France in the New World. From strangely unpromising beginnings, he grew with every emergency, and rose equal to every crisis. His whole career was one of conflict, sometimes petty and personal, sometimes of momentous consequence, involving the question of national ascendency on this continent.

Willa Cather adopted Parkman's conception of Frontenac, the man from the heart of the Old World—aristocrat, intimate of princes, professional soldier—who, arriving in the New when he was past fifty, acted with the vigor and resilient adaptation to circumstance of a young Alexander and proved precisely the leader the New World required.

She followed Parkman, with some softening of the colors, in his picture of Frontenac's irascibility and contentiousness, his fiery, dominating nature, his harsh humor, his power to transmit his confidence in his invincibility; she also followed Parkman—perhaps went somewhat beyond him—in an almost tender sympathy with Frontenac's old age, his solitariness upon the rock of Quebec, his disillusionment with his associates and with his King, the frustration of his wish to die in France. It was in the last year of Frontenac's life that she set her story, and with his death it ended. Parkman's rationalism and anticlericalism had no effect upon her; of Frontenac's disputes with the Jesuits, and his determination to confine the Canadian church within the limits of an authority that was purely spiritual, despite Parkman's approving emphasis, she has little to say. She could enjoy, and repeat with a few changes for dramatic effect, his passage on Mother Catherine de Saint-Augustin's grinding a bit of Brébeuf's bone into the gruel prepared for a heretic she was attending and thus winning him for the Catholic faith. The skeptical apothecary Auclair is indignant at the entrance of such poisonous matter into a digestive tract; but though she sympathizes with his response, this passage is not characteristic of *Shadows on the Rock*.

Willa Cather's general attitude toward friars, nuns, and Jesuits, miracles and ceremonies, is in agreement with what she found in the second of her principal sources, the *Jesuit Relations*. She rejected entirely Parkman's conception of Bishop Laval, whom he disliked even more warmly than he admired the Bishop's great adversary, Frontenac. Admitting what no one could deny, the energy of Laval's nature, the genuineness of his austerity, and the perfect consistency of his life and policy with his faith, Parkman's judgment is extremely severe:

> He thought himself above human law. In vindicating the rights of the church, he invaded the rights of others and used means from which a healthy conscience would have shrunk. . . . He was penetrated by the poisonous casuistry of the Jesuits based on the assumption that all means are permitted when the end is the service of God; and as Laval, in his

own opinion, was always doing the service of God
while his opponents were always doing that of the
devil, he enjoyed, in the use of means, a latitude of
which we have seen him avail himself.

In her rejection of Parkman's view of Laval, instinctive
and complete, Willa Cather was strengthened by conversations she had with Abbé Henri Arthur Scott, the elderly
vicar of Ste. Foy, a village near Quebec. She was introduced to him by a bookseller in the city, and from the
first day when she saw him in his library, "sensitive and
kindly, reserved and discreet," as the late chief archivist of
Canada described him, surrounded by old editions of the
classics and a multitude of the best studies on modern
thought and art, she felt that she could trust his judgment
in his special subject. This was the ecclesiastical history of
French Canada. His studies had brought him a fellowship
in the Royal Society of Canada; and the respect in which
he was held in English Canada had been shown when he
had been asked to contribute the section on the history of
the Catholic Church in the eastern parts of the country to
Canada and Its Provinces, and the life of Laval to the
revised edition of the *Makers of Canada*. His book on
Laval had come out in 1926 and he was still afire with
enthusiasm for his subject. Her conception of Laval's ideas
and policies is substantially the conception that had appeared in the Abbé Scott's biography, though the effect she
gives is far more moving, for she adds an artist's insight
into the human temperament of the old Bishop. She continued to consult the Abbé Scott almost to the time of his
sudden death, in January 1931, when her novel stood complete though it was not published until the following autumn; and to him she owed a sight of many rare and
fugitive materials on which she drew for her account of the
aspect and internal politics of Quebec at the end of the
seventeenth century.

Willa Cather's Laval is in many ways an ecclesiastical
analogue for her Frontenac. He is, to the shape of his foot,
an aristocrat, a product (as a recent historian of Canada
has said) of the exalted religious revival of seventeenth-
century France, emerging from years in the mystical practices of Bernières's group at the Hermitage of Caen to

organize and energize the Canadian church; and like Frontenac he is presented as precisely the leader the New World required. Laval was right, she thought, in insisting that the parish clergy remain a part of the great community of his seminary; right, too, in making sure that the ceremonies of the Church were accompanied by the same splendors on the rock of Quebec as he had known in the cities of France; right incontestably when he intervened in civil matters in defense of moral and spiritual values. Like Frontenac he is shown in his old age, a man approaching seventy-five when the story opens, long retired from his episcopal office, shouldered aside by his theatrical successor Saint-Vallier, painfully afflicted, miserably poor, formidably kind. The worst she will concede is that "he was a stubborn, high-handed, tyrannical, quarrelsome old man," only to add: "no one could deny that he shepherded his sheep"—and that was the crux. At the close of the novel, immediately after Frontenac's death, we are invited to make a common judgment on the two men when Auclair says to his daughter: "The Count and the old Bishop were both men of my own period, the kind we looked up to in my youth. Saint-Vallier and Monsieur de Champigny [the intendant] are of a different sort." The judgment is very like the one Willa Cather had rendered on the lapse from the generation of the pioneers in Nebraska to the generation of their children. It was because she looked at Laval and Frontenac with the same spirit in which she had looked at Governor Garber when she wrote *A Lost Lady* that she was able to be more philosophic and more profound than the historian who was betrayed by his harsh rationalism into taking a minor difference for a major distinction.

Into the shaping of her novel there entered the deep and painful emotions that followed on the first death in Willa Cather's immediate family. She had spent the Christmas of 1927 at Red Cloud, and during her visit her father had a first attack of angina. In March of the next year, shortly after her return to New York, he died. "There had always been the kindest and fondest relationship between her and her father," Miss Lewis writes, "and his gentle, modest pride in her achievements, and the high esteem they had won, were one of the chief satisfactions she got from what is known as success." Willa Cather went to Red Cloud for the funeral, and supported her brother Douglass's plea that her mother, who was worn out with strain, should go with him to California for a long stay. Mrs. Cather had depended on the hidden strength of her husband more than anyone had realized; it seemed impossible for her to make a life for herself. The death of Charles Cather was not only the loss of a father; it meant the breakup of what Willa Cather had always continued to think of as her home, the household in Red Cloud. Her mind was full of her father when she discovered Quebec; she was then reviving memories of her relation to him when she was a child in Virginia and a girl on the Divide and in Red Cloud. As she thought over the story that was beginning to take shape in her mind during the months she spent on Grand Manan, the relation between father and daughter, between Euclide Auclair and Cécile, demanded the foreground.

During the early months of 1928, when her feelings were so deeply engaged by her father's illness and death, she wrote a Nebraska story, "Neighbour Rosicky," the first of the three tales collected in 1932 as *Obscure Destinies*. It should be read along with the final part of *My Ántonia*, where Jim Burden, visiting Ántonia, whom he has not seen since her marriage twenty years before, is delighted by his first meeting with Cuzak, her husband, and by the quality of life in their household. "Neighbour Rosicky" is a study of the same man and the same household taken twenty years or so afterward, in the last few months of Rosicky's life. Like Charles Cather, Rosicky is an angina victim and learns of his ailment at the beginning of winter, to die of it the next spring. His last months are full of memories of the evil things he has escaped by fleeing from the harshness, ugliness, and deadness of big cities, and of experiences of the good things he has had in packed measure by living on the land, in a household full of warmhearted, vigorous, and impulsive people, with Ántonia, who is here called Mary, as its perfect center. There is nothing simpler in Willa Cather's fiction than "Neighbour Rosicky"; the tone is quietness itself, and perfectly sustained; the emotion has a flawless purity. The choice of a friend's husband rather than of her own father as the main subject for a story into which she poured so much of what she felt about Charles Cather's life and death is a clue to the more elaborate work that she began later in the year.

When she returned to New York from Grand Manan in the autumn of 1928, Willa Cather began to write *Shadows on the Rock*. She felt almost at once that she needed to see Quebec again, and returned there alone in November for a stay of two weeks, in which she absorbed that strong feeling for the aspect of the city in autumn which was to be rendered so powerfully in the early and late sections of the novel. On this visit she ransacked bookstores and libraries, talked with historians, antiquaries, and other men learned in the past of French Canada, and returned to New York full of her subject and her eyes complaining of strain.

An ordeal even more severe than her father's death now came on her. In December she had the news that her mother, who was still in California with Douglass, had had a paralytic stroke. Willa Cather went to her at once.

The long illness of Mrs. Cather—it lasted two and a half years—had a profound effect on Willa Cather [Miss Lewis writes], and I think on her work as well. She had come to understand her mother better and better through the years—her strong-willed, imperious nature, full of quick, eager impulses—quick to resent, quick to sympathize, headstrong, passionate, and yet capable of great kindness and understanding. She realized with complete imagination what it meant for a proud woman like her mother to lie month after month quite helpless, unable to speak articulately, although her mind was perfectly clear. In Willa Cather's long stays in Pasadena, where her mother was cared for in a sanatorium, she had to watch her continually growing weaker, more ailing, yet unable to die. It was one of those experiences that make a lasting change in the climate of one's mind.

So great was Willa Cather's involvement in what her mother was undergoing that she could scarcely continue the writing of *Shadows on the Rock*. The death of her father had turned her mind on the life of the family when she was a child; and soon after her mother went to California she resolved to open the house in Red Cloud and refurbish it for Mrs. Cather's return. It was not the shabby, crowded house in which she had grown up, but a large, well-designed one in a better part of town which Charles Cather had bought after she went to Pittsburgh. She found a surprising pleasure in choosing new paper and new drapes, carefully avoiding any change in the parlor, to which she knew her mother's attachment. In one of her stays at Pasadena, where she had a cottage in the grounds of the sanatorium, she began the short story "Two Friends," finished in 1931, a study in a relationship between two intimates of her parents whom she had admired in the first years at Red Cloud. In Pasadena she began also the longer story "Old Mrs. Harris," another study of those years, the most nearly direct representation of life in the Cather household in the town's setting she ever attempted. This also remained unfinished until 1931. If she could write little of *Shadows on the Rock,* she could take pleasure in reading about the world the novel was to evoke. The difficulty in composing was perhaps the main reason why she read so extensively in the *Jesuit Relations,* La Hontan's *Voyages,* Juchereau's history of the Hôtel Dieu at Quebec, the letters of Mother Marie de l'Incarnation, from which she drew the epigraph for the novel, and a host of secondary works, among them the *Makers of Canada,* which she bought.

During the winter of 1929–30, after another visit to Quebec, which she now saw for the first time under deep snow, she worked more steadily at the manuscript. She spent the spring with her mother, and in May sailed for France. In the course of the two months she stayed in Paris she became as familiar with Frontenac's old quarter as she was with the country about Santa Fe. With Jan and Isabelle Hambourg she made her first visit to Saint-Malo, evoked so delicately in the later part of the novel, where Pondaven, the Breton captain appears. The news from Pasadena was not disquieting, and Willa Cather decided to visit again the Provençal country, which always made her light of heart. After Avignon and Marseillle she went to Aix-les-Bains, and, staying at the Grand Hotel, had the extraordinary encounter from which she drew the most perfect of her essays, "A Chance Meeting."

In the dining-room she observed with an always growing interest an old French lady, lame and somewhat shapeless, but with a head so fine that it reminded her of the portrait busts of Roman ladies. This was Madame Franklin Grout, whose translation of *Faust* had been   corrected by Turgenev, and who had edited the *Bouvard et Pécuchet* of her uncle, Flaubert. In meeting the niece of Flaubert, the "Caro" of his letters, and finding her a person whose talk of his writings joined subtlety and justice to enthusiasm, Willa Cather felt that she had been "brought up against a mountain of memories," and that the world which survived in Madame Franklin Grout held most of "her mental past." Their talks cast a special glory over the summer of 1930, and when she heard of her friend's death the next winter, Willa Cather's sense of loss went deep.

Late in September, after some days spent with Isabelle Hambourg, who had become gravely ill, she returned to America by the St. Lawrence route. I traveled by the same ship and recall as if it were yesterday her warmth of expression and vigor of movement as she looked from the promenade deck at the aspect of Quebec on a sunny October morning. Miss Lewis writes:

> The whole voyage became a sort of home-coming to *Shadows*, and the slow progress up the St. Lawrence, between woods on fire with October, was its climax—a dream of joy. It had been Willa Cather's intention to go straight on to Boston and Jaffrey; but although her luggage had gone on ahead, she instantly decided to buy warm clothes and stay at the Frontenac for a while. (During this stay she for the first time visited the Hôpital Général, and saw Bishop de Saint-Vallier's two small, poor rooms where he humbly ended his life.) Everything she experienced brought her closer and closer to her story, and when she did finally start for Jaffrey, she could hardly wait to be at her writing-table again. She wrote the last part of *Shadows* very rapidly, part of it at Jaffrey, part at the Grosvenor, finishing it December 27th.

II

It was inevitable that *Shadows on the Rock* should reflect Willa Cather's longing for what in *My Ántonia* she had called "the previous, the incommunicable past"—her personal past, the life in the Cather household when she was a child and a girl, and the life in the pioneer society to which it was related. In population the town of Quebec in the year of her story, 1697–8, was a little short of two thousand, as was Red Cloud in the years when she was growing up. To the rock had come people who like the Cathers and so many others coming to Nebraska from Virginia or New England, Norway or Bohemia, carried their gods with them. A key to much in the material and the scale in *Shadows on the Rock* is given in this passage on which a chapter ends:

> *Inferretque deos Latio*. When an adventurer carries his gods with him into a remote and savage country, the colony he founds will, from the beginning, have graces, traditions, riches of the mind and spirit. Its history will shine with bright incidents, slight, perhaps, but precious, as in life itself, where the great matters are often as worthless as astronomical distances, and the trifles dear as the heart's blood.

The trifles at Quebec are like the trifles in the Nebraska novels—old Vavrika's Tokay and Ántonia's grape arbor, the garden of the old German couple with whom Wunsch, the musician, lived, Mrs. Forrester's laugh, Mrs. Cather's strange power, in "Old Mrs. Harris," to make a beautiful occasion out of almost nothing, and Charles Cather's courtesy, in the same story, the courtesy of his grandfather on the family farm at Flint Ridge.

Beyond the rock of Quebec, as beyond Red Cloud, lay lonely farms where life was often rough and gross, and dividing them was the wild land. A lively episode in *Shadows on the Rock*, with much characterizing force, is Cécile Auclair's unhappy visit to the Harnois farm on the Île d'Orléans, where the people and the beds were dirty, the rooms smelly and stuffy, the food heavy with lard. Cécile returned home with a new appreciation of what cleansing and polishing and cooking in the best French manner meant in life, that they were a part of life without which it would not mean much to her. What Cécile felt at the Harnois' was what Jim Burden felt when in the middle of winter he went with his grandmother to the sodhouse of the Shimerdas, where the air was stifling and the food frozen or rotting, and Ántonia slept on a pile of straw in a hole in the black earth. The Burdens—who are projections of William A. Cather and his wife—accused themselves for having allowed neighbors to live so, but on their return to their own neat frame house they had a new appreciation of its "atmosphere of comfort and security." The land in *O Pioneers!* was the "great fact . . . which seemed to overwhelm the little beginnings of human society that struggled in its sombre wastes," a land that "wanted to be let alone, to preserve its own fierce strength, its peculiar, savage kind of beauty, its uninterrupted mournfulness." The forests about Quebec are an equivalent for these Nebraska prairies: in their "dead, sealed world . . . an uncharted continent choked with interlocking trees . . . European man was quickly swallowed up in silence, distance, mould, black mud." It was because Quebec, as she imagined it in the seventeenth century, had so much of what she had responded to with such force in her years on the Divide and in Red Cloud, in the Cather household and in the society of her friends, that Willa Cather moved with such sensitive ease in calling up its aspect and its spirit.

To the qualities it shared with early Nebraska, Quebec added the precious element Willa Cather had set at the center of *Death Comes for the Archbishop*. Miss Lewis writes:

> I have sometimes thought that Willa Cather's great pleasure in this Quebec visit came from finding here a sort of continuation, in a different key, of the Catholic theme which had absorbed her for two years, and which still lingered in her thoughts, after the completion of the *Archbishop*, like a tune that goes on in one's mind after the song is ended. Dickens, in his preface to *David Copperfield*, tells "how sorrowfully the pen is laid down at the close of a two years' imaginative task." I think Willa Cather never got so much happiness from the writing of any book as from the *Archbishop*; and although *Shadows on the Rock* is of course altogether different in conception, in treatment, and in artistic purpose, it

may have been in part a reluctance to leave that world of Catholic feeling and tradition in which she had lived so happily for so long that led her to embark on this new novel.

As in *Death Comes for the Archbishop,* Willa Cather chose a later rather than an early period for the novel of the French regime in Canada, and inserted a variety of narrative reminders of what life had been when the colony was more primitive. These reminders are predominantly religious: a story about the first superior of the Hôtel Dieu, Mother Catherine de Saint-Augustin, related by her successor, Mother Juschereau de Saint-Ignace; a story about the Jesuit martyr Noël Chabanel told by another Jesuit, Hector Saint-Cyr; a story of the youth and vocation of the holy recluse at Montreal, Jeanne Le Ber, told by her former love, Pierre Charron. In the earlier time religious feeling had been more intense and exalted; the intensity and exaltation have survived in the aged and retired Laval, often called in the novel (as Willa Cather may have learned from the startling hagiography of the prelate in the first edition of the *Makers of Canada*) "Monseigneur l'Ancien." With the younger personages religious feeling has become quite different: in Mother Juschereau the "vigils, mortifications, visions, raptures" of Catherine de Saint-Augustin have given place to the "sunny outrightness" of "a religious of the practical type . . . a *Canadienne,* and the woman for Canada"; Hector Saint-Cyr, an imaginary personage modeled in his personal traits and his principal adventure on the soldier priest of the Sulpitians, Dollier de Casson, is heroic and devout, but with no overtone of Chabanel's passionate spirituality; though Jeanne Le Ber is still alive when the action occurs, she has receded into a long spiritual drought.

Much more potent in setting the tone for religious feeling at the end of the seventeenth century than contrasts with the age of the martyrs and mystics that had gone before is the amosphere in the households of the Auclairs and their bourgeois friends the Pigeons and the Pommiers. In Cécile Auclair, for all her piety, her devotion to the Ursulines who had taught her, her pleasure in miracles, there was never a trace of a vocation for the religious life;

like Madame Pommier's, her religion seemed to find its center and its preferred symbol not in a virgin or a martyr, but in the Holy Family. It was because of Madame Pommier's devotion that the cobbler shop had been opened on Holy Family Hill, and nothing delighted that old lady more than when Monseigneur Laval told her "that there is no other place in the world where the people are so devoted to the Holy Family as here in our own Canada. It is something very special to us." It was something very special to Willa Cather, writing when she felt her own losses. On its superior level this devotion is parallel to the practices in cooking, cleaning, and polishing by which the house and shop of the Auclairs became such a magnet for so many diverse persons. Religion also penetrated life and made it shine with grace and poetry.

As in the Nebraska novels, but to a greater degree, the pattern of *Shadows on the Rock* depends on responses to new circumstances and a new society. Throughout the novel there is a steady movement—of which the succession of the Canadian-born farm-girl Mother Juschereau to the place of Catherine de Saint-Augustin is an early instance— from what is French to what is Canadian. The importance of this element in the narrative is confirmed by its last incident, the arrival at the Auclairs' on the day after Count Frontenac's death of the *coureur de bois* Pierre Charron, Canadian-born and critical to the point of suspicion toward all who have about them the odor of Paris or Versailles. Cécile, born on the Quai des Célestins in Paris, but brought to Canada at four, reflects: "He had not a throne behind him, like the Count . . . not the authority of a parchment and seal. But he had authority, and a power which came from knowledge of the country and its people: from knowledge, and from a kind of passion. His daring and his pride seemed to her even more splendid than Count Frontenac's."

Although there were well-to-do Charrons, traders in Montreal and associates of Jacques Le Ber, the father of the recluse (and it was doubtless because she had come across their track that Willa Cather gave Pierre their name), he is an imaginary personage. To Auclair and his wife, Pierre "had seemed the type they had come so far to find; more than anyone else he realized the romantic picture of the free Frenchman of the great forests which they had formed at home on the bank of the Seine." In terms of the Nebraska novels Pierre is that rarest of all admirable kinds, the pioneer of the second generation who had to the full the finest qualities of the first; in his case we may say those that Willa Cather found in Robert Cavelier de La Salle. Pierre is another Ántonia; the wild land is for him an ideal setting and an opportunity. His marriage to Cécile Auclair, reported in the epilogue, is something like Ántonia's: it assures us that the future, evolving in the ways of a new society will also preserve the graces and traditions of Europe.

The main exception to the movement from what is French to what is Canadian is Cécile's father, another imaginary personage, many of whose traits are taken from the first of Canadian natural scientists, Michel Sarrazin, whose collection of botanical specimens was kept at the Jardin des Plantes in Paris and who in 1699 was named a corresponding member of the Académie des Sciences. On the rock Euclide Auclair is out of his element. Left to himself, like Ántonia's father, he would have remained in a European city; both men deferred to wills that were stronger than their own. The shift from working in tapestry and playing the violin in Prague to a sodhouse and the unbroken prairie was too much for old Shimerda—he shot himself. I am not sure that Euclide Auclair would not have done the same in similarly harsh conditions; but he had Frontenac's protection, an apothecary shop in the center of the town of Quebec, and a wife and then a daughter to make the family's way of life in New France so close to what it had been on the Quai des Célestins that one had to step outside to notice the difference. There were times when the desire to return to France grew very strong, and it is significant that the final reason for Euclide's staying at Quebec was a feeling that when the great King died, France would become a terrifyingly new world. But in Quebec nothing would change. Charles Cather, who spoke with a Virginia accent and kept Southern manners to the end of his life, who was not intended for a farmer and came into town from the Divide as soon as he could, also had his longings for the gracious society he had left, and his compensations in the way of life in his own household.

The novel in which Willa Cather traveled farthest from Red Cloud drew most of its emotional power from her memories of her life there as they flooded her mind during the years when that life had finally to take its place in the irrecoverable past.

11

Winter Memories

1932–1940

OBSCURE DESTINIES
LUCY GAYHEART
THE OLD BEAUTY
SAPPHIRA AND THE SLAVE GIRL

THE DEATH OF her parents and the sale of the family house removed Red Cloud from its place in the rhythm of Willa Cather's year. Unless she was making a long stay in Europe she had "gone home," as she always spoke of her trips to Red Cloud, for a month or two every summer or early fall; often she made a second, shorter visit in the Christmas season. In the years after the Cather home was sold she was constantly asked by early friends who were still living in the village to stay with them. She never did, however; from the time when she began to be a novelist she was averse to staying with anyone who was not a member of her family, even though the hotels in Red Cloud were primitively uncomfortable. Without the visit or visits to Nebraska the entire year seemed emptier: nothing else could take their place. Roscoe and Douglass Cather were living in the Far West; and Willa Cather, who never traveled by plane, was almost dangerously exhausted by long transcontinental train journeys.

The Hambourgs were living in France; they had less money than in the early years of their marriage and seldom came to New York. There was no one in Pittsburgh whom Willa Cather cared to visit regularly. At Grand Manan, without being unfriendly, she and Edith Lewis kept to themselves; their stays on the island were intended to be a rest from the traffic and telephones of Manhattan, and its heat and harassments, not a participation in the doings of a summer colony. It was at Grand Manan, however, that Willa Cather found the nearest equivalent to her stays in Red Cloud; at her cottage she was visited on four different occasions by nieces and heartily enjoyed having them. She could be a formidable aunt, but her interest in each of the Cathers in the next generation was serious and intense. Her letters concerning them are full of perception and affection; and she would go to any pains to arrange for their coming to stay with her. At the Jaffrey Inn, in New Hampshire, where she usually spent some weeks each autumn, she was almost always at work—from the time when she first discovered Jaffrey she had been able to write and revise there more happily than anywhere else. It meant a great deal to her when Ethel Jones Litchfield decided, after the death of her husband, to leave Pittsburgh and live in New York; with Mrs. Litchfield, whom she had first met in 1902 and whom she saw almost every week, she could talk about music unreservedly and evoke many of the best happenings in the Pittsburgh years. The friendship with Mr. and Mrs. Knopf deepened with every year. It was through them that she met two writers of her own generation to whose work and personality she was drawn, Thomas Mann and Sigrid Undset.

Madame Undset had always kept a photograph of Willa Cather on her writing-table even before they had met; they had their literary careers in common and the same feeling for people and for nature. Sigrid Undset used to delight Willa Cather with her account of her continuing discoveries of American wild flowers and her forays into the field and wood to get them. And as a devout Catholic she felt, and often expressed, her admiration for the understanding way in which Willa Cather had written of Catholicism.

Still one cannot but feel that in the years after 1931 Willa Cather was erecting walls behind which she carried on a life that was essentially inward—retrospective, creative, and speculative. One main reason for her withdrawal was undoubtedly a decline in energy. Edith Lewis believes that the physical and emotional exertion in the years of her mother's illness was so great and sustained for so long a period that Willa Cather never overcame altogether its effects. She instinctively spared herself by avoiding new intimate relationships, knowing well that once she entered upon one of these, her imaginative and sympathetic nature could not be held in check. In the course of the 1930's Willa Cather did form one such relationship, with the Menuhin family; she could not have sustained many friendships so intense and so creative—no one of her years and temper could. Again and again in the letters written during the 1930's an impression and an awareness of deep fatigue appeared.

Besides the failure in energy, her withdrawal was induced by what Harvey Newbranch, her friend from college times, describes as a slow spreading of the virus of pessimism. She was out of sympathy with the world about her. The New Deal seemed to her to threaten the free activity of the strong individual by the kind of restrictive influence that seemed to her the worst of all, restriction by government. Government worked through civil servants, and civil servants she had always believed were the culls of their generation, dreary petty men who took a mean pleasure in thwarting those who had energy, daring, and originality. The age of the pioneers was quite over, and it had been succeeded by an age of routine.

She was no less unhappy about the attitude to the arts in modern American life. Even in the universities there was an emphasis on what was done by contemporaries, a growing indifference to the great performances of the past. She was asked why during her years in Pittsburgh and Allegheny high schools she had for a while taught Latin as well as English; she appreciated with a shock that her inquirer could not believe that it was because she liked Latin—the language and the literature. Teachers of English in schools and colleges were constantly writing to her about her works; and she observed that far more than half of them did not respect their own language, could not use it without gross errors, and had no sense whatever of its possibilities as an instrument. Education seemed to her to become more and more an exaltation of technology and an aid to making money. This was not education at all, she believed, and she wondered how anyone could be duped into thinking it was. Shakespeare was less and less rightly understood, inside schools and colleges and outside; and what could be said for a people that did not care about Shakespeare? The new paths of fiction in the 1930's did not seem to her to lead anywhere worth going, though she kept all her interest in what was written by those who seemed to her genuine artists, Ernest Hemingway, Thornton Wilder, Scott Fitzgerald, and, somewhat to one's surprise, Sinclair Lewis, whose pictures of Midwestern towns and cities seemed to her not only authentic but full of suggestion. There was no critic of power writing in these years, she felt: the last of the great American critics was Henry James, and the last of the good ones W. C. Brownell and H. L. Mencken.

What she wrote during the years after the publication of *Shadows on the Rock* reflected her withdrawal, the decline in her energy, and her tendency to retrospection.

II

A year after the publication of *Shadows on the Rock* Willa Cather collected three tales that stemmed from her early life and were filled with memories of Red Cloud and of her family. One of them, "Neighbour Rosicky," had been written in 1928 at the time of her father's death. The second, "Old Mrs. Harris," and the last, "Two Friends," were set down largely in the interval between completion and publication of her novel of Quebec, but the material in them had been in Willa Cather's mind since her tenth year. Her title for the volume is one of the simplest and most effective of all her titles: *Obscure Destinies.* From the portraits of Rosicky and Mrs. Harris to the two friends she remembered sitting on the sidewalk under the Western skies in the small town, the book is rich in affection for the characters and the life she depicted. Willa Cather felt that "Two Friends," with its story of their falling out over William Jennings Bryan, was a romantic kind of realism—a painter's subject, which she had tried to do in a painter's way. She told Alfred Knopf that she had in mind, as she wrote the story, the paintings of Courbet, and indeed the memory we carry away from the sketch is the static picture of the banker and the cattleman in their chairs at evening, the small town flooded "by the rich indolence of a full moon," and the young narrator (who is clearly Willa Cather) beside them listening, always listening, to their worldly talk. But if the story is as static as an old-time painting, it is filled with the emotion of the sensitive young observer and an aching nostalgia for the past.

Fine as this tale and "Neighbour Rosicky" are, they are but sketches beside the richly developed story—it is really a *nouvelle*—of "Old Mrs. Harris," which many consider Willa Cather's finest short narrative. Reflected in it we find her memories of the time when the Cathers moved from the South to the West and when their way of living was under the scrutiny of their new neighbors. With the family has come the grandmother, a figure taken for granted in the household, devoted to her daughter and grandchildren, who seem almost unaware of her benign presence.

> In Tennessee every young married woman in good circumstances had an older woman in the house, a mother or mother-in-law or an old aunt, who managed the household economies and directed the help. . . .
>
> To be sure, Mrs. Harris, and the other women of her age who managed their daughter's house, kept in the background; but it was their own background, and they ruled it jealously. They left the front porch and the parlour to the young married couple and their young friends; the old women spent most of their lives in the kitchen and pantries and back dining-room.

But in Tennessee there was the old family house and here "the little rented house was much too small for the family, and Mrs. Harris and her 'things' were almost required to be invisible." Mrs. Harris represents those qualities of quiet self-sacrificing and self-effacing heroism which Willa Cather could never resist rendering homage to in her work; as she moves through the story, accomplishing her simple little daily tasks, she is at once a shadowy figure behind the lively bustle of the new generation and also a strong protagonist. Willa Cather's use of detail and small dramatic incident was never more felicitous, whether in giving us the portrait of Mrs. Harris through the kindly eyes of the neighbor, Mrs. Rosen (drawn from Mrs. Wiener), or describing the strivings of the daughter who plans to go to the university. Such small matters as picnics and serving tea, the routine of the kitchen, or the death of the cat take on a distinct importance because they are important to Mrs. Harris, who goes about her appointed tasks, emerging from her shadowy existence only to arrange quietly with her neighbor for Vickie to have a loan to supplement the scholarship she has won that will take her to college.

> Sometimes, in the morning, if her feet ached more than usual, Mrs. Harris felt a little low. . . . She would hang up her towel with a sigh and go into the kitchen, feeling that it was hard to make a start. But the moment she heard the children running down the uncarpeted back stairs, she forgot to be low. Indeed, she ceased to be an individual, an old woman with aching feet; she became part of a group, became a relationship. She was drunk up into their freshness when they burst in upon her, telling her about their dreams, explaining their troubles with buttons and shoe-laces and underwear shrunk too small. The tired, solitary old woman grandmother had been at daybreak vanished; suddenly the morning seemed as important to her as it did to the children, and the mornings ahead stretched out sunshiny, important.

Obscure Destinies is Willa Cather's finest book of short stories and in its minute realism and sharpness of outline invites comparison with Flaubert's *Trois Contes*. The three tales are of a piece; they were the synthesis, after many years, of old experiences; and they are filled with a humanity and gentleness and feeling which demonstrated that if Willa Cather had in her two preceding novels turned to a distant past, she could still confront her own past and draw great art from it.

The stories in *Obscure Destinies* came from an impulse and a need to live again in imagination some passages in the early years in Nebraska. It was the same with *Lucy Gayheart*, the first novel to have a Nebraska setting since *A Lost Lady*. Willa Cather began to write it in the spring of 1933, in New York. She had not recovered from the strain and the losses of the preceding years; again and again she entered in the line-a-day she began to keep at this time "very tired" or "deadly tired." The early chapters, the first book, of the novel, were drafted in this exhausted mood, and no revision could free them from a heaviness, a lagging pace, for which there is no parallel in any of her earlier writings. During the summer, passed at Grand Manan, she could bring herself to work at the novel only intermittently. In the autumn, in the cool mountain air of Jaffrey, she began to feel her energy renewed; her spirits rose; and she felt, rightly, that at last she "could live with her story as she ought to do." The draft of the last book, which she always considered the best, was written as quickly and happily as anything she had ever done.

She had just begun to revise her draft when she suffered the greatest disability in her career as an author. Miss Lewis notes:

> Her right wrist began to be painfully swollen; and when she went one day to the doctor with it, he diagnosed it as a serious inflammation of the sheath of the tendon, and said the hand must be completely immobilized. From this time on she was never free from the threat of this disability, which attacked sometimes her right hand, and less frequently her left. Often for months together she had to wear the steel and leather brace that Dr. Frank Ober, the great orthopedic surgeon, devised for her; it immobilized her thumb, but left her fingers free, so that she was able with some difficulty to sign her name, or to trace a few words at the end of a dictated letter. All this meant that for long periods she was unable to do any writing—she could not even typewrite. She never tried to dictate a piece of creative work. She felt it to be, for her, a psychological impossibility.
>
> Although this affliction made the simplest acts of life, which ordinarily one performs unconsciously— taking a bath, dressing oneself, tying a knot, opening a letter—wearisomely difficult and irksome, Willa Cather rarely let it depress her spirits or affect her independence. I remember her telling once, when some one offered to help her, how when she was a very little child, and her parents would try to assist her in something, she would protest passionately: "Self-alone, self-alone!"

The recurrence of this disability, and its persistence for weeks and even months, are one of the reasons why after *Lucy Gayheart* she composed so little—only one novel and less than half a dozen shorter fictions. In the spring of 1934 she was able to resume writing and to finish the revision of the manuscript; it was used as a serial by the *Woman's Home Companion*, and appeared as a book in 1935.

Lucy Gayheart has likenesses with many of the earlier writings about Nebraska. The most evident link, and also the most intimate, is with *The Song of the Lark*. Like Thea Kronborg, Lucy is a musician, who leaves a small Nebraska town to study in Chicago, where she lives meagerly, meets a great personage in the world of music, and becomes severed from the society in which she grew up. But unlike Thea's, Lucy's distinction is not a strength of talent, her early death did not end a promising career; her distinction is a fineness of nature, an intense response to people, to life in people. What she always admired in Harry Gordon, the man who could not forgive her until she was dead, is the clue to what made her history worth telling: "He rose and fell, he was alive, he moved. He was not anchored, he was not lazy, he was not a sheep . . . he wasn't tame at the core." The quick flow of life in Lucy is caught in the beautiful introductory reminiscence of her eager, happy walk, not faltering in the winter winds or under the summer's heat. Thea Kronborg's story is that of a talent and a career, Lucy's of a personality and a love. It does not require a massive or elaborate treatment; it can be rendered as Mrs. Forrester's was, in a few incidents and a few sketches of mood, lightly and without insistence. In the early chapters there is sometimes too much insistence; the touch does not always have that swift and delicate sureness that was unfailing in *A Lost Lady*.

The relation between father and daughter that was at the center of *Shadows on the Rock* is again important in *Lucy Gayheart*. Again the mother is dead when the story opens, and again the father is out of place in the society of a town on the edge of civilization. Jacob Gayheart, a German-born watchmaker and flute-player, has the gentleness, the courtesy, the perceptive affection of Euclide Auclair and of Charles Cather. Like Auclair, by his gentleness and personal distinction he wins the friendship of men a generation younger who have in the highest degree the qualities prized in their societies—Harry Gordon is the hero of Haverford on the Platte as Pierre Charron and Father Hector St.-Cyr are the heroes of the Canadian rivers and woods. If Harry seems much less heroic, that is because the Nebraska of this novel—the action occurs in 1902 and 1903, with an epilogue in 1927—has lost the fire of the pioneer age and become almost submerged in dreary prose.

The idea of this novel had been in Willa Cather's mind a long time; she used to speak of it as *Blue Eyes on the Platte*, although when she came to write she determined that Lucy's eyes should be a startling brown—"they were not gentle brown eyes, but flashed with gold sparks like that Colorado stone we call the tiger-eye." The name of Gayheart, symbolic as names rarely were in the early novels about Nebraska,[1] was a reminiscence of a chance encounter in the days when Willa Cather was a student at the University. In early May 1896 she drove from Red Cloud to Blue Hill for a dance and spent the night talking with a young girl who had that name, a fine, delicate, sensitive creature who seemed to her pitiably unsuited to teach school in that remote rough village.

The saturation of the novel in music and song was an outcome of a new friendship, which meant at least as much to Willa Cather as her association with Fremstad in the years when she was writing *The Song of the Lark*. In the summer of 1930 during her stay in Paris she met through Jan and Isabelle Hambourg the Menuhin family— Moshe and Marutha Menuhin, their two young daughters, Hephzibah and Yaltah, and their son, Yehudi. She had always cared intensely for children, from the early days in Red Cloud when like Thea Kronborg she asked nothing better than drawing her young brother in his cart along the narrow sidewalks of the town. The Menuhins were the most gifted, the most sensitive children she had known; and it is not too much to say that she fell in love with the family as a whole, and with each member of it individually. Mrs. Menuhin and the two girls came often to see her the next winter in New York; and in the spring of 1931, when she was with her mother in Pasadena, Willa

---

[1] An exception is Wunsch, the name of Thea Kronborg's music teacher at Moonstone.

Cather often saw Yehudi, who was giving concerts in California. The Menuhin children had been brought up with an Old World strictness and did not know very much of the larger society outside their family; the friendship of Willa Cather was as exciting and illuminating to them as theirs was to her.

In 1927 Willa Cather and Edith Lewis had moved out of the Bank Street apartment, to which they had been deeply attached and where so many fruitful years had been spent; the building was being torn down, and they had no alternative. They sought refuge in the Grosvenor Hotel, at 35 Fifth Avenue, and what was intended to be a temporary *pied-à-terre* was protracted into a five-year residence. The Grosvenor was associated in Willa's mind with the painful period of the illness and death of her parents; it carried with it a sense of displacement and homelessness. In 1932 they resolved to escape from the irritations and confinements of hotel life and were able to find the space, privacy, and repose they longed for in an apartment in the quieter reaches of Park Avenue. The brightest element in Willa Cather's life in this apartment was her association with the Menuhins in the winters. During the years when she lived at the Grosvenor she had heard little opera or music of any kind; now, with the stimulus of the new friendship, it seemed she could never hear enough.

Miss Lewis notes:

> I remember the Menuhin family's winter visits to New York, in the years that followed, as a sort of continuous festival, full of concerts and gay parties; orange trees and great baskets of flowers for Willa Cather arriving in the midst of snow-storms; birthday luncheons, with Russian caviare and champagne; excursions to the opera, where she took Yaltah and Hephzibah to hear *Parsifal* for the first time; long walks around the reservoir in Central Park, when the three children all wanted to walk beside her, and had to take turnabout. They discussed very abstract subjects together—art, religion, philosophy, life. If Willa Cather had been writing *War and Peace*, I am sure she would have abandoned it to take these walks.

She had a feeling that Hephzibah and Yaltah, travelling in so many countries, and learning something of the language of each, were never going to get a thorough sense of the English language; and this worried her. She asked Marutha Menuhin if she might organize a Shakespeare Club, with no one allowed to be present except herself and the little girls. Yehudi then asked if he might come too. They began with *Richard II*, and went on to *Macbeth* and *Henry IV*. Willa Cather hunted through the bookstores of New York to get each of the children a copy of these plays in the original Temple Edition, the only one she herself cared to read; it was then rapidly going out of print.

She was greatly touched when, many years afterward, Yehudi told her he had found and bought a complete second-hand set of the Temple Shakespeare, in a shop in New Orleans.

In *Lucy Gayheart* there is a reminiscence of these sessions and of the Temple Shakespeare. After he had sung a song from *Twelfth Night*, Clement Sebastian "ran his finger along a row of small red leather volumes, and pulled one out of its place." Lucy had thought the play "a rather foolish comedy where everybody was pretending, and nobody was in earnest." She had made this gross mistake because "until she began to play for Sebastian, she had never known that words had any value aside from their direct meaning." It was the words of Shakespeare that Willa Cather cared most to talk about. Gifted foreign people would, she thought, come to a mastery of English by learning and feeling what the language was in the use of its greatest master. For the background of the historical plays she read again J. R. Green's history, which is one of the few books in her library heavily scored and marked. The lifelong aversion to Lucius Sherman's severe and misleading analysis kept her touch glancing and informal. For the rest of her life she read Shakespeare more and more, and always with greater pleasure; but she did not care to acquaint herself with recent interpretations and criticisms.

To be with the Menuhins was to live in a world of music. Willa Cather did not go to the opera as often as in her early years in New York; she thought opera had declined; but the truth was that her taste had ripened over the years and she preferred now music by itself, without the trappings of drama, and, above all, orchestral and chamber music. One of her oldest friends, Mrs. Charles Weisz, with whom she often stayed when she was passing through Chicago, recalls her saying, especially when she was unhappy, under strain, or simply fatigued: "I must have music!" It was no longer Wagner but Beethoven or Schubert that she needed; and opera, which dominated *The Song of the Lark,* is in *Lucy Gayheart* secondary to the songs of Schubert.

What was essential to the art of Clement Sebastian, the great singer in this novel with whom Lucy falls in love, is, however, precisely what was essential to the art of Thea Kronborg in her maturity, as it was essential to Fremstad's. It was the classical austerity that Willa Cather found in the playing of Josef Lhevinne, whom she met in the early thirties and whose concerts she scarcely ever missed. In the calmness and serenity of Sebastian's rendering of Schubert there was "a kind of large enlightenment, like daybreak"; and hearing him, "one felt a long distance between the singer and the scenes he was recalling, a long perspective." Art such as Sebastian's depends most of all neither on training nor on the quality of a voice, but on the personality of the performer and what that personality has made of experience.

The art in *Lucy Gayheart* is of the same kind. The defect in *The Song of the Lark* had been in the closeness of the artist to the experiences thrown into the novel, in the absence of a long perspective, a large enlightenment. It offers quite another kind of pleasure, the pleasure that is given so often in the novels of H. G. Wells: the intellectual pleasure of following a mind of unusual sensitiveness and power as it comes to terms with experience. Nothing could be calmer than the manner of *Lucy Gayheart,* and in its finest part, where Harry Gordon surveys his life, his associations with the Gayhearts and above all with Lucy, by the long perspective and the large enlightenment a new depth is given to the incidents and musings which had come before us in the earlier sections. In those sections calmness had too often lapsed into heaviness, perspective faded to indifference.

III

Most of 1935 was given to Isabelle Hambourg, who came to America in March with her husband. She was gravely ill and Willa Cather, much alarmed, arranged for her to go into a New York hospital, and made a daily visit during the three weeks she was there. Willa Cather was told at once that Isabelle could not recover. The stay in the hospital brought unexpected improvement, however, and when Jan Hambourg undertook to conduct a summer course in Chicago, Isabelle insisted on going with him. Willa Cather accompanied the Hambourgs to lighten the journey and stayed to have an eye on Isabelle during weeks when Jan was much harried by working in a place that was unfamiliar to him, and in conditions less favorable than his hopeful and mercurial spirit had expected. The Hambourgs sailed in August; Willa Cather crossed a few days later and after a few weeks in Venice rejoined them for a final two months in Paris. The mortal illness of her friend, the wasting of her beauty, the decline in her intense response to life, left a mark on Willa Cather's writings during the next few years. Isabelle died three years afterward at Sorrento. Willa Cather never saw her again.

The very title of her next book suggested a sense of the falling away of the years, the fading of the world she had known. In a foreword to *Not Under Forty* that was belligerent, and by its brevity seemed even more belligerent than it was, she construed the title as a warning that those born in the present century would find the spirit of the book outside their range. Willa Cather was sure that she and her writings already belonged to the past. And out of this past she evoked the memory of two friends, long dead, Mrs. J. T. Fields and Sarah Orne Jewett; her recollections of the Charles Street days are at the core of *Not Under Forty*, which contains also the vivid account of her meeting with Madame Franklin Grout and papers on Thomas Mann and Katherine Mansfield. The essay on Miss Jewett was expanded from a preface written in 1925 to a selection Willa Cather had made of Miss Jewett's best stories, published in two volumes by Houghton Mifflin. She had been grieved and disturbed by the neglect of Miss Jewett's writings. She was sure they were indestructible, that a few persons with perfect taste would always turn to them as she did, taking down from her shelves now this book and now another, and always judging the pictures, the patterns, the phrases as fine as they had seemed in memory or finer. The essay is the most penetrating analysis ever written of the effects in Miss Jewett's prose, and of her sense of structure in fiction. It is also rich in provocative remarks about the prevailing climate of literary taste and opinion. With an asperity unusual in her mature critical writings Willa Cather defines the sort of reader and reviewer who seemed to her to be in the ascendant: a person born in Europe or of European parentage, reared in the jumble of a large Eastern city, drenched in the theories of Freud. Such a person would be completely impercipient of everything that mattered in the stories of Sarah Orne Jewett; his judgment on them would be that of invincible ignorance. More or less consciously Willa Cather was speaking for her own writings as much as for those of her friend. She had no confidence that her art could be understood where Miss Jewett's was neglected. They had worked in the same tradition; they belonged to the same period.

How strongly she had this feeling and some of the reasons for it appear in the next story she wrote, "The Old Beauty." This *nouvelle* was composed in 1936, probably in the autumn, and in 1937 was offered to the *Woman's Home Companion*. The editor, Gertrude Lane, who had been pleased by *Lucy Gayheart* and other shorter pieces, confessed that though she would publish "The Old Beauty," it did not stir her enthusiasm. Willa Cather asked for the return of the manuscript, made no other attempt to arrange for its publication in a magazine, and laid it aside for an eventual book of middle-length stories. That book, to which "The Old Beauty" gave the title, did not appear until after her death.

The disappointment of Miss Lane and Willa Cather's decision not to send the story elsewhere are both significant of the growing distance between her work and spirit and the temper of the age in which she was living out her last years. "I think one should go out with one's time," the Old Beauty says, and in that, as in so much else, spoke for her creator.

Nostalgia for an earlier period is a feeling that runs the length of Willa Cather's mature writing from *O Pioneers!*

to the last story she finished, "The Best Years," with its title an echo of *"optima dies . . . prima fugit."* Up to 1936 she had been drawn chiefly, almost entirely, to what was creative and heroic in the past, to the breaking of "the wild land," to the preservation of what was fine in old ways by a bold adaptation to new circumstances, to the survival against huge odds of a great idea or feeling. In "The Old Beauty" she is more simply conservative: she is recalling people and a code neither creative nor heroic, not in any obvious way precious—the way of life of an upper class unaffected by art or religion, in the years of her own introduction to the world of great Eastern cities, in "the deep claret-coloured closing years of Victoria's reign." The narrator of the story, Henry Seabury, an Anglo-American, reproaches himself in 1922—the year when for Willa Cather the world broke in two—for having taken the end of the nineteenth century as an ordinary stretch in time, for having lived the years of his youth without an appreciation of what good fortune he had had in being young then rather than a generation later. It is the same with Gabrielle Longstreet, the old beauty. Her beauty had drawn about her in the last two decades of the nineteenth century a multitude of the most remarkable men of the period; she reproaches herself in 1922, and has done so since the end of the war, for having supposed that every period brought remarkable men, for having taken the homage offered as what beauty may always expect. Now she travels with a gallery of photographs, reads everything that appears about the statesmen and soldiers who had flocked to her house in London or in New York—one is clearly Earl Kitchener, another resembles Sir Charles Dilke—and enjoys, rather grimly, "living her life over again, more understandingly than she had lived it for the first time."

The story is set at Aix-les-Bains, seen by Willa Cather for the first time in 1923, and the place of her encounter with Madame Franklin Grout in 1930. Seabury, who has spent thirty years in China, has been unhappy on his return to Europe because of the almost universal changes, and lingers at Aix because there both the place and many of the visitors agree with his memories. Gabrielle stays on for the same reason. Even at Aix things happen that would not have happened in the 1890's; and it is one of these things, a very slight thing, that leads to her death. She has motored with Seabury to the Grande Chartreuse, and on the way back their car collides with one that carries two young American girls, "bobbed, hatless, clad in dirty white knickers and sweaters." Gabrielle has a weak heart, but the shock that ends her life is not the collision but the subsequent encounter with the two girls, who are at first noisy and then impudent. It was not the bruises that did for her, Gabrielle believes, but the dirty white knickers of these "creatures." This final and fatal incident—Gabrielle dies that night—issued directly from an experience of Willa Cather's, and the decisive role she gave it shows much of her own feeling about the ways of her younger contemporaries.

She thought well of "The Old Beauty." It is a finely conducted story, subdued in all its tones like the rest of her fiction in the 1930's, and with a sureness about the right dimensions and the pace that *Lucy Gayheart* lacked. It does bear the impress of age and unhappiness, but gives no ground for supposing there had been any failure in power. There was no reason why the narrowing sympathies of Willa Cather should have threatened her art: "The Old Beauty" might have been followed by a series of sensitive, unhappy, perfectly executed works expressing not only her distance from the world about her but her pleasure in imaginative recapture of an earlier time. The artist who had written *My Ántonia* in her forties might be expected to write such works as these in her sixties.

IV

What followed was one such work, the last of her novels, *Sapphira and the Slave Girl*, in which she rendered the quality of life in the Northern Neck of Virginia not in her own childhood (only the epilogue does that), but in the time when her grandmothers were young women. Willa Cather began this novel in the autumn of 1937. The strain and exhaustion that had left a mark on the earlier books of *Lucy Gayheart* had passed, though she was never to recover the energy that enabled her to write *Death Comes for the Archbishop* in two years of unalloyed happiness. It was three years since she had been at work on a novel, and she had missed the sense of unity and purpose a long fiction gave to life, and the happy companionship with creatures of memory and imagination. She had long intended to make a novel from her recollections of Virginia and from the countless stories about a yet earlier time she had heard of from older members of the family and their friends. She had promised her father she would do so. During the years when she was living in the Bank Street apartment she seldom had spoken of Virginia and it did not seem to belong to her imaginative life. The deaths of her father and mother and her own approach to old age led her to dwell with ever increasing pleasure and preoccupation on small incidents in the life of her childhood and on the stories she had heard so often. Miss Lewis recalls that when at last Willa Cather began *Sapphira and the Slave Girl* it was with her whole power and concentration.

> It was [Miss Lewis notes] a novel written against circumstance. One catastrophe after another blocked its path; the sudden death of her brother Douglass— the most bitter, I think, of all her losses; the death of Isabelle Hambourg; the second World War. . . . Even Jaffrey, which she had always found such a happy refuge, was largely spoiled for her by the great hurricane of 1938, which wrecked the woods for miles around.
>
> Against all these things, she worked at *Sapphira* with a resoluteness, a sort of fixed determination which I think was different from her ordinary working mood; as if she were bringing all her powers into play to save this, whatever else was lost. She often worked far beyond her strength. In the summers of 1938 and 1939 we stayed in New York through the heat until the end of July, because she did not want to interrupt what she was then doing. She finished the story at Grand Manan in September, 1940.

The invasion and the fall of France led her to say: "There seems to be no future at all for people of my generation." In consoling Jan Hambourg for the loss of his wife she declared that for persons like Isabelle there could be no outcome of the war which could compensate for what it had removed from the world—the buildings, the people, the habits of life and thought. She seldom spoke of

the war, and never in casual conversation; she felt it far
more deeply than she had felt the First World War; she felt
it was the end of all. Like the deaths in her own circle, and
the devastation of her ideal scene for writing, but much
more powerfully, the war bade her record her memories
while there was yet a little time.

In the early spring of 1938, accompanied by Edith
Lewis, she had gone to Virginia, and stayed for some
weeks at Winchester, to walk over the old ground and
renew her sense of what it had meant to live there. Miss
Lewis notes:

> It was as memorable an experience, as intense and
> thrilling in its way, as those journeys to New
> Mexico, when she was writing the *Archbishop*.
> Every bud and leaf and flower seemed to speak to
> her with a peculiar poignancy, every slope of the
> land, every fence and wall, rock and stream. I re-
> member how she spoke of the limp, drooping acacia
> trees in bloom along all the roadsides—how they
> had the shiftless look that characterized so many
> Southern things, but how their wood was the tough-
> est of all, and was in great demand for fence-posts.
> She found again the wild azalea growing on the
> gravelly banks of the road up Timber Ridge, and
> gathered great bunches of it. The dogwood, in the
> almost leafless woods, had a dazzling beauty that
> spring. Her delight in these things gave, I think, a
> great freshness of detail to *Sapphira*.
>
> The countryside was very much changed. But she
> refused to look at its appearance; she looked through
> and through it, as if it were transparent, to what she
> knew as its reality. Willowshade, her old home, had
> been bought by a man who had always borne a sort
> of grudge against the place; he chopped down the
> great willow trees that gave Willowshade its name,
> and destroyed the high box hedges that seemed so
> wonderful to Willa Cather when she was a child.
> The house itself had become so ruinous and forlorn
> that she did not go into it, only stood and looked
> down at it from a distance. All these transforma-
> tions, instead of disheartening her, seemed to light

a fierce inner flame that illumined all her pictures of the past.[2]

The rest was surprisingly like what it had been in her childhood. The suspension footbridge across Back Creek had gone; and the pedestrian, as is our modern way, had to expose himself on a solid structure that could carry the heavy truck, bus, and motor traffic from Winchester to Romney. At the mill farm, which is the center of the action, the mill itself was disused and dilapidated. The mill house, where Willa Cather's maternal great-grandparents once lived, had suffered little change, though the slave cabins had disappeared. The markers in the private burying-ground were still legible, though one had first to brush away the myrtle with which it was overgrown. The road from the farm to the village ran in another place, but when one reached the postmistress's house—where Mrs. Gore, Willa Cather's great-aunt, had lived—there was no great disappointment; and the other village house that appears in the novel, her birthplace—the home of her grandmother Mrs. Boak—shaded by maples, was also much as it had been. To be on the scene meant that Willa Cather could readily remount the half century that had passed since she lived there; and from many a family reminiscence, told at the farm on the Divide or in the house in Red Cloud, she knew that the district as she had known it in childhood was almost exactly as it had been a quarter century earlier, in 1856, the year in which the action of *Sapphira and the Slave Girl* occurs.

More than any other of Willa Cather's novels this is a study of manners, a picture of how a little society lived in conditions that had vanished forever, painted by the one living person who had the knowledge and could transpose it into art. A number of the personages are included not for any role in the action, but simply because they were important parts of this society as it lived on in Willa Cather's memory. Mandy Ringer, the poor-white mountain

---

[2] The house has changed hands again. The present owner has repaired it and freshened its appearance. Nothing can make up for the destruction of the willows, but some trees are flourishing in front of it, and though the approach is certainly not a thing of beauty, it is much less dispiriting than when Willa Cather refused to enter in 1938.

woman, has no role at all in the action: she is in the book to remind us that women who could neither read nor write, and who depended for sustenance on the most sketchy kind of farming, were among the most intelligent and delightful in the countryside; by her vigor and good humor in the midst of every kind of misfortune Mandy Ringer becomes a witness for the Old South. It is the same with Dr. Clevenger, the Baltimore physician who lives in Winchester because his wife will live nowhere else; he has nothing to do with the action, but every word he says, every tone in his voice, every movement of his body, is treasured as it might be if he were the hero of the novel: he is another witness for the Old South, and it is no surprise to learn that when the war came, his place was on Robert E. Lee's personal staff.

Customs are remembered with the same intensity: the waving of the fly-brush made of peacock feathers during dinners in the hot season; the cutting into thin strips of all worn-out garments and linen, the dyeing of these with logwood, copperas, or cochineal, and the weaving of them into stout carpets; the driving out daily through June to see the masses of wild laurel which covered the mountains with "drifts of rose or peach or flesh colour." Customs like these were a part of the way of life in Back Creek Valley a hundred years ago; and always there is the unspoken comment: was it not a gracious and a wise way, would it not have been a pleasure to live in that place at that time? Once the comment is spoken. The richest massing of the laurel was on the main road west of the village, where there was a double S of four great loops around hills of rock. Even when the laurels were not in bloom, this was a place of beauty. A peddler or a poor farmer passing on foot paused to rest here or "walked lingeringly"; when people in the district spoke of the double S, "their voices took on something slow and dreamy, as if recalling the place itself; the shade, the unstained loveliness, the pleasant feeling one had there." Now the loops are denuded and ugly—a mechanical civilization did not set any store by them; and presently "the destroying armament of modern road-building" will blast them away. Once people came across the Atlantic to see the laurel bloom there; but that was in another time, which Willa Cather felt to be her own.

As its title suggests, the action in the novel turns upon slavery. When Sapphira Dodderidge, whose father was a large slave-owning landholder in Loudoun County, "took a long step down" and married Henry Colbert, a miller's son and an immigrant's grandson, she decided to put the Blue Ridge between herself and the aristocratic society in which she had lived until she was twenty-four. She terminated the lease of a mill farm in the Back Creek district of Frederick County which had been on the Dodderidge land roll since the days of Lord Fairfax, and began her married life there with a score of slaves. There she appears in the novel, thirty years later, still entirely a Loudoun County aristocrat, the representative of that element in the Old South to which slavery seemed—as it did not in the Back Creek Valley—an entirely natural institution. She treated her slaves as slaves, often with kindness, often with caprice, sometimes with cruelty, always as slaves. Her daughter, Rachel Blake, trying to account for the unhappiness she had felt during all the years when she was a girl at home, and for her deep disapproval of her mother, at last remembers "how she hated her mother's voice in sarcastic reprimand to the servants! And she hated it in contemptuous indulgence." It was the voice of the slaveowner. It was because she was wholly the slaveowner that Sapphira formed the nasty and petty design that produces the central situation in the book, as it is by their attitudes to slavery that the other characters respond to this design.

Sapphira, who is in her middle fifties, is in an advanced state of dropsy and has the easy suspicions of the immobilized. On the slightest of evidence she concludes that her husband has a personal interest in a young slave girl, the golden-colored mulatto, Nancy; that he either sleeps with her or will do so, since he will not allow Nancy to be sold. Sapphira then forms her design: she invites his nephew, Martin Colbert, a known woman-chaser, and bids Nancy care for his room. Martin, like Sapphira, has the attitudes of the slaveowners in Loudoun County; he attempts, as was expected, to make the best of his windfall. Nancy's confidante is Mrs. Blake, who had added to her instinctive dislike of slavery an intellectual disapproval as she absorbed the ideas of the postmistress, a local woman, who subscribes to an abolitionist paper. It is Mrs. Blake who foils her mother and her cousin and with the help of her neighbors puts Nancy on the underground railway and sees her across the Potomac. Between the extreme positions of Mrs. Blake and of Sapphira and Martin there are many gradations. Nancy's mother, Till, Sapphira's housekeeper, does not lift a finger; trained in Loudoun County, she accepts the institution of slavery as a natural fact; but after Nancy's escape her gratitude to Mrs. Blake lasts as long as life. Sampson, the foreman at the mill, is the most intelligent and independent of the slaves (he has, however, refused his freedom); he knows what is afoot, dares to show Martin Colbert that he knows, is dissatisfied that his master, usually so clear in his responses and quick in his decisions, temporizes and appears confused.

Henry Colbert's attitude toward slavery is the most complex of all. He had grown up in Loudoun County, but his father had never owned a slave. He had always obscurely felt slavery to be wrong; and a deeply religious man—reared a Lutheran and attending the Baptist chapel in Back Creek Valley—he constantly searched the Scriptures for an answer, marking all the passages that might have a bearing with a great "S," and reading them in sequence for what reciprocal illumination they might have. Joseph had been in slavery, and Daniel, and other prophets; and their escape had been hailed, but had the experience been all loss? There were exhortations to deal with slaves mercifully, and with tolerance, but there was no exhortation to get rid of slavery itself. The Scriptures gave no answer, even when one sat up the night through, reading and meditating. He knew no other source from which he could draw an answer he could depend upon. For Nancy he had a gentle paternal feeling, something more personal, if innocent, than for any other of his wife's slaves; he hated that she should come to ruin under his roof and by his nephew. But when his daughter Rachel asks him for the money needed in getting Nancy away, just as when Sampson had asked him to interpose, the strong man is parted from his strength. What he does is pathetically unlike his usual self—he falls into casuistry. Henry Colbert will not give the money, but he tells Rachel it is in his coat, and the coat will be hanging that night beside his open window; he lies awake, but silent, until he has heard her take it and creep away. By laying the responsibility on her, not only does he require her to become a thief, he provokes a complete breach between Rachel and Sapphira.

The evil of slavery is shown by its effects on individuals. There is an evidence of Willa Cather's persisting indifference to politics in the wide inaccuracy of her reference to the date when the Fugitive Slave Law was passed; for the legal and political aspects of the institution she has no interest. Her interest is in what slavery has done to harden Sapphira and Martin, to inhibit Till's maternal feelings, to take the edge off Sampson's will, to drive the slave girl into exile, to paralyze the conscience and stultify the intelligence of Henry Colbert. These are the disasters that have the foreground; there are others, episodically represented—a slave who loses his wits because the girl he loves is taken to Baltimore, a family of poor whites pigging it on the mountains because they will not take work that would put them side by side with colored people. No one is the better for slavery, and only those who oppose it root and branch are safe from its poison.

The tract from the past rendered in *Sapphira* has upon it the great spreading stain of slavery, and from the stain the action arises. The reader is often persuaded to forget the stain—the picture of slavery is framed in leisure, grace, peace, and happiness. Because of the frame *Sapphira* does not affect one in the manner of a problem novel. The problem is exhibited with no minimizing, but the other traits of life in Back Creek Valley before the War between the States are also exhibited not to deepen one's sense of the problem directly or by contrast, not to obliterate the problem—but without relation to the problem. The people in the valley were in no way remarkable—the last phrase in the novel is Till's and depends perhaps on a Loudoun County set of values: "here where nobody was anybody much"—but Willa Cather cared for them, as Till had always done, though like Till she thought it was better to live somewhere else. She cared for them as she cared for the people in "The Old Beauty," because in their way of life there were qualities that belonged to the age in which she had been young and that had disappeared in the age in which she was growing old. Now she no longer wished to contemplate the heroic moments in American life—the moment when the French made a civilization in the Canadian wilderness, the moment when the Southwest was at its apex, the moment when the wild land of Nebraska took

the first impress of the pioneer. Now it was enough to
evoke quite ordinary moments from the past; and these too
had vanished, taking with them a burden of beauty for
which there was nothing to compensate.

V

The retrospective mood of the last books coincided with a
rereading of all her works as Willa Cather prepared them
for the substantial, ornate "Library Edition" that Houghton Mifflin Company brought out during 1937 and 1938.
There were twelve volumes, to which was added *Sapphira
and the Slave Girl* in 1941. To reread her work was to
relive her creative life and, rediscovering the work of her
youth, she sought to bring it up to the level of her maturity. Willa Cather freely revised the first pages of *My Ántonia* and the last part of *The Song of the Lark*. To the
latter she attached the brief preface she had written for the
1932 edition, explaining that she was well aware of the
book's defects and in particular the way in which the story
drops to a flat indeterminate ending. She might have said
that life is often like this; but she defined the real reason
for what she felt was an imbalance in the work when she
said that "success is never so interesting as struggle—not
even to the successful." Once Thea Kronborg's career ends
in victory, everything else is anticlimax.

There were other changes in the edition. "A Death in the
Desert" was dropped from *Youth and the Bright Medusa*,
as well as the Christina Rossetti epigraph. *Not Under
Forty* was meekly renamed *Literary Encounters*, and the
defiant prefatory note that gave the book its original title
was eliminated. The dedication of *One of Ours* to her
mother and of *April Twilights* to her father were omitted,
perhaps because her parents had died so recently that all
dedication to them now seemed meaningless. She had already removed Jan Hambourg's name from the dedication
of later editions of *A Lost Lady*, and the book remained
undedicated here; she retained the dedication to him of
The Professor's House, while *O Pioneers!* remained inscribed to the memory of Sarah Orne Jewett, and *The Song
of the Lark* to Isabelle McClung. And finally she altered
the chronology of her work. Although written after *Alex-*

ander's Bridge, O Pioneers! received first place in the collection. She had once said in an article entitled "My First Novels (There Were Two)" that *O Pioneers!* was spontaneous and *Alexander's Bridge* contrived. In the end she could perhaps claim that of her two "first" novels, the novel about Alexandra Bergson was really the first.[3]

3 Issued in 1937 were (I) *O Pioneers!* (II) *The Song of the Lark,* (III) *Alexander's Bridge* and *April Twilights,* (IV) *My Ántonia,* (V) *One of Ours,* (VI) *Youth and the Bright Medusa.* In 1938: (VII) *A Lost Lady,* (VIII) *The Professor's House,* (IX) *Death Comes for the Archbishop,* (X) *Shadows on the Rock,* (XI) *Lucy Gayheart* and *My Mortal Enemy,* (XII) *Obscure Destinies* and *Literary Encounters.* In 1941: (XIII) *Sapphira and the Slave Girl.* A number of the sets were autographed and issued as the "Autograph Edition."

12

Epilogue: *a Cadence, a Quality of Voice . . .*

1941–1947

THE SEVEN YEARS that remained to Willa Cather after the publication of *Sapphira and the Slave Girl* were an epilogue to her career as a writer. Only two stories were completed, one no more than a sketch. A third, more ambitious but not intended as a full-length novel, was never brought beyond a fragment of a rough draft.

Throughout these years Willa Cather was in poor health. During her lifetime she had been relatively free from illness, save for a period in childhood when she had what may have been a mild attack of polio which affected her leg for some time, and periods when she suffered from extreme nervous fatigue; but not until 1940 did she have an illness that sapped her vitality. It was a condition to which she could not become accustomed. The vigorous woman who thought nothing of a twelve-mile walk on her Canadian island or an afternoon stroll around Central Park, now found herself reduced to comparative inaction. Work was impossible, and much of the discouragement of her last seven years had this simple physical origin.

She was ill in a world that was crumbling about her. To one who had lived through 1914–18 the experience of the new war was not unfamiliar; but now she was nearing seventy and the ever present sense of catastrophe was much harder to bear. As Hitler's bombs crashed ruin on places long loved in Europe, and America was increasingly regimented for a total war effort, Willa Cather felt that the German dictator was smashing not only the Old World but also the last vestiges of freedom in the New. The war, she told her younger friends, was hardest on older persons. The young, after all, had no beautiful past to regret. What brought the war close to her was correspondence with men in the armed forces. Most of her novels were republished in the rectangular army editions that could easily be carried in a soldier's pocket, and men in lonely outposts read her and wrote to her. She could not leave their letters unanswered, even though it taxed her strength to reply. And often she found herself writing as well to grieving parents when some of her correspondents fell in action. Nothing in the war stirred her so much as the liberation of her beloved France; and Joseph Kessel's account of the underground in *Army of Shadows* moved her to write enthusiastically to Blanche and Alfred Knopf, who published it, and to endorse the book (a rare thing for her) as telling "incident by incident, sacrifice by sacrifice, the courage and the constancy (and the resourcefulness) of all the unconquered and unbought people of France."

She was in ill health when she made her last trip across the continent to see her brother Roscoe in 1941. Her hand was in a brace and she was in a state of exhaustion. During the 1930's she and Roscoe had rarely met, but their letters, charged with the memories of the years, had brought them closer and closer together. Of all her brothers and sisters, he was the one who had been nearest to her, the one who understood her nature and her work the most fully. Willa Cather felt such a need to be with him now—he was suffering from a heart ailment—that despite her physical discomfort she traveled to San Francisco during the summer's heat, pausing only briefly at Chicago for much needed rest. Miss Lewis recalls that both Roscoe and his wife thought that Willa Cather looked "very frail." Nevertheless the reunion was a happy one and her hand improved sufficiently during her stay in California to enable her to remove the brace. She could not shake off the sense of fatigue, however, and rather than face the heat of Manhattan she journeyed on to British Columbia and spent a vacation at Victoria, where she did little but sit in the garden and read. She returned to New York in early autumn and promptly entered the French Hospital for a rest. This was her last long journey and the last time she saw Roscoe. He died in his sleep four years later. Willa Cather got the news while vacationing at Northeast Harbor, where she had just completed "The Best Years," a story intended for him and filled with memories of their common Nebraska childhood. She had been four when Roscoe was born and he figured in all her family memories, early and late. His passing was for her a time of deep heartbreak; in letter after letter to friends she could talk only of what he had meant to her. They had taken long trips together on horseback and in buck-wagons through the Northwest and Southwest before motor roads had been cut through the mountains. On one such journey Isabelle McClung had accompanied them. Willa Cather, alone of the three, now survived.

During the winter and spring of 1942 she showed signs of increasing illness and in April she began to run a high fever. At Presbyterian Hospital a gall-bladder condition was diagnosed; and at the end of July she re-entered this hospital for an operation. Her convalescence was slow and she never regained her former health. In her letters she speaks in particular of her loss of weight and of the way in which her clothes no longer fitted her.

Because of the war it was impossible for her and Miss Lewis to return to their North Atlantic retreat at Grand Manan, and during these last years they finally found that the Asticou Inn, at Northeast Harbor in Maine, provided the most congenial summer surroundings. It was here that "The Best Years" and the brief sketch "Before Breakfast" were written, the latter a kind of *De senectute* in fictional form, an admission that "Plucky youth is more bracing than enduring age," but at the same time an assertion that however old one may be, life doesn't really change; if old age brings its trials and life has had its difficulties, the process of living is still a challenge and a delight. The elderly man who is set to musing about these matters by a geologist's chance remark about the hundred and thirty-six million years of life of the island where the tale is set—an island like Willa Cather's—contemplates a snowshoe hare nibbling clover, reaches for his eyedrops, and leaning back his head to use them, glimpses the morning star. Lucy Gayheart with all life before her had looked at it in the evening sky feeling that recognition had flashed between her and its twinkling distance "that joy of saluting what is far above one was an eternal thing." So had it been for Willa Cather at Dieppe as the kite rose, and in Washington Square as the pigeons wheeled out of the dust; and now the elderly man, his head tilted back to receive the eyedrops of age, observes Venus. "Serene, impersonal splendor. Merciless perfection, ageless sovereignty. The poor hare and his clover, poor Grenfell and his eyedrops!" Like Willa Cather in the months after her operation he feels "limp." And he muses that man has "his little hour, with heat and cold and a time-sense suited to his endurance."

II

She might thus, at threescore and ten, muse on time's flight, but unlike other writers she had the distinct comfort of not outliving her reputation. Her books continued to sell and to be read; her public continued to grow; translations were made in many lands. There was a constant clamor from anthologists to republish her and every now and again some movie-producer would discover her novels and want to film them. One producer dreamed of a great panoramic *Death Comes for the Archbishop* (doubtless in technicolor) and another sought to obtain rights to *The Song of the Lark*. Willa Cather disliked being anthologized and disliked almost as much being used as a school text; she told Alfred Knopf that she felt literature was so badly taught now in the schools that children would grow up with unpleasant memories of being forced to read her writings, instead of discovering them for themselves. As for the dazzling offers from Hollywood, she had had her one experience with the Warner production of *A Lost Lady* and that sufficed; in her will she expressly prohibited theatrical or cinematic treatment of her fiction. Her artistic integrity was not for sale to the highest bidder to be turned into "supercolossal" films, and her reason was simple: she did not want her name attached to dialogue written by some person whose name and ability she did not know and to a product that would not be hers but that of many hands. It offended her artist's sense, her belief in herself as a literary craftsman. She had worked in a great medium after taking years to master it and saw no need to be transposed into any other. This law she made absolute also for radio. She permitted her work to go into Braille for the blind, but not to be recorded for them, fearing that through a reading of it in this way it might some day be broadcast surrounded by commercials. She relented only to repeated requests from composers to set her early poem "Spanish Johnny" to music, and a number of settings were made. Her concession to the machine age, where art was concerned, was to the phonograph. It was a great comfort to be able to play recordings of great singers and the quartets of Beethoven. Music remained a passion to the last.

Honors continued to come. In 1944, her seventieth year, she was awarded the gold medal of the National Institute of Arts and Letters. She had been honored once before, by the Academy, in 1930, with the Howells medal for fiction, and in 1933 had received the first annual Prix Femina Américaine for *Shadows on the Rock*. Now the totality of her work was being crowned. What made the occasion of the presentation (on May 19, 1944) particularly joyous for her was the presence on the dais of S. S. McClure, who at the same time received the Institute's order of merit for his services to literature. Those who were in the audience still remember the spontaneity with which Willa Cather spread out her arms and gave the veteran editor and her one-time boss a public hug as she met him on the stage. Also receiving awards on this occasion were Theodore Dreiser and Paul Robeson, the latter for "good diction on the stage."

The Institute honor was the last of a series that began as far back as 1917 with an honorary degree from her own University of Nebraska, followed in ensuing years with similar degrees from Michigan, Columbia, Yale, and New York universities and later California, Creighton in her home state, and Smith College. In June 1931 she received an honorary degree from Princeton at the same time as Colonel Charles A. Lindbergh, Frank B. Kellogg, and Newton D. Baker, but, said the *New York Times*, the conferring of the Doctorate of Letters on Willa Cather "seemed to attract the greatest attention." This was a tribute alike to her art and to the fact that she was the first woman to receive an honorary degree from the university.

III

There remained at the end certain of the steadfast friends of other years, the loyal companionship and devotion of Edith Lewis, and the visits, when they were in New York, of such long-standing musical intimates as Myra Hess or the Menuhins, now grown to maturity. High among these friends were Blanche and Alfred Knopf and Ethel Jones Litchfield. Knopf still, as during all the years, carefully remembered festive occasions, such as birthdays and of course Christmases, and sent Willa Cather the rare sherries and vintage wines she relished; he had from far back ministered not only to her artistic sensibilities and literary interests but to her highly developed palate. There had been times when, from her summer's isolation at Grand Manan, she would suddenly appeal to him, sometimes by urgent wire, for candy or for such comestibles as wild rice, tins of Italian tomato paste, and supplies of garlic to be artfully compounded into a *risotto* washed down by an appropriate wine. Knopf had always respected to the full Willa Cather's tastes and had never made demands on her for the publicizing of her work, knowing her aversion to public encounters. There had also been a common interest in the manufacturing problems involved in her books. From the time of her *Home Monthly* days the smell of print and the problems of the composing-room were familiar to Willa Cather. More often than not it was she who dictated the kind of type to be used, demanding, for instance, that *Lucy Gayheart* be set in exactly the same type face as *A Lost Lady*; or choosing the Monotype Old Style No. 31 in which *Death Comes for the Archbishop* was set because, in her rationale of printing, she felt this particular book had to have the air of being printed on a country press for old people to read. Legibility was therefore all-important. Her decisions were always deliberate and carefully made. When objections were raised that the dialogue in *Shadows on the Rock* was stiff and stilted she explained that this had been her intention; she had translated every conversation in her mind back into French, to give to the readers the effect of characters talking the Quebec French of 1697.

During a quarter of a century what began as a cordial business relationship between publisher and author had long ago become a mellow friendship of shared interests and social occasions (Willa Cather for instance attended regularly the annual reception the Knopfs held for Serge Koussevitsky after his opening Boston Symphony concert in New York). To Knopf fell also the never ending process of warding off from Willa Cather demands for speech-making and attendance at innumerable functions, which are the inevitable lot of the successful writer. Above all, Knopf had promptly published her work, defended it in the marketplace, and helped maintain and augment her reputation with all the resources of a modern publishing house. To the last she was grateful for his loyalty and care and for his deeply founded belief that "close personal and friendly bonds . . . should hold publisher and author together."

Sigrid Undset continued to come over from Brooklyn, where she lived, for an occasional dinner with Willa Cather, and of the younger generation a warm friendship had developed with Stephen Tennant, an English artist and writer who had written to her about *A Lost Lady* when he was still a student at the Slade School in London. The son of Lord and Lady Glenconner and a nephew of the late Lord Asquith, he had known many of the older writers in England—Yeats, Hardy, Barrie—as well as some of the newer, including Virginia Woolf. When in America, he would have long talks with Willa Cather, and often he brought her personal messages from her transatlantic colleagues. It was he who wrote the preface for the posthumous volume *Willa Cather on Writing*.

Mrs. Litchfield, whom she saw regularly during her last winter as she had done for a number of years, remembers the grace and spirit of Willa Cather's talk, the unaltered ritual with which she entertained her intimate friends, her continued interest in music and books and food; there were sometimes casual meals in restaurants and leisurely, if now abbreviated, walks in Central Park. At the end of March 1947 there was a morning in which Yehudi and Hephzibah Menuhin came to see her with their children a few hours before sailing for England. They were going to give a series of popularly priced concerts. Willa Cather had known them for sixteen years and, as did her nieces, they filled the apartment on Park Avenue with the voices of youth. She thought that the beauty in the natures of the Menuhin children transcended mere "giftedness," and she confided to one correspondent that she would rather have almost any other chapter of her life left out than the Menuhin chapter, which had brought her so much happiness. At the end of that morning the Menuhins quietly slipped on their things, the appointed cabs were waiting, and they drove away. This was the last time they saw Willa Cather.

Of these last months Miss Lewis writes: "During the

winter and spring of 1946–1947 up to the time of her death she never lived the life of an invalid; she went out nearly every day, walked, read a great deal, dictated letters, saw a few friends, attended to all the small chores of life. Her interest in things, her talk, were full of life and spirit. It was only her bodily strength that failed."

Twelve days before the end she talked of her plans for the summer. She had begun to think of a trip to the West, but there was a hope of doing some writing again; the cottage at Northeast Harbor seemed to her most likely to meet her best needs. On April 24 she remained late in bed and had her lunch brought in to her. She chatted of a number of things with Miss Lewis and then fell into a sleep from which she awoke in midafternoon complaining of a severe head pain. Death came for Willa Cather with a single swift step at about four o'clock on that day. Four days later she was laid to rest, as she had asked, in the quiet burial ground of Jaffrey, in New Hampshire, in the shadow of Mount Monadnock, in the stubborn soil of New England.

IV

"To note an artist's limitations is but to define his talent," Willa Cather once wrote in discussing Sarah Orne Jewett. And she went on to make a highly significant distinction between *reportage* and creative writing, by which I suppose she meant imaginative writing. "A reporter," she observed, "can write equally well about everything that is presented to his view, but a creative writer can do his best only with what lies within the range and character of his talent." What she may have had in mind were the criticisms that had been addressed to her repeatedly in American journals in which reviewers accused her of neglecting the world around her by writing only of the past. There has been for a long time a tendency among book-reviewers to lecture novelists for "turning their back" on this subject and on that—as if the novelist must create his novels on prescribed subjects like reporters sent out to cover a disaster or a political meeting. The great novelists have always been those who wrote about the world to which they were drawn and which they deeply experienced and not those who "collect" what passes for "local color" and then "work up" a subject. Willa Cather had neither the capacious imagination of the Balzacian, the Dickensian, or the Jamesian novelist nor a gift for elaborating fictional panoramas; she deliberately arrived at a novel unfurnished, almost bare by comparison with the fiction of her immediate predecessors. She had no capacity or desire to construct tight and intricate plots. She was not a writer of "love stories"; indeed "love," in the conventional literary sense, scarcely figures in her novels. These are not, perhaps, strictly the limitations of the artist; they *are* distinctly the things she was not. She limited herself to a narrative of people seeking to master their environment, to farm-folk or missionaries or colonists, or, at the opposite pole, to artists (and mainly singers), seeking in their fugitive world to maintain their integrity amid the tensions of modern life. The passion in her books is for the process of living and conquering, for preserving things as they are; and the intensity in her books rises from her own feelings about her people. Motive and image, carefully organized in compact, dramatic statement, are central to her narrative.

Willa Cather was unyielding—sometimes belligerently so —in her refusal to accept change. Yet by some curious alchemy of the spirit her inflexibility was transmuted into the very core of her art. Her ultimate symbol was the stratified, immovable rock, "the utmost expression of human need"; and this is understandable when we think of her, in the end, as a kind of monolith of rugged individualism, an exalter of the pioneer and the builder. The enduring rock knows only the slowest change; it yields only to earthquake or the blast of man-made explosive. Willa Cather's inner malaise in a world that underwent violent change during her lifetime caused her to look ever backward at what was enduring. "It has changed less than most places," Flaubert's niece remarked to Willa Cather at Aixles-Bains, where they had their chance encounter. She remembered the remark. She spoke of herself as having written certain of her essays in *Not Under Forty* "for the backward, and by one of their number," suggesting that the forward-looking, who were under forty, were perhaps in the truest sense the most backward. In the sketch "Before Breakfast" the note of joy at the end is that Grenfell finds "Nothing had changed. Everything was the same. . . ."

To look forward meant acceptance of the ephemeral things of daily life and acceptance too of the inevitable wear of the decades. It meant growing old. Therefore Willa Cather looked only to where there had been youth and high hope and bright beginning; her novels are in effect a reverie, a "remembrance of things past." Her famous remark about the world breaking in two was made as she neared her fiftieth year and the rock of her life had been blasted with the dynamite of the First World War. A new generation of little goblin men had succeeded the pioneers. The past could give Willa Cather a sense of consorting with the heroic men, a sense of clarity and order undiscoverable in the rushing present. In the past, as Sir Max Beerbohm once observed, all is "a work of art free from irrelevancies and loose ends. There are, for our vision, comparatively few people in it, and all of them are interesting people. The dullards have all disappeared—all but those whose dullness was so pronounced as to be in itself for us an amusing virtue. And in the past there is so blessedly nothing for us to worry about. Everything is settled. There's nothing to be done about it—nothing but to contemplate it and blandly form theories about this or that aspect of it."

In "the precious, the incommunicable" past there was nothing for Willa Cather to worry about. The eternal flux could be frozen and immovable, unchangeable. The Rock stands as it always has stood; the cliff dwellings survive; the ancient men have wrought and their handiwork remains even after they and the vanities of their daily lives have perished. Between the tight society of French Canada (symbolized by the Rock of Quebec, and the steep old streets of the Catholic city) and the placid pre-Civil War society in Back Creek, Timber Ridge, or Hayfield there was an affinity that Willa Cather could appreciate; the order, the hierarchic, the parochial society, where the game of life is played according to hard and fast rules, with no tolerance of change or nonconformity, as Willa Cather well knew. She had been one of the nonconforming in her youth; yet in the later years she found in that society certain eternal values that seemed to transcend its intolerance.

This love for the ordered and regulated mode of life in a small society sprang undoubtedly in part from the violence of Willa Cather's early uprooting from Virginia to the Divide, so that ever after she felt acutely what it means to be torn from cherished things and transported to scenes unfamiliar and wild. Willa Cather's childhood pilgrimage, and her adult pilgrimage eastward, could make her sensitive, and it did, to those pilgrims who had come from the Old World to a new land; and she could experience in all its intensity their longing for things left behind in their forsaken worlds. There was also the reverse of this: in the New World order was being created out of chaos, a new life replaced the old. Trees transplanted were nourished and grew in alien soil. One has only to remember the role that gardens play in Willa Cather's work to understand this. To have been brought up on the sprawling prairie had given her a deep fondness for the small cultivated plot, the well-kept garden that is also a well-kept work of art. She always remembered how the Germans in the West planted trees and hauled water and labored to make them flourish. Garden succeeds garden: the Troll Garden, the garden at Uplands, the Wunsch garden, Ántonia's grape-arbor, the evil garden at Ácoma, the professor's French garden set in the Middle West. . . .

> The Professor had succeeded in making a French garden in Hamilton. There was not a blade of grass; it was a tidy half-acre of glistening gravel and glistening shrubs and bright flowers. There were trees, of course; a spreading horse-chestnut, a row of slender Lombardy poplars at the back, along the white wall, and in the middle two symmetrical, round-topped linden trees. Masses of green-briar grew in the corners, the prickly stems interwoven and clipped until they were like great bushes. There was a bed for salad herbs. Salmon-pink geraniums dripped over the wall. The French marigolds and dahlias were just now at their best—such dahlias as no one else in Hamilton could grow. St. Peter had tended this bit of ground for over twenty years, and had got the upper hand of it.

The transplanting of graces and traditions, like the transplanting of trees, was in fact a bringing of the unchanged, the old, into the new; not only was something of the past kept alive in the process, but it grew and flourished and took on new life. So the transplanted Bohemians and Swedes and French and Germans sought to recapture what had gone before in the midst of the wild land.

Willa Cather wanted life to be an arranged garden, she liked an *achieved* order; and this inevitably meant the conquest of disorder. The emphasis must be on the word *conquest*, for Willa Cather's books were built around the central theme of her own life—"the passionate struggle of a tenacious will." Her heroes and heroines were Alexanders and Alexandras whose names were synonymous with conquest, and it is no accident that of all of Plutarch's lives, little Cécile reads in the evenings at Quebec the life of Alexander the Great; and when, in Pittsburgh, Willa Cather wrote an essay on her actress friend Lizzie Hudson Collier, she gave the article the Meredithian title of "One of Our Conquerors." Her stories are stories of conquest; sometimes there is defeat, but mostly there is the timeless victory of the spirit. To conquer meant to rise above the petty men, the little conniving spirits, the baleful goblins of this world, always whittling greatness down to their own spiteful mediocrity. She, Willa Cather, had conquered by tearing herself away from the inarticulate vastness of Nebraska and rendered it articulate in a competitive and brutal world. "What I cared about," she wrote in her late preface to *The Song of the Lark*, "and still care about," she added, "was the girl's escape; the play of blind chance, the way in which commonplace occurrences fell together to liberate her from commonness." But what Willa Cather forgot to mention was that Thea had been uncommon and endowed with great inner resources, which would ultimately lead her to what James once spoke of as the artist's "free possession of himself." The fortuitous circumstances had been there in Willa Cather's life as well—Mr. Ducker, Dr. Tyndale, the eagerness and curiosity that attracted certain professors to her, the chance meeting that led to her escape to Pittsburgh, that other chance meeting which led to her friendship with Isabelle McClung, the interest of Sam McClure in her first tales. Above all, there had been—and this was not fortuitous—the way in which she had learned by the costly process of trial and error that what mattered most was "the loyalty of young hearts to some exalted ideal, and the passion with which they strive."

That passion is written into all her books. Within the

heroic personages she created, leading simple lives, there was the tension and emotion with which she was able to suffuse so many of her pages; the feelings well up almost imperceptibly into the acute experience that Brownell recorded on his first reading of *My Ántonia* or Mr. Justice Oliver Wendell Holmes when he wrote to Willa Cather that she had the "gift of the transfiguring touch." If we retain the image of the Rock and Willa Cather's devotion to the unalterable, we must recognize that her great gift was her capacity to observe and record the shadows on her own spiritual rock and endow it with light and color and a play of feeling. Her unfinished fragment describing the effect of light on adobe walls in the south expresses this. The artist, she wrote, cannot paint the sun or the sunlight, "he can only paint the tricks that shadows play with it, or what it does to forms," and, she adds, it is not even that so much as "some emotion they give him, some man-made arrangement of them that happens to give him personal delight." At bottom, she said, all the artist could give was "the thrill of his own poor little nerve." She ventured the belief that in the end some great artists outgrow their own art; "the men were bigger than the game." Tolstoy did, and Leonardo. "When I hear the last opuses, I think Beethoven did." In *The Tempest* Shakespeare gave the "awful veiled threat" that he too felt "he had outgrown his toys, was about to put them away and free that spirit of Comedy and Lyrical Poetry and all the rest he held captive—quit play-making and verse-making for ever and turn his attention—to what, he did not hint, but it was probably merely to enjoy with all his senses that Warwickshire country which he loved to weakness—with a warm physical appetite. But he died before he had tried to grow old, never became a bitter old man wrangling with abstractions or creeds. . . ."

Willa Cather never wrangled with abstractions or creeds, never struggled with politics or the pressing history of the front pages. She was concerned with the concrete process of observing life. In her later years, however, a note of bitterness crept increasingly into her work. It came first as a vigorous note of criticism: her sense that new generations were adulterating the pioneer spirit, possessing neither the standards nor the values of those who had gone before. The pioneers were creators. What had followed was a decline in creativity. The pampered new generation waxed fat on the capital created by the old without adding anything new save cluttering machinery, baubles that could not really replace the old valued things and were soon enough relegated to basement or attic as a child discards obsolescent playthings. Willa Cather had no use for a gadget civilization. "You Americans are always looking for something outside yourselves to warm you up and it is no way to do," the Bohemian boy tells Claude in *One of Ours.* In the old countries "we learn to make the most of little things." What Claude discovers in the life of the Erlich family in Lincoln is that "they merely knew how to live . . . and spent their money on themselves, instead of on machines to do the work and machines to entertain people." And Eusabio, speaking of the railroad from Gallup to Santa Fe in *Death Comes for the Archbishop,* observes: "Men travel faster now, but I do not know if they go to better things."

Men indeed traveled faster, as Willa Cather saw in her old age. They had soared from the earth into the astronomical spaces, and Willa Cather was no longer sure even of the freedom of the skies; there were moments when her tone became petulant and merely irritable not only against those who had watered down American life but against change itself, the inevitable flow and forward movement of the years. It was then that the strong voice, which could be addressed against decay and corrosion, faltered and at times became shrill. She could no longer face with equanimity a group of callow and unfeeling girls in knickers, as in *The Old Beauty,* without identifying them with the destruction of the world of grace and politeness she had known, rather than with perhaps some part of the Willa Cather of Red Cloud and Lincoln who had affected unconventional attire and sought to *épater les bourgeois.*

Posterity will overlook, I think, the moments of petulance and irritation and recognize that Willa Cather's picture of American achievement and its subsequent metamorphosis into a technical and material gadget civilization was a view from an artist's great height of transition from the nineteenth to the twentieth century, the obliteration of early promise and man-made deeds by the impersonal machine. And posterity will also recognize that in her extraordinary craftsmanship, as in her vision, she achieved an enduring artistic synthesis of this transformation of a country and a way of life.

What we have gained by her craftsmanship is, above all, a beautiful lightening of the novel form. From George Eliot's time down to ours, the load upon the novel has been steadily increasing until in works like *The Financier* or *The World of William Clissold*—to choose examples from two of Willa Cather's contemporaries—the form broke beneath the stress. For the popular fiction of a semi-serious sort, and for fiction that aspires to distinction without fully attaining it, the characteristic formula has been during the past quarter of a century the memoir of a crowded life, abounding in rather crude sexual experience and with somewhat hasty reflections on education, industry, the social system, coming to a climax in a melodramatic ethical regeneration or else in an equally melodramatic recognition of life's futility, the entire story often crowded with violence and brutality. Examples of such fiction, written for the day, or at best for the decade, will be in everyone's mind. In most of them character and story are mere props and are handled with an almost unbelievable clumsiness; structure and tone are scarcely considered; and in style the model appears to be the manner of the more lively foreign correspondent or the court reporter. Against such a degradation of the art of fiction to mere journalism Miss Cather's craftsmanship stands out with an alien definiteness and firmness of beauty.

Her vision is of essences. In her earlier novels the essential subject, a state of mind or of feeling, was enveloped in the massiveness of the conventional modern realist novel. It was there, but it was muffled. Then she saw that if she abandoned the devices of massive realism, if she depended on picture and symbol and style, she could disengage her essential subject and make it tell upon the reader with a greater directness and power, help it to remain uncluttered in his mind. The things that pass, the things that merely adhere to states of mind and feeling, she began to use with a severe and rigid economy. Her fiction became a kind of symbolism, with the depths and suggestions that belong to symbolist art, and with the devotion to a music of style and structure for which the great literary symbolist strove, Pater and Moore and the later Henry James. What she cares for in humanity and in nature many sensitive and cultivated people have cared for in every time. She was aware of this. Amid the discouragements of her last years, her belief could never be shaken that whatever the war had done to the past—the destruction of the Tolstoy memorial by the Nazis, the breaking up of the estate of Madame Franklin-Grout—it could not destroy the works themselves. Time and circumstance and indifference might disperse the material relics of a writer, but they could not annihilate what the writer left of himself or herself in books. Sarah Orne Jewett came alive every time Willa Cather took one of her volumes from the shelf. *The Pilgrim's Progress* had survived the centuries. The enduring works needed no justification for their continued existence. "One might say," Willa Cather had written in her essay on Miss Jewett, "that every fine story must leave in the mind of the sensitive reader an intangible residuum of pleasure; a cadence, a quality of voice that is exclusively the writer's own, individual, unique. A quality which one can remember without the volume at hand, can experience over and over again in the mind but can never absolutely define, as one can experience in memory a melody, or the summer perfume of a garden."

"A cadence, a quality of voice . . ." and what this voice, so singular and intense, tells us in the case of Willa Cather is that America was created not only by sheer vitality projected from the Old World, but by a heroism alike sensitive and perceptive; that it took men and women of large imagination and unbending faith to achieve a pioneer greatness which a later generation accepted without comprehending. Her theme, as Henry Seidel Canby has said, was unique in our formative time, "the overflow of vigorous men and women from the Old World into the new country, after one thousand years of stability." To write of it Willa Cather described the arc in reverse, and having learned the world she discovered that she knew the village. Of American artists she was the first who wooed the muse in her particular wild land, and because it was an authentic muse, the art is authentic and pure, almost classical in form, built of the rocklike materials that endure.

Acknowledgment

E. K. BROWN traveled widely and talked to many persons in the process of piecing together the record of Willa Cather's creative life. One clue led to another, and long before the end he was carrying on an extensive and exacting correspondence. In going over his voluminous notes and papers I have found the names of a number of persons to whom he was clearly indebted for generous assistance at various stages of his research, and I give them here neither in alphabetical order nor indeed in any special sequence, but as I come upon them. He was particularly indebted to Mariel C. Gere; Elsie Margaret Cather; Mary Virginia Mellen; William Linn Westermann; Helen McAfee; Mrs. Robert W. Millar; George Seibel; James R. Shively; Norman Foerster; Earl A. Dimmick, superintendent of Pittsburgh Public Schools; the late Dr. George W. Gerwig of the Allegheny Central Board of Education; the late Benjamin D. Hitz; Mrs. W. W. Ray; Mrs. W. A. Sherwood; Mr. and Mrs. Sydney Florance; Ferris Greenslet; Mrs. L. C. Dillon; Louise and Olivia Pound; Mrs. Forman; Miss Sarah Bloom; Ned C. Abbott; George Kibbe Turner; and Napier Wilt, of the University of Chicago. A generous grant from the Carl and Lily Pforzheimer Fund facilitated the necessary travel and searches in libraries for much buried material.

In completing the work I had the assistance of a number of persons who had also aided Brown, and the gratitude here expressed is therefore on my behalf as well as his—to Mrs. Ethel Jones Litchfield; F. B. Adams, Jr., of the Pierpont Morgan Library; Elizabeth Shepley Sergeant; Miss Rose Demorest, of the Carnegie Library of Pittsburgh; and

Preston Farrar. In especial I single out Dorothy Canfield Fisher, who with great patience and unvarying promptness answered in full detail all my queries concerning Willa Cather's early years in Pittsburgh and abroad; without her copious notes and generous searching of her papers and memories, that portion of this biography would lack much of the precise detail it now possesses. I wish also to express thanks to Mrs. Jessica Cather Auld, Mrs. E. H. Anderson, A. S. P. Woodhouse, Ernest Sirluck, Morton Dauwen Zabel, and Mrs. Edward K. Brown for assistance given me in the difficult task of taking up and completing an unfinished work. Harry Finestone, a graduate student at the University of Chicago, who worked under Professor Brown, generously supplied material from a thesis he is preparing on Mrs. Cather's Pittsburgh years. I am indebted also to my wife, Roberta Roberts Edel, for her guidance in matters pertaining to her native Nebraska.

E. K. Brown would have specially singled out for his thanks Alfred A. Knopf, Miss Cather's publisher of many years, for the interest he displayed in the project from the outset. This interest was proffered just as generously to the solution of the problems I encountered in completing the book. He placed his archives at my disposal and in every way facilitated my task.

Miss Edith Lewis's contribution to a project she first conceived and to which she gave its essential design is amply attested by the passages of reminiscence which she set down for E. K. Brown and which he incorporated in his text. What cannot emerge for the reader of the book, however, is the fine quality of attention and loyalty she brought to bear on the research problems and to the questions we brought to her. No small detail was too insignificant to be pursued and evaluated. In the fullest and friendliest sense of the word, Miss Lewis must be considered as a collaborator, alike generous and devoted, in this book.

L. E.

Bibliographical Note

THE WORKS OF WILLA CATHER

April Twilights, 1903.
The Troll Garden, 1905.
Alexander's Bridge, 1912.
O, Pioneers! 1913.
The Song of the Lark, 1915.
My Ántonia, 1918.
Youth and the Bright Medusa, 1920.
One of Ours, 1922.
A Lost Lady, 1923.
The Professor's House, 1925.
My Mortal Enemy, 1926.
Death Comes for the Archbishop, 1927.
Shadows on the Rock, 1931.
Obscure Destinies, 1932.
Lucy Gayheart, 1935.
Not Under Forty, 1936.
Sapphira and the Slave Girl, 1940.

THE NOVELS AND STORIES OF WILLA CATHER were published as a "Library Edition" in 13 volumes (Boston: Houghton Mifflin Company; 1937–41). Unless otherwise indicated, all quotations are from Willa Cather's work included in this collected edition and conform to the edition's text. *April Twilight and Other Poems* (New York, 1933) is a new edition of the 1903 volume with several poems omitted and others added. Reprints include *Alexander's Bridge* (Boston, 1922) with a preface by the author; *O, Pioneers!* (Boston, 1929) in the Riverside Library; *The Song of the Lark* (New York, 1932) in the Traveller's Library with a preface by the author; *One of Ours* (New

York, 1926) with an introduction by Stanley T. Williams and *Death Comes for the Archbishop* (New York, 1931, in the Modern Library, and also New York, 1945). A number of Miss Cather's novels have been translated into Dutch, German, French, Czech, Japanese, Swedish, Danish, Norwegian, Spanish, Hungarian, and Italian. English editions exist of a majority of the works.

Posthumously there appeared *The Old Beauty* (New York, 1948), containing three stories left completed at the time of Miss Cather's death, and *Willa Cather on Writing* (New York, 1949), with a foreword by Stephen Tennant. During Willa Cather's lifetime there were a number of de luxe and limited editions of some of her novels and a limited signed edition of her poems. A list of first editions is to be found in Jacob Blanck: *Merle Johnson's American First Editions* (fourth edition, New York, 1942). A listing of secondary items is contained in Fred B. Millett: *Contemporary American Authors* (New York, 1940, pp. 289–92). Frederick B. Adams, Jr.: "Willa Cather, Middle Years: The Right Road Taken," *Colophon* (New Graphic Series, I, 1939, No. 4, 103–8) contains comment and data on editions. See also the bibliography in *Literary History of the United States* (New York, 1948, III, 436–8.)

Students of Willa Cather will find that a search of the journals for which she wrote during her years at Lincoln and later in Pittsburgh will yield much material concerning the young Willa Cather serving her apprenticeship in letters. In particular the files of the *State Journal* and the *Courier* in Lincoln and the *Leader in Pittsburgh*, 1897–1901, are filled with examples of Miss Cather's energetic journalism and early critical attitudes. James R. Shively in *Writings from Willa Cather's Campus Years* (*Lincoln*, 1950) brought together much early material as well as recollections from her classmates. The Pittsburgh *Home Monthly*, 1896–7, contains a considerable body of miscellaneous writing, but due attention must be paid to the fact that Miss Cather was here producing, in accordance with strict editorial requirements, material often distasteful to her and designed to fit the publisher's special concept of what a "family" magazine should be.

The short-lived *Library*, published during 1900 in Pittsburgh, contains some twenty items by Willa Cather, some pseudonymous, and the column "The Passing Show" in the

Lincoln *Courier*, appears from October 23, 1897 and weekly thereafter, with some interruptions, until April 30, 1898; it is resumed January 7, 1899 and again weekly, with occasional interruptions, until May 12, 1900. The files of the newspaper also contain stories, poems, miscellaneous contributions, and reprints of some of her contributions to magazines.

A number of Willa Cather's stories, published in the magazines and recorded in the periodical index, were never republished by her. Notable among these are "The Enchanted Bluff" (*Harper's Monthly*, April 1909); "The Bohemian Girl" (*McClure's*, June 1912); and "Uncle Valentine" (*Woman's Home Companion*, February-March 1925). Her key essay, "The Novel *Démeublé*," first published in the *New Republic* (April 12, 1922), has been reprinted a number of times and is to be found both in *Not Under Forty* and in *Willa Cather on Writing*. For the *Nation* (September 5, 1923) she wrote "Nebraska: The End of the First Cycle." This was reprinted in *These United States*, edited by Ernest Henry Gruening (New York, 1923).

In 1933, in reply to increasing demands for biographical data concerning Miss Cather, Alfred A. Knopf published a twenty-eight page pamphlet which contained a biographical sketch, an English estimate by Alexander Porterfield originally published in the London *Mercury*, March 1926; Robert Morss Lovett's review of *Death Comes for the Archbishop*, originally published in the *New Republic*; Willa Cather's letter to the *Commonweal* on how she came to write this novel; an unsigned review of *Shadows on the Rock*, originally published in the *Irish Press*, January 22, 1932; Miss Cather's letter to Governor Wilbur Cross concerning this novel, originally published in the *Saturday Review of Literature*, October 17, 1932; a *Manchester Guardian* review of *Obscure Destinies*, December 16, 1932 and an estimate of Miss Cather's fiction by Frank Kendon, which first appeared in *John O'London's Weekly*. The pamphlet also contained an abridged bibliography.

It is significant that most of the reviews used in this pamphlet were from British pens. This was not because of any special preference of Mr. Knopf's or Miss Cather's for them. Although the American public had unhesitatingly accepted her novels, American criticism, preoccupied with the jazz age of the twenties and the depression in the thirties, had lagged seriously in appreciating and comprehending the art of Miss Cather. A finer perspective prevailed on the other side of the water. The earliest American estimate of significance was a discriminating article by Lloyd Morris, "Willa Cather" in the *North American Review* (CCXIX, 1924), and the first significant literary portrait was sketched by Elizabeth Shepley Sergeant in *Fire under the Andes* (New York, 1927, pp. 261–82).

Other estimates include Thomas K. Whipple: *Spokesmen* (New York, 1928, pp. 139–60); René Rapin: *Willa Cather* (New York, 1930, in the "Modern American Writers" series); Rebecca West: *The Strange Necessity* (New York, 1931, pp. 215–28); Louis Kronenberger, in *Bookman* (LXXIV, 134–40, October 1931); Harry Hartwick: *The Foreground of American Fiction* (New York, 1934, pp. 389–404); Lionel Trilling, in Malcolm Cowley, ed.: *After the Genteel Tradition* (New York, 1937, pp. 52–63); Carl Van Doren: *The American Novel* (New York, 1940, pp. 281–93); Alfred Kazin: *On Native Grounds* (New York, 1942, pp. 247–57); Maxwell Geismar: *The Last of the Provincials* (Boston, 1947, pp. 153–220); Edward A. and Lillian D. Bloom: "Willa Cather's Novels of the Frontier," *American Literature* (XXI, 71–93, March 1949). David Daiches: *Willa Cather: A Critical Introduction* (Ithaca, N.Y., 1951) is the most recent critical estimate to appear.

Reminiscences of Miss Cather's life in Pittsburgh are to be found in *These Too Were Here*, by Elizabeth Moorhead (Pittsburgh, 1950, pp. 45–62), and "Miss Willa Cather from Nebraska," by George Seibel, the *New Colophon*, Vol. II, Part 7 (1949), pp. 195–208. John P. Hinz in "Willa Cather in Pittsburgh," in the *New Colophon*, Vol. III (1950), pp. 198–207, has appended a bibliography covering the novelist's extensive pseudonymous writings during this period. Light on "Willa Cather's Call on Housman" was shed by Carl J. Weber in *Colby College Quarterly*, Series II, No. 4, pp. 61–4 (November 1947).

Mildred R. Bennett's *World of Willa Cather* (New York, 1951) is devoted largely to the writer's Red Cloud years.

E. K. Brown's first estimate of Willa Cather appeared in the *University of Toronto Quarterly*, July 1936 (V, 544–66); his essay in the *Yale Review*, "Homage to Willa

Cather," September 1946 (XXXVI, 77–92). He also contributed a note on the Benjamin Hitz Collection of Cather Material in the *Newberry Library Bulletin* (Chicago, December 1950, pp. 158–60). His third in the series of Alexander Lectures delivered at the University of Toronto, in *Rhythm in the Novel* (Toronto, 1950), contains a discussion of *The Professor's House*, pp. 71–8.

Index

DISCUS BOOKS

DISTINGUISHED NON-FICTION

THEATER, FILM AND TELEVISION

ACTORS TALK ABOUT ACTING Lewis Funke and John Booth, Eds.	15062	1.95
ANTONIN ARTAUD Bettina L. Knapp	12062	1.65
A BOOK ON THE OPEN THEATER Robert Pasoli	12047	1.65
THE CONCISE ENCYCLOPEDIC GUIDE TO SHAKESPEARE Michael Martin and Richard Harrier, Eds.	16832	2.65
THE DISNEY VERSION Richard Schnickel	08953	1.25
EDWARD ALBEE: A PLAYWRIGHT IN PROTEST Michael E. Rutenberg	11916	1.65
THE EMPTY SPACE Peter Brook	32763	1.95
EXPERIMENTAL THEATER James Roose-Evans	11981	1.65
FOUR CENTURIES OF SHAKESPEARIAN CRITICISM Frank Kermode, Ed.	20131	1.95
GUERILLA STREET THEATRE Henry Lesnick, Ed.	15198	2.45
THE HOLLYWOOD SCREENWRITERS Richard Corliss	12450	1.95
IN SEARCH OF LIGHT: THE BROADCASTS OF EDWARD R. MURROW Edward Bliss, Ed.	19372	1.95
INTERVIEWS WITH FILM DIRECTORS Andrew Sarris	21568	1.95
MOVIES FOR KIDS Edith Zornow and Ruth Goldstein	17012	1.65
PICTURE Lillian Ross	08839	1.25
THE LIVING THEATRE Pierre Biner	17640	1.65
PUBLIC DOMAIN Richard Schechner	12104	1.65
RADICAL THEATRE NOTEBOOK Arthur Sainer	22442	2.65
SOMETHING WONDERFUL RIGHT AWAY Jeffrey Sweet	37119	2.95
TO DANCE Valery Panov	47233	3.95

GENERAL NON-FICTION

ADDING A DIMENSION Isaac Asimov	36871	1.50
A TESTAMENT Frank Lloyd Wright	12039	1.65
AMBIGUOUS AFRICA Georges Balandier	25288	2.25
THE AMERICAN CHALLENGE J. J. Servan Schreiber	11965	1.65
AMERICA THE RAPED Gene Marine	09373	1.25
ARE YOU RUNNING WITH ME, JESUS? Malcolm Boyd	09993	1.25
THE AWAKENING OF INTELLIGENCE J. Krishnamurti	45674	3.50
THE BIOGRAPHY OF ALICE B. TOKLAS Linda Simon	39073	2.95
THE BOOK OF IMAGINARY BEINGS Jorge Luis Borges	11080	1.45
BUILDING THE EARTH Pierre de Chardin	08938	1.25
CHEYENNE AUTUMN Mari Sandoz	39255	2.25
THE CHILD IN THE FAMILY Maria Montessori	28118	1.50
THE CHILDREN'S REPUBLIC Edward Mobius	21337	1.50
CHINA: SCIENCE WALKS ON TWO LEGS Science for the People	20123	1.75
CLASSICS REVISITED Kenneth Rexroth	08920	1.25

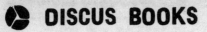

DISCUS BOOKS

DISTINGUISHED NON-FICTION

THE CONCISE ENCYCLOPEDIC GUIDE TO SHAKESPEARE Michael Rheta Martin and Richard A. Harrier	16832	2.65
CONSCIOUSNESS AND REALITY Charles Museous and Arthur M. Young, Eds.	18903	2.45
CONVERSATIONS WITH JORGE LUIS BORGES Richard Burgin	11908	1.65
CORTES AND MONTEZUMA Maurice Collis	40402	2.50
DISINHERITED Dave Van Every	09555	1.25
DIVISION STREET: AMERICA Studs Terkel	22780	2.25
EINSTEIN: THE LIFE AND TIMES Ronald W. Clark	44123	3.95
ESCAPE FROM FREEDOM Erich Fromm	47472	2.95
THE FEMALE IMAGINATION Patricia Meyer Spacks	28142	2.45
THE FEMINIZATION OF AMERICAN CULTURE Ann Douglas	38513	2.95
FRONTIERS OF CONSCIOUSNESS John White, ed.	48850	2.95
GAY AMERICAN HISTORY Jonathan Katz, Ed.	40550	3.95
GERMANS George Bailey	44917	2.95
GERTRUDE STEIN: A COMPOSITE PORTRAIT Linda Simon, Ed.	20115	1.65
THE GREAT POLITICAL THEORIES, VOL. I Michael Curtis	23119	1.95
THE GREAT POLITICAL THEORIES, VOL. II Michael Curtis	49858	2.50
THE GREEK WAY Edith Hamilton	37481	2.25
GROTOWSKI Raymond Temkine	12278	1.65
THE HEBREW GODDESS Raphael Patai	39289	2.95
HENRY JAMES: Five Volume Biography Leon Edel	39636	14.75
HOMOSEXUAL: LIBERATION AND OPPRESSION Dennis Altman	14214	1.65
THE HUMAN USE OF HUMAN BEINGS Norbert Wiener	21584	1.95
THE INCAS Garcilaso de la Vega	45542	3.50
INTERPRETATION OF DREAMS Freud	38828	2.95
THE LIFE AND DEATH OF LENIN Robert Payne	12161	1.65
THE LIFE AND WORK OF WILHELM REICH M. Cattier	14928	1.65
LIFE IN A CRYSTAL PALACE Alan Harrington	15784	1.65
THE LIFE OF JOHN MAYNARD KEYNES R. F. Harrod	12625	2.45
LOUISA MAY: A MODERN BIOGRAPHY Martha Saxton	48868	3.50
MALE AND FEMALE UNDER 18 Nancy Larrick and Eve Merriam, Eds.	29645	1.50
POE, POE, POE . . . Daniel Hoffman	41459	2.95
MAN IN THE TRAP Elsworth F. Baker, Ph.D.	18809	1.95
MAWSON'S WILL Lennard Bickel	39131	2.50
	(2) DDB	2-80

DISCUS BOOKS

DISTINGUISHED NON-FICTION

MOZART Marcia Davenport	45534	3.50
NATURE OF POLITICS M. Curtis	12401	1.95
THE NEW GROUP THERAPIES Hendrick M. Ruitenbeek	27995	1.95
NOTES OF A PROCESSED BROTHER Donald Reeves	14175	1.95
OF TIME AND SPACE AND OTHER THINGS Isaac Asimov	24166	1.50
DELMORE SCHWARTZ James Atlas	41038	2.95
THE RISE AND FALL OF LIN PIAO Japp Van Ginneken	32656	2.50
POLITICS AND THE NOVEL Irving Howe	11932	1.65
THE POWER TACTICS OF JESUS CHRIST AND OTHER ESSAYS Jay Haley	11924	1.65
PRICK UP YOUR EARS John Lahr	48629	3.50
PRISONERS OF PSYCHIATRY Bruce Ennis	19299	1.65
THE LIFE OF EZRA POUND Noel Stock	20909	2.65
THE QUIET CRISIS Stewart Udall	24406	1.75
RADICAL SOAP OPERA David Zane Mairowitz	28308	2.45
THE ROMAN WAY Edith Hamilton	33993	1.95
SHAHHAT: AN EGYPTIAN Richard Critchfield	48405	3.50
SHOULD TREES HAVE STANDING? Christopher Stone	25569	1.50
STUDIES ON HYSTERIA Freud and Breuer	16923	1.95
THE TALES OF RABBI NACHMAN Martin Buber	11106	1.45
TERROR OUT OF ZION J. Bowyer Bell	39396	2.95
THINKING ABOUT THE UNTHINKABLE Herman Kahn	12013	1.65
THINKING IS CHILD'S PLAY Evelyn Sharp	29611	1.75
THOMAS WOODROW WILSON Freud and Bullitt	08680	1.25
THREE NEGRO CLASSICS Introduction by John Hope Franklin	49452	2.75
THREE ESSAYS ON THE THEORY OF SEXUALITY Sigmund Freud	29116	1.95
TOO STRONG FOR FANTASY Marcia Davenport	45195	3.50
TOWARDS A VISUAL CULTURE Caleb Gattegno	11940	1.65
THE WAR BUSINESS George Thayer	09308	1.25
WHEN THIS YOU SEE, REMEMBER ME: **GERTRUDE STEIN IN PERSON** W. G. Rogers	15610	1.65
WILHELM REICH: A PERSONAL BIOGRAPHY I. O. Reich	12138	1.65
WOMEN'S ROLE IN CONTEMPORARY SOCIETY	12641	2.45
WRITERS ON THE LEFT Daniel Aaron	12187	1.65